Killer Analytics

WILEY AND SAS BUSINESS SERIES

The Wiley and SAS Business Series presents books that help senior-level managers with their critical management decisions.

Titles in the Wiley and SAS Business Series include:

For more information on any of the above titles, please visit www.wiley.com.

Killer Analytics

Top 20 Metrics Missing from Your Balance Sheet

Mark Graham Brown

WILEY

Library of Congress Cataloging-in-Publication Data:

Brown, Mark Graham.
    Killer analytics : top 20 metrics missing from your balance sheet / Mark
Graham Brown.
        pages   cm — (Wiley and SAS business series)
    Includes index.
        ISBN 978-1-118-63171-3 (hardback); ISBN 978-1-118-69173-1 (O-book);
        ISBN 978-1-118-73778-1 (e-book); ISBN 978-1-118-73780-4
        1. Organizational effectiveness—Evaluation. 2. Performance—
Management. 3. Industrial efficiency—Evaluation. I. Title.
HD58.9.B762 2013
658.4'034—dc23
                                                             2013017382

Printed in the United States of America

10 9 8 7 6 5 4 3 2 1

This book is dedicated to my wife,
Holli Brown.

Contents

Foreword

Insights and knowledge lead to better decisions and it is those better decisions that lead to improved business performance. Companies that outperform their peers are those that underpin their decisions by facts, data, and analytics. I call those companies intelligent companies and believe *Killer Analytics: Top 20 Metrics Missing from Your Balance Sheet* by Mark Graham Brown will help any business become more intelligent. More intelligent analytics are no longer a nicety to have but a required core competence that enables any company to compete in today's data-driven world. Enterprises without the right analytics will simply be outsmarted by their competitors and left behind.

In the past, the challenge for intelligent companies was to find data, any data, to shine some light on current performance and inform decision making. It often involved creating simple ways of counting things in order to get better insights and understanding of the business. Today, the challenge is picking the right metrics from the ever-growing mountain of data. We no longer have a data shortage, we have the opposite: a data explosion. Just digest this recent quote from Google's executive chairman Eric Schmidt: "From the dawn of civilization until 2003, humankind generated five exabytes of data. Now we produce five exabytes every two days . . . and the pace is accelerating."

Under this backdrop of ever-growing data volumes it becomes more critical than ever that companies are able to distill information down into meaningful insights. What I love about this book is that it goes beyond the oversimplified descriptions of metrics I see every day and digs deeper into analytics that provide real business insights. It provides managers with powerful ways of combining data points— qualitative and quantitative, past, present, and future—into indices and analytics approaches that generate more intelligent insights.

My own experience of working with many of the world's best-known enterprises shows the need for books like this one. Every day I see companies that are drowning in data while thirsting for insights. Most companies experience information overload where managers get bombarded with data, key performance indicators, and metrics, often presented in phone directory–type reports and cluttered management dashboards. What companies don't need are more metrics; instead they need fewer and, more important, smarter analytics that really help them answer their most critical business questions. I call them key performance questions and believe they are crucial to better information and analytics. For each analytics approach presented in this book, Mark provides a list of questions they will help answer. This is an excellent starting point for choosing the right metrics and analytics approaches for any business.

The other phenomenon I see in practice is that companies have invested in business intelligence, dashboard, or analytics software solutions with the hope of providing managers with better insights and decision-making tools. The problem is that many simply automate the reporting of the oversimplified metrics and then wonder why there is so little payoff. In the information technology (IT) world, the phrase "Garbage in, garbage out" is well known, and it couldn't be truer for performance reporting and analytics solutions. This book will help companies sift through their mountains of data, separate out the garbage, and find the relevant metrics to inform key decisions. Any company with existing dashboard, business intelligence, or analytics solutions can use this book to give it the focus it needs for reporting.

At the Advanced Performance Institute we have just completed the world's largest study on how companies measure and manage business performance. Responses from over 3,000 companies covering most regions of the globe show us that the majority of companies are still struggling with measuring and analyzing business performance. However, those that do it well gain valuable insights, make better decisions, and ultimately outperform their competitors. As part of the research, we created a maturity model that allows us to categorize how mature companies are in their approaches to measuring, analyzing, and managing performance. We found that most companies fall into one of two categories:

1. **Data and facts**. Where companies have facts and data, but the collection and usage of data is ad hoc, sporadic, and uncoordinated, leading to very limited insights.

2. **Information**. Where companies collect data and produce reports or dashboards in a more structured approach, which leads to some useful information.

However, the most mature companies and those that clearly outperform others use performance data to make better operational and strategic decisions and develop strategic foresight and predictions for the future. Those companies leverage their data analysis to look into the future through predictive analytics. The good news is that most analytics approaches described in this book are forward looking and predictive of future financial performance.

What's interesting, we also identified a number of things companies at the highest level of business performance management maturity have in common. So, what differentiates so-called intelligent companies from not so intelligent companies? Here is the list of seven factors:

1. Companies combine traditional measures of performance such as net profit margin, EBITDA, or economic value added with analytics approaches that are more dynamic and use wider and larger data sets—exactly the type of analytics introduced in this book!

2. Companies integrate strategic and operational approaches to create a closer link between the strategic business outcomes and the operational drivers of performance. Again, a point well supported in this book.

3. Companies focus more on the here and now as well as the future, rather than the past. Traditional metrics look backward while more sophisticated analytics approaches leverage the ability we have today to bring in real-time measures and predictive analytics tools. Another point made in this book.

4. Companies create a real focus on data quality to ensure that the input into their analytics approaches and performance metrics are reliable. Those at the highest level of maturity proactively manage data-quality throughout the organization. References

to the need for good quality data are made in many places in this book.

5. Companies use technology to support their analytics and performance reporting. Instead of turning it into an IT project, companies use IT systems and tools effectively to provide integrated platforms with the ability to perform predictive and big data analytics and enable companies to visualize relevant information in interactive graphs and reports delivered to decision makers via mobile devices or over the Internet.

6. Companies use analytics and metrics to improve internal decision making and not primarily to showcase externally how well they are doing. There is a difference in the type of metrics and analytics approaches used to really understand your business and identify the things that need attention compared to those that just exist as a box-ticking exercise. The analytics in this book are not simply there to generate a good marking message but will help companies identify many of the real performance issues.

7. Companies achieve real buy-in for analytics and performance reporting right throughout the organization—from the boardroom to the shop floor. A lack of buy-in for analytics often stems from the fact that the wrong measures are being used and irrelevant data is being shared. People at all levels of the organization will only buy into analytics and take some ownership for it if it is valuable to them and if it is generating insights that will lead to better decisions and improved performance. The purpose of this book is to achieve exactly that.

I am sure that like me, you will find this book extremely useful, practical, and engaging. It will enable you to enhance the portfolio of analytics and metrics in your company with more insightful and relevant ones in order to become a more intelligent and high-performing enterprise.

Bernard Marr,
Chief Executive Officer, Advanced Performance Institute,
author of *The Intelligent Company* and
*Key Performance Indicators: The 75 Measures Every
Manager Needs to Know*

Preface

Leaders need a constant stream of information to steer their organizations down a path of success. Being able to detect little problems or challenges before they escalate into bigger ones is a key requirement for managing organizational performance.

Too many managers today rely on anecdotal data or no real data at all, with only lagging financial and operational measures to look at to see how things are going. This book is not about measuring financial performance. There are plenty of books about that. It is rare that I encounter an organization that does not have good solid operational and financial metrics. This book is about measuring the stuff that most organizations struggle with. The ultimate goal in most organizations is financial success: growth, profits, share price, and return on investment are certainly important, but many other things are prerequisites to achieving those financial goals. Reviewing financial and operational performance against targets is extremely important. However, the root causes of failures or missing your financial targets are usually other dimensions such as dissatisfied customers, unhappy employees, external factors, poorly performing suppliers, legal and regulatory issues, or failure to bring in quality new customers.

KEY QUESTIONS

This book is about how to develop composite or analytic metrics that provide answers to the following questions that cause sleepless nights for leaders:

- Are we encouraging our people to develop innovative products, processes, and services?
- Are we effectively managing our supply chain and maintaining good relationships with suppliers and partners?

- Are we performing well on key corporate projects and initiatives?
- How well are the various improvement projects, teams, and committees working to actually improve organizational performance?
- Are we managing and minimizing risks?
- How are we doing at managing the pipeline or sales process to bring in quality customers and clients?
- Are we tracking key external measures and events that directly influence our performance and decision making?
- How are we doing at being an environmentally conscious organization?
- Are we able to demonstrate achievement of key nonfinancial outcomes for customers and stakeholders?
- How are we doing at managing relationships with our customers?
- What do customers say on social media about our products, services, and organization?
- Are we providing consistently excellent service to our customers?
- How many customers did we make mad today and how mad did we make them?
- How are we doing at supporting our country and the economy?
- Are we consistently a good corporate citizen and behaving in an ethical manner?
- Do we have the right mix of talents and skills for today and tomorrow's work?
- Do people enjoy working with our organization and are they happy in their jobs?
- What is our real corporate culture and set of values and is it what we want it to be?
- How much time are employees actually spending doing what we hired them to do?
- Do we have a healthy workforce and do we encourage wellness?

WHO THIS BOOK IS FOR

If you are interested in the answer to any of these questions, then you will find some value in this book. Not all 20 index metrics I discuss are going to be of interest to all organizations. My hope is that you will find three to five that really resonate with you and that you develop data collection methods and start tracking them. This book is not just for corporations or businesses; many of these metrics apply equally to health care organizations, government, military, and others. My clients run the gamut, and most organizations have more in common than they think. For example, they all have customers and employees, and they all care about financial results.

This book is also not just for big organizations. Many of the indices discussed have been used in organizations with as few as 50 employees, up to those with over 100,000. This book is also not just for metrics specialists or executives. I have worked with department managers, supervisors, and all levels of staff to develop analytic metrics that provide data on important performance dimensions.

DOWNSIDE OF METRICS

The problem with any performance measure is that you get what you measure, so you have to be very careful to make sure that whatever you are tracking drives the right behavior from your employees. The beauty of analytic or index metrics is that gaming and cheating become far less likely, as employees would need to influence a number of different submeasures in order to get the overall index to move into the "green" or target zone. Another downside that I frequently hear about is the cost. Yes, measurement costs money, and that money could be spent on other things like producing products, treating patients, or delivering services. However, without data, you don't know how well you are doing at any of those things. I am very sensitive to this in my own business and have wasted time tracking metrics over the years that ended up either being inaccurate or not really telling me anything that helped me manage the business better.

What is ironic is that many organizations have no problem dropping a couple of million for a management program that is supposed to improve performance, like knowledge management or customer relationship management, but balk at measuring the success or failure of any of those programs.

Metrics can be gamed, including financial ones. However, by tracking a suite of different measures that address different dimensions of performance, managers are more likely to get an accurate view of the health of their enterprise. Even though I am a huge proponent of objective performance data that can be tracked daily and weekly, I also acknowledge that sometimes observing and trusting your gut is a great way to see what is going on. If you have ever seen that show called *Undercover Boss*, you will realize the power of observational data. Bosses pose as entry-level employees and see what it is really like to be a worker in their company. Most come away in tears and learn more about their organization in a few days of watching and listening than they could from reports on 50 analytic performance measures. Observational data is critical and needs to be collected on a regular basis. Most leaders in big organizations just do not spend enough time where the real work is done. My client AltaMed, the largest community health care organization in California, requires that all medical officers spend a third to half their time in the clinics practicing medicine rather than going to meetings at corporate.

Sometimes the best way to measure something is just to talk to people and ask them questions. Numbers are critical but only tell half of the story—words are just as important. I call this "How's it going?" data. This kind of information can be very inaccurate when most people tell the boss what he wants to hear, but assessing performance by asking questions can help supplement reports on the quantifiable metrics I discuss here. Studies are also an important way of measuring a dimension of performance. We might have an annual employee engagement survey or have an auditor come in and evaluate our sustainability program once a year. Studies provide both words and numbers and tend to include some quantifiable data. The big problem is that you can't manage a variable that is collected once a year. All of the analytic metrics I present in this book are indices that can be tracked on a daily, weekly, or at least monthly basis.

HOW THE BOOK IS ORGANIZED

There are three parts in the book, with eight chapters in the first part, seven in the second, and five in the third. In each chapter you will find sections on why the measure is important, how it benefits an organization, and how to measure the factors that go into the analytic. In each case, a generic model of the index is presented, which will mostly need to be customized for your own organization. I find that most of my clients do not want a cookie-cutter approach created by a consultant. They want to have some ownership in deciding what gets measured and how. However, I find it always helps to show them a generic "straw man" analytic as a starting point so that can modify it to suit their own needs. Not only does this create buy-in from your staff, but the metrics are always much better because they have been tailored to your industry, company, and availability of data.

SUPER ANALYTICS

Another way of using this book is to combine a number of the indices into "super analytics" that provide a broad assessment of similar areas of performance. Some of my clients like this approach of having four or five big gauges on their daily scorecards that tell them about the following areas of performance:

- Financial
- Operational
- Customer and stakeholder
- People

Data is then stacked in layers, with warning lights to tell leaders to drill down deeper into the super analytics to see what measure is showing the problem and where it is happening. The beauty of this approach is that leaders have fewer than six high-level health metrics to track, each with a wealth of detail underneath them that can be viewed on an as-needed basis. The following graphic shows the hierarchy of performance data in a consumer products company.

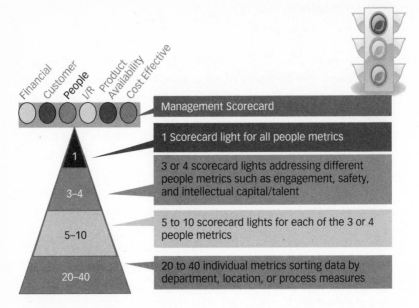

Some examples of super analytics that you might create are as follows:

Responsibility Super Index

Risk index

External factors index

Sustainability index

Outcomes index

American index

Corporate citizenship index

It also might be possible to combine some formula or singular metrics along with a couple of composite or index metrics to create some super analytics:

Future Performance Index

Opportunity management index

Percent in revenue from new customers index

Innovation index

Risk index

Customer Index

Customer engagement index

Social network index

Opportunity management index

Customer rage index

Customer loyalty index

Customer satisfaction index

THE INTELLIGENT COMPANY

If you have not read the foreword, I encourage you to do so. Author Bernard Marr is clearly one of the thought leaders in the use of analytics to help organizations become more intelligent enterprises. I asked Bernard to write the foreword because I think this book serves as a good companion for his two recent books, *Key Performance Indicators: The 75 Measures Every Manager Needs to Know* (Pearson, 2012) and *The Intelligent Company: Five Steps to Success with Evidence-Based Management* (Pearson, 2010). Having accurate data on any dimension of performance is only the first step toward improving it. A scale never makes anyone lose weight, but it is a good tool to track the success of your efforts to do so. Intelligent companies take the time to try to collect quantifiable data on things that are very important but difficult to measure. They also use that data to analyze problems and declining trends and to evaluate actions and strategies in real time to get the organization back on track.

Acknowledgments

I wish to thank my current and recent clients who have given me the opportunity to apply the concepts in this book and develop analytic metrics:

CRREL: Dr. Lance Hansen, Dr. Bert Davis, and Roy Cooper

Pfizer: Anthony Ramagnole and Jennifer Peck

AltaMed: Daniel Ruiz, Patricia Ziegler, and Lipika Choudhury

City of Los Angeles: Grace Benedicto, Robert Sainz, and Manny Sanchez

L.A. Fire Department: Greg Apodaca, Richard Caplan, and Mark Clark

Nestlé Purina: Ken Dean and Dr. Adam Pollard

Introduction: What Are Predictive Analytics?

You've probably heard or read something about analytics, which are a hot topic these days with finance and IT types. You are probably also a little confused about what analytics are and how they might be useful to your organization. The world of finance is characterized by tracking and studying individual statistics like sales revenue and costs as well as ratios like assets and liabilities, or overhead costs and total costs. While these are important statistics, analytics are more sophisticated numbers used to track and predict future performance in a business.

Organizations spend a lot of time and money measuring the past. Pretty much all traditional financial metrics (sales, profits, costs, adherence to budget, stock price, etc.) are measures of the past. Most nonfinancial metrics are also measures of good and bad things that have already happened: lost customers, accidents, new accounts landed, acquisitions completed or sold, employee turnover, overtime hours or costs, customer complaints, patients discharged, and so on. The good thing about measures of the past is that the data tends to have high integrity. In other words, there is no uncertainty when an employee quits, a customer closes her account, or we buy another company. Past-focused metrics tend to be based on reality and hard to deny.

LEARNING FROM PAST MISTAKES

The problem with this type of performance measurement is that it is too late to do anything about it. When I canceled DirectTV and signed up with Verizon Fios, it was too late for DirectTV. Sure, the company tried to lure me back with better prices than they had offered when I was a loyal customer for years, but this made me hate them even more. One thing is certain: DirectTV knows that they lost a customer. Data on measures of past incidences like this can be useful to collect and analyze to try to prevent future problems. If we bought a company that ended up being a dog, we can analyze how the decision was made, and perhaps be more careful the next time an acquisition target comes onto our radar. If we lost a customer or employee, we can determine the reasons for those losses and try to improve next time. Learning from one's mistakes can be very effective but also very expensive. Having a performance measurement system that includes only measures of the past ensures that an organization is always in a reactive mode, doing damage control when there are problems. The typical organizational scorecard includes 80 to 90 percent past-focused metrics. These organizations are always looking in the rearview mirror tracking things that have already happened and trying to solve problems that have already occurred. It is possible to combine a number of lagging metrics into an index to help predict future performance on another measure. Psychology teaches us that the best predictor of future behavior is past behavior. Therefore, a measure of how often you stayed in a Marriott hotel over the past 12 months might be a good predictive metric for future Marriott stays. This singular metric might become an even better predictor if it is combined with other past metrics like use of Marriott points for free stays, customer satisfaction, and Marriott dining experiences. Data might show that the most likely customer to stay in Marriotts in the future is one who has frequently stayed in Marriotts over the last year, eaten many meals there, filled out multiple surveys indicating satisfaction, and made use of Marriott Rewards points for free stays. This analytic is composed entirely of lagging metrics (number of stays, money spent on food, customer satisfaction levels, and free days and stays at Marriotts) and could be used to predict the future likelihood of this customer continuing to spend money at Marriott properties the next year. The problem with metrics like this is that they are never 100 percent accurate as predictors. Human beings are fickle creatures, and how we spend our money may change with time. I was very loyal to Starwood properties when I was doing a lot of work in St. Louis for a couple of years and spent many nights in the Westin there. However, when my contract in St. Louis ended, I found myself working in cities that did not have any Starwood hotels, so I started staying in Marriott properties. I was always really happy with Starwood, as I have been with Marriott, but my spending and loyalty are determined by the location of my clients, not my past experience with the brand.

ORGANIZATIONAL CHOLESTEROL

The problem with measuring heart attacks is that a lot of people who have them don't survive. It is clear that a person who has a heart attack has cardiac problems, but this is an expensive, painful, and perhaps deadly way to learn about a health problem. A better way to measure health is to track predictive factors that lead to heart disease and manage those measures, rather than simply to count heart attacks. Most physicians today believe that the ratio of high-density lipoprotein (HDL), or good, to low-density lipoprotein (LDL), or bad, cholesterol is a better predictive measure than simply the total of HDL plus LDL. In fact, people with HDL of about 60 milligrams have been found to have very low risk of heart disease. Monitoring blood sugar may be a better measure of predicting and preventing diabetes than simply counting the number of people with diabetes. Tracking waist size and body mass index and weight have proven to be good predictors of future hip and knee problems. Huge advances have been made in community medicine that allow doctors, insurance companies, and the government to predict the likelihood that a population will experience health problems in the future.

I don't see many organizational cholesterol metrics, but instead I do see mostly heart attack metrics. Those few predictive metrics are most often flawed and not supported by research or are based on data that cannot be trusted. For example, surveys are most often used to try to predict customer and employee loyalty. People who complete surveys tend to be ones who are really satisfied or really dissatisfied—if you are ambivalent, you probably don't bother filling out the survey.

USES OF PREDICTIVE ANALYTICS

Predictive analytics are being used by a wide variety of organizations to improve planning, decision making, and marketing. Some of the specific uses are detailed in the following sections.

Managing Risk and Preparing for Disasters

Insurance companies are supposed to be masters of predicting and preparing for risks, so it was shocking when insurance giant AIG had to ask for a bailout to avoid going under. Apparently even insurance companies can be surprised and caught unprepared to deal with economic or other types of crises. Of course, greed tends to be more powerful than fear, so companies often assume great risks because of the great potential for rewards. The banking crisis of the last few years in the United States and Europe has caused entire industries to rethink the way they measure and assess risk, and reevaluate what levels are appropriate to balance other factors such as growth and profitability. Good analytics can provide better business intelligence about existing and projected future risks and an organization's level of preparedness. With all the violent weather we have been having the last few years as well as acts of terrorism, it has become more and more important for organizations to get a reading on how well prepared they are for disasters. There are all sorts of risks besides bad weather that might go into a risk analytic. For an oil, pharmaceutical, or medical devices company, legal risks are a huge factor that must be considered. Judgments in recent years have exceeded $1 billion, which could cripple all but the largest of organizations.

Predicting Customer Loyalty

Waiting for a customer to leave to measure loyalty is an expensive way to track loyalty. Today's most successful organizations have conducted extensive research to uncover the factors that impact consumer loyalty to their products, services, and brand. Asking customers to predict their future loyalty turns out to be a waste of time, because most people do not do a good job of predicting their future actions. We might predict we will be a loyal Lexus customer until we see that new Jaguar and read the reviews and then trade the Lexus in for the new Jag. If I were Lexus, I would want to know what factors I could measure about a consumer's relationships with a car and the company that might predict his or her loyalty. If Lexus found out that a certain segment of its customers considered sexy styling slightly more important than a car's reliability, those customers might be more easily lured away by an attractive new body style. If they found that another segment of Lexus owners is more concerned with price and value, those consumers might be lured away by the new top-of-the-line Hyundai. Predictive analytics can be extremely useful not just in measuring future customer loyalty but in ensuring it. Many of the studies I have seen on predicting loyalty or likelihood of future purchases are based on survey questions asking people if they are more likely to purchase a product or service in the future. Unless you are 100 percent dissatisfied with a product or service, a survey question like this is not likely to be a good predictor of future loyalty.

My wife and I went to a great Neapolitan pizza restaurant, Gjelena, in Venice, California, for my birthday, and the food, ambiance, and service were outstanding. I wrote a stellar review on Yelp, indicating that this was the best Neapolitan pizza I had eaten outside of Pizzeria Bianco in Phoenix (rated number one in the United States) and Keste, which is rated number one in New York City. Sadly, we have not been back in nine months. Getting a reservation takes about 30 days and driving to Venice is a pain. In this case, satisfaction did not predict my future visits and spending even though I was 100 percent satisfied. It seems as though dissatisfaction is a better predictor that you will not buy a product or service again than satisfaction is a predictor that you will do so. My wife and I went to another gourmet pizza place in Los Angeles that was rated as the best new restaurant by *Los Angeles* magazine and we hated it. We never went back. The food, service, wine, and atmosphere were all bad. In this case, dissatisfaction was a clear and accurate predictor of a lack of loyalty and future spending.

Suggestive Selling

Analytics are used to customize recommendations to customers, increasing sales. Music sellers like the iTunes Store suggest other artists and songs you might like based on your most recent purchase. Amazon does the same thing, and their recommendations have helped me find a few new authors whose books I like. These recommendations also help Amazon sell more books. The analytics used to do this suggestive selling are fairly simplistic, like counting beats per minute for songs, but companies are becoming more sophisticated at combining a number of individual factors into more comprehensive analytics that are more accurate. If a web site recommends a book or song that you end up hating, you will probably not trust these recommendations in the future. However, if every recommendation is right on and you love the song, book, or whatever is recommended, you are more likely to accept this advice in the future for purchases. Thus a good analytic might comprise whether I purchased a recommended book or song, my history of buying things recommended in the past, and my review of the recommended purchase.

Attracting and Keeping Talented Employees

Most of the biggest organizations today spend a lot more on payroll than they do on machinery, suppliers, and raw materials. In a company like Apple, manufacturing is done by outside vendors, but key processes like research and development (R&D), marketing, and retail sales are handled by Apple's own army of geniuses. Some forward-thinking organizations have developed predictive analytics that help them assess the future performance of new employees, as well as the likelihood that they will stay with the company. A consumer products company I worked with has dramatically improved the caliber of their new hires and reduced recruiting costs by using predictive analytics to score job applicants. That same organization is also able to predict the likelihood of turnover of certain categories and individual employees based on predictive analytics. Google has found that eight key management behaviors correlate with managers' success and high levels of employee engagement. The eight behaviors are anything but a surprise (e.g., "provides coaching," and "empowers versus micromanages"), but now Google has some pretty strong evidence that certain behaviors are important for managers to exhibit on a regular basis. These same data can be used to assess the performance of managers, which Google does every six months. Some authors suggest that employee engagement depends on the person, not the job or work environment. Their research suggests that some people are likely to be engaged employees and some are not, so careful selection is the key to having an engaged workforce. While I agree that there is some truth to this, I also think engagement has a lot more to do with the job and work environment. I can recall many organizations like ARCO and Alcoa that had big groups of highly engaged engineers. They loved their jobs and had very high levels of engagement until they became managers or supervisors. Engagement levels dropped almost immediately when they had to deal with people issues and could no longer work on the cool engineering projects.

Targeted Marketing

Predictive analytics can be used to segment customers of one product or service and develop a targeted marketing pitch tailored to their interests and likelihood of purchase. A mail order catalog might buy the mailing list of a similar catalog and use that list to send its own catalog. The use of analytics to map out tastes and consumer preferences can help ensure that your marketing dollars are not wasted on mass e-mails or catalogs sent to thousands of people who will mostly delete them or throw them away. Analytics can also be used to help identify influential people to market your product or service to, in the hope that they will promote it to others. Virgin Airlines gave free round-trip airline tickets from Toronto to Los Angeles or several other cities to a couple hundred influential individuals who were identified using an analytic called a Klout score.

Product Differentiation

R&D in many big pharma firms today must "sell" their new products to business units, thus ensuring that the research function is closely aligned with the needs of consumers and the business. One I worked with has an analytic that looks at drug differentiation. Each new drug being proposed gets a differentiation score based on its unique properties and how it is different and better than any competing drugs. Technology companies use the same types of analytics to determine if their new product is going to be a real game changer like the iPhone or the iPad both were when they were released. These differentiation indices can help predict the sales and overall success or failure of a new product and rely on having good intelligence about existing and planned competitor offerings. The more dimensions on which your product or service is unique, the higher the score, and the more likely the company is to invest money in its design and marketing.

ANALYTICS VERSUS FORMULAS VERSUS SINGULAR METRICS

The easiest way to measure anything is just to count something. We can count dollars in sales, number of accidents, heartbeats, weight in pounds or kilograms, goals in soccer, new accounts, completed projects, and all sorts of things in our personal or work lives. Counting metrics are always preferred because they are simple and objective. Keeping score in both bowling and golf simply involves counting, whether it's counting the total number of pins knocked down or the number of times you hit the ball before completing the course. Simple, right? Most sports are based on counting metrics, with some judgment for variables like balls, strikes, or fouls. Most metrics in business, government, and health care are based on counting: number of patients seen, flights completed, hotel rooms booked, days without an accident, transactions completed, products shipped, products sold, money in costs or profits, billable hours, or reports developed. Measuring performance with singular metrics is always the preferred approach. The problem is that most of what is easy to count may not matter too much. In the words of Albert Einstein:

> Not everything that counts can be counted, and not everything that can be counted counts.

The second type of metric is a formula. We see all kinds of formulas used in business and nonprofits. Most are X/Y comparisons, such as assets/liabilities or sales/costs. Ratios of all sorts are found in financial statements as well as in measures of human resources (percent turnover, average performance appraisal scores, etc.), IT (average time to resolve trouble calls, percent milestones met on projects, etc.), customer service (percent on-time deliveries, percent returns, percent repeat business, average survey score, etc.), and operations (revenue per room, average restaurant check, inventory turns, etc.). Every industry has its own unique metrics that are usually some type of formula. Airlines track seat miles, banks track share of wallet, and hospitals track infections and mortalities. Formula metrics are easy to compute and well understood by most employees. If you can develop some key ratios like these examples to track every day or week, it is easy to monitor performance. If your entire suite of performance measures consisted of singular and formula metrics, measuring and managing performance would be easy and there would be no need for expensive business intelligence software. The problem with singular and formula metrics is that most of them are measures of the past, and rarely do they alone provide answers to important business questions.

An index or analytic metric allows you to combine unlike units of measurement on a single dimension of performance. A predictive analytic metric we all know something about is our credit or FICO score. Lenders calculate a score from 400 to 800 points based on a wide variety of counting and formula metrics such as ratio of income to monthly expenses, number of late payments, money in available credit, money in monthly expenses, net worth versus liabilities, and other factors. Each of these and other variables is given a percentage weight based on their importance in determining someone's creditworthiness.

The FICO score is believed to be a better predictor of creditworthiness than any singular or formula metric by itself. The value of such a composite number is that lenders don't need to review 30 to 40 individual numbers or ratios to determine a person's creditworthiness. Your car dealer can access your credit score online and provide an instant decision on whether to give you a car loan and the percent interest you will pay. Savvy consumers have learned that canceling a credit card with a zero balance and $5,000 limit makes their credit score go down rather than up. This seems a little counterintuitive, but money in available credit is one of the variables that goes into the FICO score. The challenge with analytic metrics is that they are harder to understand and usually require software for data analysis. A navy shipyard I worked with spent several years getting managers to use and understand their scorecard that was populated with analytic metrics, until the leader changed and the new commanding officer went back to tracking a few singular and formula metrics like overtime hours and milestones met on maintenance projects.

TIME PERSPECTIVES

Regardless of whether your metrics are analytics, formulas, or singular, they can represent measures of either the past (lagging indicators) or the future (leading indicators). All measures are actually a measure of either the past or present, but a leading indicator is usually something that you would not care about by itself. You only care about cholesterol because it predicts heart disease. Blood pressure is a similar leading or future-focused metric. There is no pain with high blood pressure, but this measure predicts other health problems like strokes and heart attacks. Lagging metrics or past-focused measures tend to be water under the bridge. In other words, nothing can be done about them now. The employee already quit, the budget is spent, or the deadline was missed. Lagging metrics are good or bad things that have already occurred. The only way this data is useful is to avoid future problems or repeat past successes. Leading indicators, on the other hand, are very useful to track and manage aspects of performance linked to success or for the identification of minor problems so that they can be addressed before they become severe. Detecting a slight level of dissatisfaction from a customer is much more useful than waiting until the customer is so angry that they give their business to one of your competitors. A scorecard or collection of performance metrics for an organization should ideally consist of about 75 percent leading and 25 percent lagging metrics, and most of the metrics for executives should be analytics that drill down through many layers of detail and individual submetrics. Data is stacked in layers like a pyramid. Top-level analytics at the peak of each pyramid indicate "red," "yellow," or "green" performance. Further analysis and drill-downs are only necessary when top-level measures show yellow or red performance. Supplementing your traditional lagging financial and operational metrics with some good predictive analytics can go a long way toward allowing organizations to become more agile and lessen the number of surprises you encounter.

PAST, PRESENT, AND FUTURE

Another approach that is even more comprehensive is to include past, present, and future metrics in a single analytic. For example, a financial health index might include a past measure of revenue from last month, a present measure of dollars and aging of accounts receivable, and a future measure of orders or proposals. A health index might include family history (past), current health statistics (present), and knowledge of nutrition and exercise techniques (future). The challenge in coming up with good future-focused metrics is to ensure they are correlated to the past and present success measures. You might find, for example, that knowledge of nutrition and exercise is not at all correlated with eating healthy or engaging in regular exercise. Therefore, knowledge of nutrition and exercise would be a false indicator that does not link to improved health. Most businesses don't have the time, patience, or expertise to conduct controlled studies that identify links between predictive and lagging measures. Consequently, they often rely on the research of others or anecdotal evidence and logic. Many strategy maps I've seen that are supposed to document causal relationships between leading and lagging outcome metrics are nothing more than a nice diagram of assumptions and opinions.

ANALYTICS ARE SUPERIOR TO INDIVIDUAL METRICS

The following are the top nine reasons analytics are superior to individual metrics:

1. **Improve data integrity**. Measuring a dimension of performance like risk, customer engagement, or financial health is complicated, and good performance is determined by a variety of individual factors. Rarely is an important dimension of organizational performance accurately assessed by looking at one or two individual measures. Ask any chief financial officer what are the key measures of financial health, and you are likely to hear a long list of variables that need to be measured. Ask your doctor what are the two or three best indicators of your overall health, and you are likely to get another long list. In order to accurately measure broad areas of performance it is critical to include a number of different metrics in your analysis.

2. **Minimize total number of metrics reviewed**. Research on a balanced scorecard conducted by American Productivity and

Quality Center (APQC) suggests that no executive should regularly review more than 20 high-level metrics. The problem with having to review 50-plus charts every month is lack of focus. No one can keep track of that many variables, and the likelihood of missing important factors increases, as does the tendency to micromanage. If most of the executive-level metrics are analytics, executives can regularly scan 10 to 15 high-level gauges to see how the organization is performing and then drill down into details when necessary.

3. **Minimize cheating and game playing**. Employees quickly figure out how to make performance look good on a few key metrics if that is the focus of their bosses. Real estate agents being measured on customer satisfaction only hand out surveys to satisfied clients. Car dealers offer incentives for good scores on J.D. Power surveys. Salespeople inflate sales projections to achieve arbitrary targets. They sell customers stuff they don't really need because they get measured and compensated on sales and margins. Cheating and manipulation is still possible with analytic metrics that are composed of four to six submeasures; it just becomes much more difficult. If the analytic includes both leading and lagging metrics, it also is harder to cheat because different strategies are likely to be required for improving each of the individual measures. Not revealing the exact formula for computing the analytic (as with a FICO score) also further minimizes deliberate manipulation or cheating to make performance look good.

4. **Keep management focused on the big picture**. One of the big problems with leaders who review 50 to 100 charts every month is that they tend to get down in the weeds too much. I've sat in countless monthly review meetings where leaders spend way too much time looking at detailed charts on measures that are way down on the hierarchy of important things executives need to track. Meeting time runs out before they get a chance to review major dimensions of performance because too much time has been spent discussing lower-level measures and micromanaging the details of how to improve performance.

Part of the job of leaders is to detect and solve small problems before they become bigger problems, but most of the time they should be managing the forest rather than analyzing the leaves on the trees.

5. **Improve forecasting and projections**. Most scorecards I've reviewed contain individual or counting metrics that are measures of the past. While it is important to learn from the past, it is more important to predict and prepare for future events. Predictive analytics allow organizations to detect minor past problems and correct them so that big future problems are prevented. Waiting for a customer to leave or an employee to quit is an expensive way to learn about performance problems. Predictive analytics allow organizations to more accurately forecast the future behavior of markets, customers, competitors, and employees. If banks and mortgage companies had better risk analytics, they might have predicted the banking crisis of recent years.

6. **Avoid wasting time on measures that show good performance**. When data is stacked in layers that roll up to high-level analytics it is unnecessary to review the graphs and tables showing good performance. Data is reviewed in a hierarchical fashion from top to bottom if the top-level analytic shows there are problems with lower-level individual measures. Many clients have found that monthly review meetings take less than half the time they used to with analytic metrics and more time is spent analyzing and solving problems than listening to presenters drone on with hundreds of PowerPoint charts or unreadable spreadsheets. By focusing the meeting on areas of performance needing improvement, the emphasis is more on diagnosing and improving performance than on a "show and tell."

7. **Focus employees on a few key metrics**. Employees in an aircraft maintenance and overhaul company get daily feedback on a few key measures, like the project management index, which balances cost, quality, and schedule with differential weights depending on customer priorities, and billable

hours, which is an individual metric. FedEx and Jet Blue both focus employees on three key dimensions of performance:

1. People—employees and other members of the workforce

2. Service—customers

3. Profit—shareholders who care about financial performance

   Having a few key analytic metrics can make it easy for employees to track how they are doing, and having three or four ensures the proper balance in focusing on different stakeholders and dimensions of success. In fact, FedEx takes this "People-Service-Profit" model all the way from the hourly workforce on up to the CEO. Of course, he monitors a lot more than three metrics, but they all fall into these three categories.

8. **Review past, present, and future perspectives in a single metric**. Some of the best analytics include a mixture of leading or predictive metrics (e.g., diet, exercise, stress), present-focused metrics, (current weight, blood pressure, body mass index [BMI], HDL/LDL cholesterol), and lagging metrics (genetic factors, previous health problems). The best way to measure any dimension of performance is with an analytic metric that incorporates all three time perspectives. By combining a number of indicators into a single analytic it is possible to get a more holistic view of performance. The performance of any dimension is determined by looking at both past performance indicators and predictive indicators. Leading indicators are the most useful for predicting and managing performance, but lagging indicators tend to have the highest data integrity, so a combined view of both tends to be the most useful.

9. **Find correlations between leading and lagging measures**. It all starts with a hypothesis that some random variable or factor is predictive of an important outcome. Someone suggests that engaged employees tend to predict higher levels of customer satisfaction. Or someone suggests that lowering admission standards on GPAs will lead to more revenue from tuition. Finding links between two individual variables with singular metrics is fairly simple research, but rarely is one factor completely predictive of a key outcome. In spite of how strong a

link there is between high levels of HDL cholesterol and heart disease, this factor on its own is not enough to be a good predictor. In fact, a recent article I read suggests that there are 17 key metrics that have been found to be at least somewhat predictive of heart disease, with some better predictors than others. If one were to construct an analytic metric comprised of these 17 metrics weighted based on their importance, this would likely be a very accurate predictive measure of the likelihood of someone getting heart disease. Further research could then be done to determine if there is a stronger correlation between this analytic metric and heart disease compared to any of the singular metrics that make up the analytic. Understanding correlations like this enables organizations to fine-tune their analytic metrics to better predict organizational performance.

MYTHS AND FACTS ABOUT ANALYTICS

Here are some common myths and facts about analytics:

Myth: Analytics hide important facts about organizational performance by only providing a summary of overall performance.

Fact: The best business intelligence and data visualization software includes both an overall view of performance showing red, yellow, or green, a trend line, and a warning light that lets the viewer know that one of the subsidiary metrics is yellow or red, or trending in the wrong direction. With a few simple keystrokes, reviewers can drill into the data to see minor problems and diagnose their causes. The fact is that an analytics-based scorecard like this makes it more likely to detect minor problems since the data reporting screens alert viewers when they need to drill deeper into the data that makes up the high-level analytic. Without the warning light feature one needs to drill down into several layers of subsidiary metrics to make sure that the overall analytic measure is not hiding something.

Myth: You need to learn and memorize complicated formulas in order to use analytic metrics to review and manage organizational performance.

Fact: Analytics we use in everyday life like our FICO or credit score help us manage our finances and predict the likelihood that we will obtain credit, and no one I know understands the formula for computing a FICO score. I use my real age number I get from the analytic Realage.com to monitor and manage my health without having to consult my doctor or understand the exact formula used to compute my "real age" versus my chronological age. People need to understand the basic factors that make up an analytic, but they certainly don't need to know the exact formula.

Myth: Your workforce needs to be highly educated to be able to understand analytic metrics.

Fact: Many of my clients have mostly analytic metrics on scorecards for teams of employees, and they monitor them daily. Many of these organizations have large groups of employees with less than a high school education, and they understand the measures and what they mean. Younger Brothers Construction builds components for houses and buildings, and has a scorecard that is posted daily for employees that includes many indices such as a safety index, quality index, and productivity index. Employees understand how their job performance makes each of the gauges move, and most like getting daily feedback on how their teams performed. Another client has hundreds of employees in a call center handling insurance claims, and workers have no problem understanding analytics that look at customer service and operational efficiency. You don't need a staff of PhDs or engineers to make use of analytic metrics, nor do you need to understand the formula for computing the analytics for the data to be useful information.

Myth: It is best to keep searching for the ideal individual statistic that provides the best measurement of a performance dimension than to combine a bunch of stuff into a summary index, watering down the meaning of the metric.

Fact: If there was some magic statistic we could track that would tell us everything we need to know about the health of ourselves or our organizations, that would be the best choice, as opposed to developing complicated analytic metrics. However, every one of these metrics that were thought to be the holy grail of performance measures has turned out to be not quite as revealing or predictive as we initially thought. C-reactive protein is a factor measured in your blood that assesses the amount of inflammation in your body, which is a predictor of all sorts of diseases and health problems. It turns out this analytic has fallen out of favor with many doctors since inflammation is only one of many factors that needs to be measured to assess health. Total cholesterol was once thought to be the best number to use to assess a person's likelihood of getting heart disease. Once again, it turns out that other factors need to be factored into the equation, such as BMI, glucose, blood pressure, and HDL/LDL ratios. In business, Net Promoter Score (NPS) was hawked as the one magic number organizations could track that would measure customer satisfaction and predict customer loyalty. But many firms have moved away from tracking NPS as their only measure of customer satisfaction because the majority of people don't fill out surveys (even if they are one question), and sometimes extremely satisfied customers are not loyal. The bottom line is that running an organization or even managing your own health is extremely complicated and it is unlikely that you can monitor and manage performance by tracking a few simple statistics. Hence there are only two choices: monitor and track hundreds of individual measures, or try to roll them up into a dozen or so high-level analytics. The latter is the only reasonable choice.

Myth: Analytics are not sensitive enough to move much because all the different subsidiary measures tend to cancel one another out as one improves and another gets worse.

Fact: This is a valid concern that is commonly experienced with analytic metrics. Pay off your $12,000 Visa bill for the first time in two years and get rid of your car lease, and your overall credit score barely moves up at all. Take a daily aspirin and decrease your "real age" by two years, whereas diligent exercise and healthy diet might only reduce it by five years. The secret to constructing a good analytic is that it is sensitive enough to move up or down based on highly weighted variables and move only a little with changes in measures that are of lesser importance. Tuning the weights of individual metrics in the analytic often requires some research up front and quite a bit of trial and error. Periodic studies help you adjust weights and add and delete metrics as appropriate. The bad news about performance measurement is that measures need continual evaluation and improvement. New variables and techniques for collecting data are being developed all the time, so it is important to keep your metrics current with the latest discoveries and research. Software can help improve data analysis with analytics. Business intelligence programs can be set so an alert occurs if there is a change in level or trend in any of the submeasures in an analytic. Actuate has had this feature in their software for more than 10 years. SAS software also includes warnings for changes in subsidiary measures that make up an index or analytic.

ANALYTICS USED FOR STUDIES VERSUS ONGOING PERFORMANCE MEASUREMENT

A health care client learned through the voice of customer research that men and women want different things from their health care providers. One of men's biggest concerns was speed. Men do not want to go to the doctor in the first place and their number one priority is getting in and out of there as quickly as possible with a prescription or some other solution to their problem. Women, on the other hand, care less about how fast they get in and out, but care about whether they have time to describe all their symptoms to the doctor, understand that doctor's communication, and get answers to all their questions about side effects, treatment options, and so on. This study might lead to the development of different standards for cycle time for male and female patients that could be monitored easily without an analytic. This same organization might do another study to investigate the hypothesis that adhering to cycle time standards for male and female patients correlates to higher levels of patient satisfaction. If this proves to be a valid hypothesis, this information might be helpful in constructing a patient satisfaction index that includes both a survey and a measure of total cycle time, with different standards for male and female patients.

Studies are very useful for testing hypotheses and finding links between one factor and another. Studies sometimes result in a change in a product or service that does not need to be monitored over time—you just do it. For example, when airlines found out that leg and seat room did impact loyalty and repeat purchases from airline customers, airlines like American and United created sections in the plane with more leg room and slightly larger seats. They don't have to continue to monitor the seat size and leg room, they just change the seats on the planes—done. What they do need to monitor is whether the additional room still links to loyalty. Southwest Airlines just made an announcement that they are going in the opposite direction by reducing seat size, pitch, and leg room. EasyJet and similar airlines in Europe is talking about making everyone stand on short flights just like passengers do on a subway. The point is, when your research indicates that certain variables will impact business performance, you change your product or service and closely monitor whether the desired outcomes really occur. Studies of links between two variables might lead to the creation of new measures and/or targets to continuously monitor performance. For example, a hospital that won the coveted Malcolm Baldrige National Quality Award found that a key phrase spoken by patient care personnel had a big impact on patient satisfaction: "Is there anything I can do today to make you more comfortable?" Not surprisingly, most patients had no problem responding to this question: "Yeah, either get me out of here or quit waking me up every hour to do something painful to me." The study resulted in training for patient care personnel, but also required continual monitoring to make sure that staff asks the question of every patient every day. Getting an employee to engage consistently in a new behavior usually requires much more than training and is certainly a lot harder than installing new seats in an airplane.

Most of the articles I read about analytics are more about using them for studies to do things like predict customer buying behavior. While these studies are really useful and important, so is ongoing monitoring of analytic measures to ensure compliance with the new process or change that leads to a positive outcome. Too many organizations that conduct these sophisticated analytic studies still rely on simplistic singular metrics to evaluate ongoing performance. Analytics are useful for both purposes. This book is about 20 different analytic metrics that are useful for ongoing monitoring of performance versus simply conducting periodic studies. Many of these metrics will not be important or appropriate for your organization, and I certainly don't recommend using them all. A good scorecard will include a mix of a few past-focused singular metrics like sales, profits, customers served, and so on, combined with a number of ratios or percentages and four to six good analytics or index metrics.

Some of the metrics in this book may not go on your chief executive officer's (CEO) scorecard but may find their way to other people's scorecards. An ongoing performance measure that is tracked weekly with complicated analytic metrics might only be tracked monthly and with simpler metrics for the CEO. For example, a human resources (HR) vice president I worked with had a comprehensive analytic that looked at the quality of new hires. The CEO just wanted to track the percent of time he hired his first choice, which was one of the submetrics in the new hire analytic. The more information you need about a particular performance dimension, the more comprehensive the metrics tend to be.

PART
ONE

Operational
Analytics

CHAPTER 1

The Innovation Index

WHY AN ORGANIZATION MIGHT TRACK THIS

Questions Answered

- Are creative people attracted to an organization like ours as possible employees?
- Does our culture reward creativity and risk taking?
- Do we hire creative people versus those who always follow the rules?
- Do we have work processes for encouraging creativity?
- Do we have multiple mechanisms for people to submit ideas for new things and improve old things?
- How much of our financial success can be attributed to innovation?
- Do we have efficient processes for operationalizing innovations and getting them to market quickly?

Why Is This Information Important?

If you look at most fields, the most successful companies in those fields are the innovators. Southwest Airlines is a true innovator in the airline business, coming up with a different strategy for an airline that remains successful years later in spite of many copycat airlines that have attempted to rip off their strategy. United has twice tried to come up with their own version of Southwest and both are gone. Remember United Express or Ted? United Express still exists, but it is no longer a direct

23

competitor to Southwest. Coming up with a great and innovative idea is certainly a good way to start a new business, but it often does not take long for a competitor to come along and copy your product or approach. Bose is a company I worked with that is really good at innovation. Some of their products, such as the little cube speakers, the noise-canceling headphones, and the Bose Wave, are still successful and were considered major innovations in audio when they first came out. Other companies have similar and lower-priced products in all of these categories, but most of us still prefer the original—Bose. I almost considered a Samsung Galaxy when my iPhone 4 was in need of replacement, but I ended up sticking with Apple and going for the iPhone 5, which I love. Once again, the innovator won out over the copycat.

Innovation is elusive. Some organizations have a number one hit and never have another one. They come out with one good product that runs its course and are never able to come up with another hit. In the music business, it is hard enough to get one chart-topping song, but doing so year after year for decades is close to impossible. For every Beatles that comes along there are thousands of one-hit wonders. They may even get a Grammy for Best New Artist, and by the next year we have forgotten all about them. For every Monopoly there are hundreds of games that get discontinued after the first season. For every Ralph Lauren or Giorgio Armani who have had more than 30 straight years of success in fashion, there are hundreds of designers whose collections never even make it beyond one short season. Watch for their latest fashions at your local TJ Maxx selling for pennies on the dollar.

Like any other dimension of performance, innovation needs to be precisely measured and managed. Managing costs is pretty straightforward. Managing production or delivery is pretty straightforward, as is measuring these two functions. Measuring and managing innovation is incredibly difficult. Like human capital and some of the other performance dimensions discussed in this book, there are some dimensions of organizational performance that everyone agrees are linked to growth, revenue, and profits, but no one can agree on how to measure them. This does not stop organizations from trying to measure and encourage innovation, however. Most of the metrics I've seen miss the mark. They either are not good measures of innovation or they are good measures but we can't trust the integrity of the data.

WHAT IS IMPORTANT ABOUT INNOVATION?

People. When you look at organizations known to be really good at innovation, you often find that a huge part of their success is based on hiring the right people. Think of the value of Steve Jobs at Apple, and how a single person can make a big difference.

Imagine if you had 2,030 Steve Jobses or potential Steve Jobses? Google and Microsoft both focus on hiring smart people. People with degrees from Stanford, Harvard, MIT, and other top universities are probably really smart, but not necessarily creative and innovative. On the other hand, some smart people find college boring and drop out. You also find that some very creative people never went to college, let alone MIT. You would probably also find that some really creative people don't score well on intelligence tests and perhaps were C students in school. Any measure of innovation surely needs a people component to it, but rarely is this the case. If there are people measures at all, it is something dumb like the percentage of people who attended your three-day innovation workshop. I am not sure creativity and innovation are even trainable. I guess you could take a completely noncreative person and make them a notch or two better with some training, just like I could take any 20 of your employees and teach them basic guitar skills in a few days. However, none of them are likely to become competent guitar players, and among the thousands of competent guitar players out there, very few can write a good song, and one in a million can write a hit song. Rather than hire smart but not necessarily creative people, it makes more sense to hire people who already have a high degree of creativity and have already written a hit song, or at least have the ability to do so.

Environment. If you visit all the usual benchmarks like Google, Pixar, Apple, Amazon, and Facebook, you will see that their work environments tend to differ from the typical cubicle farm in the middle of each floor with offices around the perimeter. You will see open workspaces, meeting spaces without traditional conference rooms, bright colors, lots of flipcharts and whiteboards scattered about, bulletin boards for posting visuals and ideas, small workspaces tucked in random corners, pool tables, Wii consoles, and all sorts of other things that would look a little out of place in most corporate environments. You might also get the feeling from being in an environment like this that the company really embraces diversity. In other words, there are a lot of different types of people working here, and they all look different. In fact, some of them are downright weird. You might also see an environment where a sense of humor seems to be part of the atmosphere. You might actually hear lots of laughing at work. Both my brother and sister-in-law work for companies like this. My sister-in-law works for Google and has done so for most of her career, and my brother Paul works for a Silicon Valley firm called Duarte Design that puts together major PowerPoint presentations for big meetings. Nancy Duarte's claim to fame is the presentation she developed for Al Gore on global warming, "An Inconvenient Truth." Her firm helps other organizations develop compelling visual-based presentations like this. Both companies (Google and Duarte Designs) have work environments that do not look anything like what I was seeing when working with big traditional companies in New York or Chicago. This type of workplace design is actually quite common in Silicon Valley, however, starting with leading companies like Fairchild and Intel. Hire the right people and put them in a creative environment, and you are already at least 50 percent there in creating an innovation-friendly workspace.

Culture. Related to environment but different is your organization's culture. I talk about how to measure culture in Chapter 18, and some of that information may be relevant here as well. Some organizations have a culture that rewards risk taking and creativity and some do not. Hiring creative people and putting them in a loft with bright colors and no offices will only lead to innovation if the culture encourages this. I remember working with IBM years ago at their old 590 Madison Avenue building in New York City. The company was in the process of trying to change the work environment to encourage more innovation and get salespeople to spend more time with customers. Several floors of the building were converted to an open environment where employees could sign in, plug in their laptops, and use a workspace, but no one had assigned offices. Meetings occurred in informal conference rooms and the latest furniture from Herman Miller was scattered about in bright colors and retro designs. The place looked really cool and modern. The problem was that it was still IBM. This was after top management had relaxed the blue suit, white shirt dress code, but it was still IBM. IBM is certainly known for some great innovations, but it is also known for being very conservative and kind of stodgy.

New furniture and a loft office space by themselves will not change the culture. Few companies I have worked with embrace failure as an opportunity for innovation. In fact, the culture of most companies is that you are one bad decision or failed project away from the unemployment line. Part of having an organization that is good at innovation is having a culture that encourages it. That means it is okay to fail. How many times did that Dyson guy say he redesigned his vacuum before settling on one that works? How many failed inventions did Thomas Edison have compared to successful ones?

Processes. Organizations that are good at innovation are also not bogged down with committees, procedures, approvals, and lawyers whose main focus is to prevent the company from taking a risk. Managing risk is certainly important, and I outline how you might go about measuring risk in Chapter 5. However, speed is usually a major factor. While working with Ericsson back in the day when it made cell phones, I recall that the new product development cycle took about twice as long as Nokia's. By the time Ericsson came out with a new phone it was old news. Seen many Ericsson cell phones lately? It sold its cell phone division to Sony years ago, but I don't recall seeing many Sony cell phones lately, either. Processes have a huge bearing on innovation and the ability to get products to market quickly. Organizations known to be good at innovation have work processes that make it easy for employees to submit ideas, get feedback on those ideas, and perhaps turn the ideas into prototype new products and services. Rapid innovation is an important business trend right now, because you have to jump on opportunities quickly before the market window closes or some competitor gets there before you and scoops up the market. Part of work processes that relates to innovation is focus. One of the big points of Steve Jobs's approach to running Apple was that the company had a singular focus. The iPad consumed almost all of the employees' attention and resources for new products until the products were released. Apple does not try to release 20 to 30 new products each year like some technology companies do. It tends to do one big one every year or two and make sure it is a game changer. The new iPhone 5 with personal assistant Siri is a pretty big improvement over the 4 or 4s versions. However, the first iPhones were the real game changers. There was nothing remotely like them at the time. Focus is part culture and part processes. Some companies just have focus as part of their DNA, whereas others always seem to struggle with this. My clients that grapple with focus seem to be afraid they won't succeed if they don't continue working on 25 new things at once.

TYPES OF ORGANIZATIONS WHERE THIS METRIC IS APPROPRIATE

There are a lot of organizations that do not need an analytic measure that looks at innovation. For many successful companies out there innovation is not a key success factor. Copying someone else's business model or strategy and doing it cheaper can be a very effective approach. A lot of smaller companies, for example, wait for the big corporations to do their market research and start building a new store or location before competitors start building one nearby without having to pay for any market research. I read that this is how Motel 6 builds new motels. It waits until Holiday Inn or a low-end Marriott property starts construction and then Motel 6 finds its own site nearby. There are a lot of organizations that just need to do their job and not worry about being creative or innovative. Innovation certainly has its place in health care, and there have been many innovations in recent years in treatments. However, if you are running a chain of 20 urgent care clinics you probably don't need to start measuring innovation. Just become more efficient and effective at seeing and treating patients.

The organizations that need this metric are certainly technology companies, creative businesses like advertising, publishing, filmmaking, architecture, music, or even software. Many traditional manufacturing businesses probably need to measure innovation as well. Even a pet food company like Purina gets a big percentage of its revenue and growth from new products. Automobile companies certainly need innovation, as do aircraft manufacturers, hotels, restaurants, and even some health care providers. Research organizations and retail stores certainly need to be innovative, and many successful franchises came from some pretty important innovations. In short, there is a much longer list of organizations for which this metric is needed than those who don't need it.

HOW DOES THIS IMPACT PERFORMANCE?

Like many of the analytics described in this book, the impact of innovation is huge. Look at Henry Ford's assembly line. This innovation changed the world, as did the light bulb, microprocessor, phonograph, telephone, computer, and iPhone. Innovation is thought to be one of the major factors that fuels the U.S. economy. Americans certainly did not invent all the good products that have come out in the last 50 years, but we did invent a lot of them, and continue to do so. Some cultures, like those in Indonesia, the Middle East, and China, that are good at manufacturing struggle with how to get their industries to be more innovative. Innovation is the difference between success and failure in many industries. HBO is almost always the winner of stacks of awards for TV programming because of great and innovative movies and series like *The Sopranos*.

Innovation clearly impacts revenue, since many companies get a big chunk of their sales from new products and services. Innovation has a major impact on stock prices. Hearing about a new drug that your company has in Phase II testing can make stocks soar if results are positive and the drug is a game changer. Innovation impacts employee engagement in a big way. If people are encouraged to be creative and come up with new ideas, and the company actually listens to some of their ideas, work can be a lot more rewarding. Innovation often has a big impact on market share and profit as well. What percentage of the market do you think Apple has with its various iPods compared to other manufacturers of portable music devices? Remember when Sony first came out with the Walkman? Everyone bought one of those as well, and no one wanted a knockoff Walkman, even if it was cheaper. How about Viagra? Pfizer had 100 percent market share, and because there was no competition the company could charge whatever it wanted for many years. How about Trader Joe's? It created an entirely new category of grocery store, and many of its innovative products cannot be purchased anywhere else. Trader Joe's continues to grow by leaps and bounds, and has no real competition. They don't try to be Kroger, Publix, or Safeway, or Whole Foods, either. The worst thing that happened to Safeway/Vons in Los Angeles is that it let its workers stay out on strike for many weeks. Consumers who had never considered shopping anywhere else tried Trader Joe's, loved the products, and loved that they could get four bags of groceries for the price of three at Vons. Many never went back and became loyal Trader Joe's customers.

Innovation impacts just about every other measure on your scorecard if you are an organization that depends on it for your success.

MOSTLY WORTHLESS INNOVATION METRICS

As with culture, human capital, and customer relationships, innovation is really hard to measure and manage. The measures that are objective and easy to count are the ones I usually see, but they are always lagging indicators. The typical innovation metrics include:

- Sales number from new products or services
- Percent market share from new products or services
- Growth in revenue from new products or services
- Number of new products or services launched
- Profit amount and percentage from new products or services
- Innovation premium

According to *Forbes* magazine, the innovation premium is a measure of how much investors have bid up the stock price of a company above the value of its existing business based on expectations of future innovative results (new products, services, and markets).[1] This one sounds a little shaky to me, since it is not possible to determine if news of future innovations is the single factor that drove up stock price.

These are all good lagging financial measures that are worthy of consideration for inclusion in an innovation index. However, relying on only these measures is foolish, because they are all backward-looking metrics and you can't manage the past. Realizing this, some companies have made attempts at measuring some leading indicators. Some of the less useful ones I have seen are:

- **Attendance at innovation training**. There are a couple of problems with this one. First of all, I am not sure creativity and innovation are trainable. Second, measuring training by counting butts in seats is not a measure of whether people learned anything.

- **Innovation teams**. Counting the number of teams working on developing new products, services, or processes does not tell you anything except that you have a lot of meetings and teams.

- **Milestones met on innovation projects**. This one could be okay if schedules are aggressive and focused on getting something to market or implemented quickly. Sadly, this is not often the case. Project managers set their own milestone dates and get measured on the extent to which they hit their own self-imposed deadlines. Ericsson always looked really good on this one when they were taking twice as long to design new phones as Nokia.

- **Ideas submitted by employees**. Companies like Toyota have gotten a lot of press for a culture of having each employee think of a way to improve the company or products every day at work. The company must get thousands of ideas every day and I bet most of them end up in the trash. However, there are probably a few gems in there as well. My concern is that with so many ideas submitted every day, the gems are a lot more likely to be missed. Easier to find a needle in a small pile of hay than a big one.

COST AND EFFORT TO MEASURE

The cost of constructing a good innovation analytic in most companies is low. Many of the variables that go into an innovation index are already being tracked somewhere in the organization. Most of the financial measures of sales and profits from new products and services are certainly being measured, as is a set of research and development (R&D) metrics like patents, successful product launches, consumer feedback regarding new products and services, market share, and other lagging output and outcome measures. What do not exist that might take some effort and cost to measure are things like the extent to which you are hiring innovative people, the degree to which your culture encourages innovation, and how effective and efficient your processes are for driving innovation. These factors could drive the cost and scale of effort up to a medium level. However, I recommend starting with a fairly simple analytic and making it more sophisticated with time as you learn which variables best predict your overall success.

HOW DO I MEASURE IT?

As with some of the other analytics I discuss in this book, a good way to think about what metrics to include to measure innovation is to make sure they are a mix of leading and lagging indicators. The lagging indicators all tend to be objective, important, and easy to count, and that is true for innovation measures as well. I like to further sort the leading measures into:

- **Inputs**. The major inputs to the innovation process are market research, customer feedback, competitor data, information on new technologies or findings, tools, equipment and resources, goals, and information on company direction. Other inputs for innovation might be problems or specific requests brought to R&D to solve by marketing, engineering, manufacturing, and other departments. For example, when Pfizer found out the-number of people who suffer from chronic pain, the top executives learned a lot about the size of the market for an effective pain drug. When they also found out that the average person sees many doctors and tries four to six different treatments for their pain, they learned that there was a huge need in the marketplace for an effective pain treatment. Another major category of inputs for the innovation analytic is people. Hiring smart, talented, and creative people is a huge input that needs to be measured. Assessing a possible hire for creativity or innovation should be done via a combination of behavioral interviewing, review of past accomplishments at previous jobs (e.g., painted 18 works that sold for over $25,000 each and were exhibited in major New York City and Paris galleries), and any kind of creativity instrument testing you feel has validity. Both the hiring and retaining of creative people need to be measured. It is important also to update your data on existing employees. We all know people who were incredibly creative in their younger years, but who have settled into middle age and a secure job, and may have lost that creative edge they once had. This does not happen to everyone—look at Bob Dylan or Paul McCartney—but it does happen to a lot of people. Assessing an existing employee on past innovations from 20 years ago is worth something, but what have they done for you lately?

- **Processes**. A number of processes go into the innovation function: coming up with new ideas, evaluating ideas, writing proposals, making presentations, attending meetings, conducting research, developing prototypes, testing and evaluating, documenting findings, preparing publications, developing project plans, communicating and deploying new technologies, and obtaining funding. All these processes could be excellent and very efficient, or just the opposite. One of the key process measures that should be part of your analytic is cycle time. This is what killed Ericsson's innovation process—it took too long. Measuring the total cycle time as well as the cycle time from point A to point B and point D to point E are important. Another key process metric that might be considered is the extent to which the innovation process has been followed. This is more important in some industries than others. In the pharmaceutical industry there is strict protocol for Phase I, Phase II, and other types of trials and testing that must be done before a new drug is released to market. This is important for the Food and Drug Administration (FDA) to ensure that the product is safe. Several pharmaceutical firms have almost gone out of business because of liability lawsuits from drugs that had a negative impact on some patients. Following a regimented and disciplined process for developing and testing new products is a type of metric worth considering for inclusion in your innovation analytic.

- **Outputs**. R&D produces a number of outputs that can be measured, including patents, papers, publications, prototypes, study results or data, project plans, grant applications, proposals, new products, and new knowledge or technologies. Depending on the nature of your business, innovation outputs might also include counting things like new products introduced, new services, renovated products or new versions of old products, new markets penetrated, new uses for products developed, and so on. Outputs are things that you can count that relate to the innovation process. Some are more leading indicators like patents, and some are more lagging indicators like new products sold, but both are types of outputs that could be counted. For an existing product an output metric might be the number of new features added. If you compare the 2003 Corvette with the 2013 Corvette, you are likely to see a number of new features. Another output metric might be the number of times you are first in the industry to include some feature in your product or service. Being the first airline to let you book a ticket online might have been a pretty innovative accomplishment years ago. Being the first airline to let customers comment on their flight experience via Twitter versus a long and complicated survey might be an innovation as well. An output metric might be the product/service differentiation index discussed in Chapter 12.

- **Outcomes**. Outcomes are things the organization values that usually involve the behavior of those outside the organization. Outcomes are certainly all the key financial metrics mentioned earlier like sales and profits from new products. Market share for new products is also a key measure that looks at the impact of your product or service in the marketplace. Outcomes could also be greater loyalty from your customers or a strengthening of your relationship. See Chapter 13 for more information on measuring the strength of the relationship you have with your customers. Outcomes might consist of awards or rankings done by prestigious publications or organizations. Outcome measures might also focus on nonfinancial measures such as cost reductions, improvement in product or service quality, improved efficiency, or greater yield.

FORMULA AND FREQUENCY

The overall formula for an innovation index is that it consists of leading (input and process) and lagging (output and outcome) indicators and that the leading indicators have been proved to link to the lagging ones. In other words, avoid superstitious input and process measures that may look logical but are unproven. The straw man to begin with is as follows:

Input metrics	30%	
People	15%	
Market data	10%	
Opportunities	5%	
Process metrics	20%	
Cycle time	10%	
Process discipline	10%	
Output metrics	20%	
Number of units sold	5%	
Patents or new intros	5%	(number of new products or services developed)
Differentiation	5%	
Number of new customers	5%	
Outcome metrics	30%	
Revenue—new stuff	7%	
Profit—new stuff	8%	
Market data	8%	(market share, customer loyalty, etc.)
Internal	7%	(cost reductions, improved quality, improved productivity, etc.)

VARIATIONS

As with many of the analytics in this book, there are a wide variety of ways to calculate an innovation index depending on the level of sophistication of your business and the type of industry you are in. The previous model is still a good overall design that balances predictive and lagging indicators, but variations occur in the individual metrics under each category and their weighting. At one company, for example, the outputs they count are innovations (new products) and renovations (old products that have been reinvented). The degree of renovation is also measured so that it counts more to completely redesign the product than just improve the packaging. Another good outcome metric I have seen is the number of game-changing products. Viagra or the iPod would both be good examples. These products created an entirely new category of product that did not exist before. Another outcome measure that could be considered is the one suggested by *Forbes*: an innovation premium that looks at the impact of innovation on stock price.

TARGETS AND BENCHMARKS

Targets for both the overall index and the individual submetrics depend on many factors, but the most important is the degree to which your industry and organization is dependent upon innovation for its success. What I find not useful is setting targets for the number of innovations. If you set a target for 10 new products per year you will get 10 new products and all of them could have marginal value. I prefer setting overall outcome targets and letting the R&D, marketing, and other people figure out how to meet those targets. For example, if you set an overall target that 30 percent of sales comes from new or improved products, achievement of that target might come from one breakthrough blockbuster new product or from 15 slight enhancements to existing products. Setting quotas for the number of ideas or new things does not tend to work well. Many musicians never have another hit after they get a record contract stating that they need to come out with a new album every year.

BENEFITS OF DATA

Innovation is a performance factor that is vital to a lot of a companies' success. It is something many organizations invest millions in and have only lagging indicators to measure its effectiveness. Drug companies spend literally billions researching and testing new drugs, only to sometimes find out at the very end that the product has too many side effects and won't be approved by the FDA. Innovation is a dimension that is extremely difficult to measure and manage, but doing so can have a dramatic impact on the bottom line.

NOTE

1. Hal Gregersen and Jeff Dyer, "How We Rank the World's Most Innovative Companies," *Forbes*, September 5, 2012, www.forbes.com/sites/innovatorsdna/2012/09/05/how-we-rank-the-worlds-most-innovative-companies.

CHAPTER **2**

The Supply Chain Index

 WHY AN ORGANIZATION MIGHT TRACK THIS

Questions Answered

- How important is each of our suppliers to our overall business performance?
- Do we have trusting relationships with our most important suppliers?
- Are we monitoring and managing the relationship we have with suppliers?
- Do suppliers value our business and think we are living up to our part of the business relationship?
- Are we minimizing supplier and partner risks?
- Are suppliers consistently performing up to our expectations on key measures of quality and distribution?
- Are we getting good value from our suppliers and do the prices we pay allow them to make a fair profit?
- Are suppliers controlling key process variables to ensure high-quality goods and services?

Why Is This Information Important?

This question should not need answering if you look at the percentage of your overall costs that go to writing checks to suppliers and partners. When I worked with Air

Products and Chemicals in Allentown, Pennsylvania, they spent more money on suppliers (66 percent of their costs) than any other single factor, including their own labor. When I worked with Alcoa, they spent a huge portion of their operating expenses on energy, equipment, and raw materials. Hospitals depend on doctors to do most of their patient care, and doctors are not hospital employees except in a minority of places like the Mayo Clinic. Supplier and partner performance impacts just about every measure of performance in your organization. My wife and I were disappointed recently because the wild salmon we looked forward to ordering at our favorite restaurant was sold out—the supplier had not delivered any that day. Having bad suppliers can also impact productivity and engagement if employees depend on these suppliers for needed tools and materials. Supplier performance also impacts your risks and brand image. Iams pet food got a black eye a few years ago when pets died from eating food that contained a tainted raw material Iams got from one of its suppliers. It also cost them a lot of money recalling the pet food and investigating the root cause of the problem.

Many organizations today have a global supply chain and are impacted by world events such as natural disasters, weather, political unrest, material shortages, and poor workmanship. Events like the food crisis of a few years ago had a major impact on consumer food prices. Big retailers like Walmart refused to pay suppliers more and pass on price increases to consumers even though some raw materials increased in price as much as 600 percent. This caused tension between the food retailers and the food manufacturers, who are both looking to make a profit. Tracking down the root cause of product and service delivery problems requires some good detective work and investigation of the long chain of suppliers that goes into most products today. Tracking simplistic metrics like order accuracy and on-time delivery just does not cut it in today's hypercompetitive world that demands an agile, lean, and customer-oriented supply chain. Suppliers themselves are also getting pickier about who they sell to. A company I worked with that sold pigments to a variety of industries, including automotive, figured out that their worst customers were GM, Ford, and Chrysler. Not only were the Big Three demanding, but the company barely made any margin on the product it sold to them because of constant pressure to reduce prices. The pigment company eventually told them to take a hike and find a new supplier—"And by the way, you have to buy your own Super Bowl tickets this year as well." Managing the relationship you have with key suppliers is just as important as managing the relationship you have with customers and employees.

TYPES OF ORGANIZATIONS WHERE
THIS METRIC IS APPROPRIATE

This is one of the rare metrics in this book that is appropriate for just about any size and type of organization. Some big government organizations are run by mostly contractors. Savannah River, a huge Department of Energy (DOE) site in Aiken, South Carolina, has a handful of federal government employees overseeing the work of thousands of contractors. The same is true of Knolls Atomic Power Laboratory in New York, which is run by Bechtel but overseen by the Navy, Nuclear Regulatory Commission, and DOE. The government even has an acronym for this (imagine that!): GOCO—government owned, contractor operated. My friends Dino and Lia, who own my favorite Italian restaurant and a pizza place by the beach, have to rely heavily on their suppliers. They have big company Sysco deliver some of their food items, but buy other foods from local fish and produce suppliers. They send out the staff uniforms for laundry services and have a company that helps with advertising. Even though they are a small business, they need to regularly monitor supplier performance.

My client AltaMed is the largest community health care system in California, with 44 clinics in Los Angeles and Orange Counties and about 2,000 employees. After doubling in size in just six years, the organization decided to manage its growth in demand by setting up a division called the Independent Practice Association (IPA). This network of independent providers has its own doctors and clinics willing to see AltaMed patients. This greatly expanded the organization's capacity to deliver health care without its having to open more clinics and hire more people. Of course, for the quality of service to be as good as what patients get in the AltaMed-owned and AltaMed-managed clinics, IPA physicians, clinics, and staff have to be carefully selected and monitored on a regular basis.

In summary, if your organization spends at least 25 percent of its operating expenses on outside partners or suppliers of any type, you need to consider this metric. Even if suppliers make up a minor part of your costs, you might also consider this metric if the goods and services you buy from suppliers have a huge impact on the quality of your products, services, or outcomes.

HOW DOES THIS IMPACT PERFORMANCE?

The customer does not care about your supply chain and who is responsible for what. All they know is that you sold them something bad. If I buy something at Target that breaks as soon as I get it out of the package, I'm taking it back to Target and blaming them for buying such junk and selling to me. If I get food poisoning from a restaurant, I am blaming them, not their fish supplier. The product or service customers are buying includes whatever you had to buy to make the product or deliver the service. When I fly to Chicago and then take a puddle jumper to Norfolk, Virginia, I don't really care that the commuter aircraft is operated by another carrier and is not really United. It says "United" on my ticket and it is painted on the plane, so from my point of view as a customer it is United Airlines.

The suppliers you choose to partner with directly impact just about every measure of performance in your company. They certainly impact key financial metrics like sales, cash flow, and profit margins. Suppliers also impact your costs and productivity if a late shipment delays your manufacturing schedule. Suppliers have a big impact on employee engagement. Having to constantly monitor and threaten poorly performing suppliers causes a lot of stress for employees, and they may have to take the heat for it. Switching cheese suppliers at my favorite pizza place elicits a complaint and a small tip to the delivery person, who had nothing to do with picking the supplier. Only after owner Larry got enough negative feedback from customers and employees did he agree to go back to his original cheese supplier.

COST AND EFFORT TO MEASURE

If you are only going to track a few operational metrics like delivery and defects, this will be really simple and low-cost, but also of limited value. Many of the metrics I propose for this analytic are currently not being tracked by many large organizations, so that means that it will require some time and effort to come up with reasonable and practical data collection strategies. The more challenging metrics will be those that assess supplier relationships, risks, processes, and the health of your portfolio of suppliers. Of course, even though the cost is high, so is the value. Being able to better manage the performance of your suppliers with good data can have a huge positive impact on many aspects of your performance and prevent many downside risks.

HOW DO I MEASURE IT?

A good supplier performance or supply chain index includes the following types of data:

- Supplier engagement and relationships
- Supplier portfolio
- Supplier performance
- Supplier processes

Supplier Engagement and Relationships

Just as relationships with employees and customers need to be measured and managed, so too do relationships with suppliers. Many large organizations don't even think about this, given that they are the customer and have the upper hand on suppliers. However, as I mentioned earlier, suppliers can fire you just as you can fire them. Sometimes a customer is just not worth the effort. I had one client that decided it was not worth it to sell to Walmart even though it meant giving up a huge volume of sales. I know of a number of companies that refuse to sell to the government—too much red tape, scrutiny of their work and invoices, low margins, and long wait times to get paid. There are two parts to a good supplier engagement index. The first part is a scale of 1 to 10 or 1 to 100 where you rate the supplier based on its importance and desirability to you. Some of the factors that determine how you score a supplier include:

- Importance of the supplied good or service to your business
- Availability of good or service from others
- Ease of working with the supplier—factors like flexibility
- Location of supplier
- Stability and success of supplier

- Capacity to handle your needs
- Knowledge of your business and needs
- Minimal risks
- Performance history—how well they have done in the past at meeting your demands
- Rank against their key competitors in quality and brand strength

This attractiveness rating is typically done on the top 20 or suppliers that make up 80 percent of your external costs. It is also important that the ratings are done at least quarterly, because the status of suppliers changes, as does their business performance. Building a new plant that increases capacity might increase their attractiveness to you, whereas filing Chapter 11 would definitely lower their rating.

The attractiveness ratings are going to be used later to set specific targets for the level of engagement or relationship that is desired. The second part of this metric is an assessment of the level of your relationship with the supplier. Again a 1–10 or 1–100 scale is used, with a 100 or 10 indicating a true business partner that you have worked with for years, and a company that is almost part of yours. The highest rating also means that you give a lot of business to this supplier and have done so for years. They may be your only supplier for this good or service or are certainly your biggest one. A lower-level relationship score would indicate a backup supplier that you only buy from when you can't get what you want from your tier-one and tier-two suppliers. Factors that go into assessing the relationship with suppliers include:

- Satisfaction levels on both sides
- Amount of business given to a supplier
- Supplier dependence on you as a big customer and you on them as a big supplier
- Length of time your two firms have worked together
- Stability of key personnel on both sides (turnover means a lower engagement level)

- Availability of suitable alternatives—how many customers are there like you and suppliers like them that could do as good of a job?

- Growth or decline in revenue or units you purchase from the supplier

- Price of divorce for either side—how hard would it be for them to find a customer like you or for you to find a supplier like them?

The concept of the last factor is that it is sometimes smarter to stay with the partner you have if divorce will be expensive and you know the alternatives out there are much worse than your current husband or wife. The same may be said of suppliers and customers. Part of the reason to work on a relationship rather than end it is that it is easier and less expensive to stay with an existing supplier and there may not be alternatives out there that are as good. Just like the attractiveness factor, relationship or engagement level needs to be assessed at least quarterly and preferably monthly. Keep in mind that you are not doing this with thousands of suppliers, just the top 20 or so.

Supplier Portfolio

A measure that is important for managing your risk is the makeup of your portfolio of suppliers. Diversity and risk minimization are what is important here, just like in your investment portfolio. The number of suppliers you have for key goods and services is also a factor to consider when assessing your portfolio. You never want to have just one, and many organizations have primary, secondary, and tertiary suppliers so that they always have a backup plan. If you work for a government organization, different categories of diversity are also important for your portfolio. Small businesses, women-owned businesses, disabled vet–owned businesses, and minority-owned businesses are important for a government to make sure it is balancing its dollars and providing some advantage to more disadvantaged or underutilized supplier types. You need to set individualized targets for all the different diversity factors important for your suppliers, and then measure the extent to which you have achieved the perfect portfolio by balancing all of these factors.

Supplier Performance

This is the type of data most organizations track on a daily and weekly basis, and these are typically fairly objective metrics for which specific targets can be set and agreed on. Some of the metrics to consider for this section of the supplier index are:

- Order cycle time
- On-time delivery
- DPMO (defects per million opportunities)
- Fill rate
- Inventory turns
- Stock outs
- Backorders
- Accurate orders
- Unit costs
- Warranty claims
- Come-backs—repeat service work
- Change orders
- Cost increases

Ideally you will develop a standard set of metrics that are used for all suppliers from which you purchase raw materials, parts, and components, and a set of metrics to assess the performance of service suppliers.

Supplier Processes

Some organizations do not inspect supplier products but ask to monitor key process variables while the supplier is manufacturing the product or performing the service. These process measures have been proven to correlate to output and outcome measures, so it saves the buying organization time and money that would have to be spent on inspections. Other process measures might focus on social responsibility, like not using pesticides, paying growers a living wage, and using renewable farming techniques. Process metrics might also focus on using environmentally responsible approaches, or on ethics and governance. Process measures might also examine factors like capacity utilization, screening of their suppliers, and managing the business so as to ensure profitability and survivability. Partnering with a bank or insurance company that is taking too many risks makes it less likely that your financial partner will be around next year. Process measures are the most individualized types that will vary greatly depending on what you are buying. Labor contracts where you are buying contracted staff might look at the processes the supplier uses for recruiting and selection as well as for managing the people.

FORMULA AND FREQUENCY

Calculating the health of your supply chain involves assessing a variety of different supplier performance factors as well as the relationship between your firm and theirs. Partnering with the right suppliers is also an important factor to consider in the index. The following formula is a straw man supply chain index that can be customized to match your own situation:

Supplier relationships and engagement	30% (Actual versus desired engagement level based on attractiveness and importance of supplier to your operation)
Supplier portfolio	15%
Diversity factors	5%
Backups	5%
Risk factors	5%
Supplier performance	35%
Quality	10%
Distribution and delivery	10%
Value and cost	10%
Flexibility	5%
Supplier processes	20%
Business processes	5%
Sustainability processes	5%

Manufacturing or	
service processes	5%
Ethics and corporate	
responsibility	5%

VARIATIONS

One variation is simply to spell out everything that both sides will do in a detailed service level agreement, or SLA. The metric is then simply a degree to which the targets in the SLA have been achieved each month. Each SLA has different metrics and targets, but there is just one overall metric that senior management looks at that tells them how key suppliers are performing. Another variation is just to measure the last two categories of measures—supplier processes and supplier performance. This is a good alternative for a smaller firm that does not have the need or the resources for a more complex metric. Both factors would be weighted at 50 percent so that the index is a good balance of leading and lagging indicators.

TARGETS AND BENCHMARKS

Individual targets need to be set for individual suppliers and individual submetrics. With one supplier you might expect better than Six Sigma performance on a key quality measure, and with another, 2 percent returns or quality problems could meet your standards. Targets for engagement levels depend a lot on what your desires are. You may have one supplier that is currently on probation and is a level 2 out of 10 on your scale. Your goal might be to get rid of the supplier entirely and replace it with someone new. On the other hand, your goal with another supplier might be to move it from a level 7 to a 9 on the 10-point relationship scale. Targets for your portfolio measure are also going to vary depending on mandates by the government and other factors. Deciding on how to set targets for the supplier chain index will require detailed analysis and collection of both baseline data and some comparisons on key submetrics that you can benchmark with others.

BENEFITS OF DATA

The benefits of having frequent and comprehensive data on supply chain performance are enormous. Not only will this information help you to better manage your suppliers and partners, but it will help improve their satisfaction with you as a customer. Getting frequent measurement of predictive factors such as supplier processes and the relationship between your two firms will also allow you to take a proactive role in managing that relationship to ensure your continued business success.

CHAPTER **3**

The Project Management Index

 WHY AN ORGANIZATION MIGHT TRACK THIS

Questions Answered

- Are we on schedule on a handful of key projects leaders need to monitor?
- Are we producing quality deliverables or products from this project?
- Will the projects' customers be happy with our performance?
- Are we staying under budget and managing costs?
- Is the scope of the project being managed properly to avoid scope creep?
- Are we following the project plan and using a disciplined project management process?

Why Is This Information Important?

All organizations spend some amount of their time and money on projects. Projects are usually clearly defined activities designed to produce an outcome or product. Typical projects include:

- Purchasing and installing new hardware and software
- Building or remodeling facilities

- Developing new HR programs such as training programs, compensation, or recognition
- Buying another company
- Performing maintenance on major equipment
- Designing and launching a new marketing and advertising strategy
- Developing and implementing a new communications strategy
- Changing the culture
- Purchasing new equipment

Projects are an important and expensive part of work for all organizations. For some organizations I have worked with, like Bechtel or the Army Corps of Engineers, or consulting firms like Deloitte, all their work is projects. Because each project is unique, many organizations have no data on them, they simply rely on verbal reports and custom presentations prepared on each project. In other words, if an executive wants to know how a team is doing getting a project done, she has to ask the project manager a bunch of questions and rely on verbal data. This might be fine if there were one or two big projects that the leaders are overseeing. However, in many large organizations there are too many projects to keep track of this way, and verbal report data is often very unreliable. Project managers always want the boss to think their project is going well. Another common error is to rely not simply on verbal reports or "How's it going?" data but rather on a single metric that looks at one dimension of performance. For most this metric is milestones met. Project managers defined the milestones in the first place, and when they see they are not going to meet one they often reset the due date and then everything is back on schedule. Focusing on a single metric like the schedule drives the wrong behavior as well. If all you measure is whether a due date has been met, corners will often be cut or overtime money spent to make sure the task is completed by the due date. Another common project management metric I see is a ratio of percentage complete with money spent. This is actually better than just looking at milestones or schedules, but it has its problems, too. The money spent is usually a hard and objective number that is difficult to dispute. However, percentage complete is usually a subjective assessment that can easily be manipulated in order that the work completed matches the dollars expended.

So, most existing data on projects is seriously flawed. Many organizations rely on verbal reports that are easy to spin because there is no way for executives to know all the details concerning a project. Tracking a few singular metrics like schedules or milestones or percentage completed to money expended can be easily manipulated as well. Having a comprehensive set of metrics for each project does not work for executives, either, because that means reviewing details of a dozen or more high-level projects to determine their status.

TYPES OF ORGANIZATIONS WHERE THIS METRIC IS APPROPRIATE

This metric is a must for any engineering or consulting organization where all their work is projects. It is probably also important for construction organizations regardless of whether they are building power plants, office buildings, or homes. Any organization that works mostly on projects needs to have this metric so they can easily track all of their projects without having to get separate reports on each one. R&D organizations also mostly do projects and need to have this metric on their dashboards, as do many support departments like information technology and marketing. Okay, what about service, manufacturing, health care, universities, and government organizations? Well, most of them spend some percentage of their time working on projects as well. Hospitals might be converting to electronic medical records or implementing the Baldrige model, which can be viewed as projects. Manufacturing companies are often purchasing and installing new equipment, building new plants, and repurposing factories for other uses. Service organizations like hotels, restaurants, airlines, delivery services, and repair facilities work on big projects as well. In short, this metric is important for any medium to large organization and imperative for those organizations that mostly do projects.

HOW DOES THIS IMPACT PERFORMANCE?

If you are an engineering, consulting, or R&D organization, your performance on projects impacts all other measures on your scorecard, including revenue, profits, customer satisfaction, and employee engagement. Project management organizations like Bechtel, known to be one of the best, need to have real-time balanced measures on how each of their hundreds of projects are being managed. However, even exemplary project management personnel cannot manage the details of 50 to 100 projects. Even trying to monitor the details of 10 projects can be overwhelming. If your organization spends a minimum amount of time and money on projects, your performance on this measure still can have a major impact on many performance measures. For example, I worked with several California State University campuses while they were converting to PeopleSoft. The conversion involved streamlining and improving many of the processes prior to installation of the software. This effort required many months of work and was viewed as a major distraction for many of the staff—and that was just one project. They all knew that things would supposedly be better once the new system was up and running, but they would have to endure a lot of pain to get there. Consequently, the levels of employee engagement in their jobs and the "distraction index" described in Chapter 19 probably turned yellow or red during the course of this project. Another client (Thrivent) was changing and improving all of their operational processes in preparation for a new enterprise resource planning (ERP) system. EDS was in there with a big team doing the project over the course of several years, but there was a big team from Thrivent involved as well, and the project affected the jobs of hundreds of people.

Important projects that are not managed well can have a devastating impact on an organization. Good performance on a project can also have a big positive impact on a number of different measures, or at least the avoidance of any declines in performance. My community health care client AltaMed recently completed construction of a new corporate headquarters building. The company had been renting space on several floors of a nearby office building. The new three-story building was completed early and under budget. The project was very well managed and the move from the rented offices to the new headquarters went off without a hitch. People moved over in several groups as the new facility was ready, and over the course of a few weeks everyone was settled into the new facility with little impact on productivity or other factors. In this case, the project management index on the chief executive officer's (CEO) dashboard looked bright green because the construction project and the others that made up the index were all going well. This high-level analytic that told him everything was going well prevented the CEO from having to micromanage any of the projects.

COST AND EFFORT TO MEASURE

The cost of constructing a project management index will be either low or high. In organizations that just do projects, they often have project data loaded in project management software that tracks milestones, deliverables, expenditures, and other factors. When I worked with the navy's shipyards, they had detailed project plans and budgets, and databases were in place that tracked cost, quality, and schedule on each project. Creating the project management index for the commanding officer was just a matter of having him decide whether he wanted all of the projects in the index (he did) or just the larger ones such as aircraft carriers. Creating the project management index for a navy shipyard like the one in Norfolk, Virginia, or in Pearl Harbor, Hawaii, was fairly simple and low-cost. At one government R&D lab I worked with, the cost was not high because the director elected to only include about four or five big projects in the index. One big project is called the "Master Plan," a multiyear effort to change the campus to get rid of old buildings that are not useful or too expensive to maintain, build new offices and testing facilities to suit the current and future work mix, and change the whole layout of the campus to make it more pedestrian-friendly. There is a detailed project plan for this master plan, and data exists that could be built into the index. The lab works on literally hundreds of R&D projects at any one time and some of them are very small (e.g., an analysis done by one researcher that is completed in a week), whereas others were quite large and involved partnerships with universities and other entities. For the most part, none of these projects were managed using any kind of project management software. Some of the projects were so small that they did not even have a project plan. Consequently, the data on project milestones, expenditures, and deliverables would take a lot of work to track and we would likely get pushback from the researchers, who are used to having a great deal of autonomy. Thankfully, the boss did not want to include all the organization's projects in his index, only the ones that he personally wanted to track.

Another client had a database on milestones or schedule and on costs and expenditures, but they did not have any data on quality, customer satisfaction, or other factors that they thought were important. Consequently, it ended up being a lot of work figuring out a system for measuring quality and customer satisfaction on a project and incorporating that data into the project management index. The factors for determining whether this is a lot of work and money are:

- Number of projects that are included in the index.
- Existence of project management software and data.
- Number of different metrics included in the index.

HOW DO I MEASURE IT?

Every project management analytic I have ever helped a client construct includes three lagging measures of a project's success:

1. **Budget**. The first submetric is designed to tell the project team whether they are staying within budget as they make progress in completing project tasks. A different but related metric I often see is percentage of budget spent divided by percentage of project completed. This is supposed to predict whether the project is likely to run out of money in the future, but as I mentioned earlier, percentage complete is subject to data integrity problems.

2. **Quality of deliverables**. The second submetric is a measure of defects or quality problems with the outputs or deliverables that get produced during the course of a project. The quality metric often drills down to a number of lower-level metrics that might be measures of accuracy, completeness, or following prescribed standards. The customer's level of satisfaction with major deliverables can also become part of the quality measure. This need not be a survey, but it could be as simple as the customer's sign-off on certain products (drawings, specifications, designs, etc.).

3. **Schedule**. The third submetric is a measure of milestones being completed on time. The most common way of measuring the schedule is to calculate the percentage of milestones met. This is actually a poor metric because milestones are usually not equal in importance—if you just track whether a milestone was met, the metric does not take into account the degree of lateness. In other words, an unimportant milestone that was missed by a day counts the same as a major milestone that was missed by eight

weeks. Better alternatives include days late or some weighting factor assigned to each milestone based on how critical it is for project success.

PROCESS AND CHURN: TWO ADDITIONAL METRICS TO CONSIDER IN A PROJECT MANAGEMENT ANALYTIC

The problem with measuring only budget, quality, and schedule to evaluate the success and progress of a project is that they are all *lagging* metrics. In other words, you have to have already gone over budget or missed the deadline or had some defect for data to be recorded. All three are measures of the past. Therefore, it is wise to include at least one *leading* indicator in the project management analytic. A few examples from client case files illustrate how this can be done.

Measuring Process

The Sacramento District of the Army Corps of Engineers (ACOE) put a lot of thought into the project management analytic it developed for its new scorecard, because the analytic represented most of the work being done. One thing that concerned the ACOE about the district was that project managers often did not plan and manage their projects systematically. Part of the reason for this was that the staff had a great deal of experience and was more comfortable just "winging it." A dimension the ACOE wanted to include in the analytic was a measure of the degree to which a systematic process was followed. In addition, the ACOE felt that the process submetric would always be given a weight of 30 percent, so that even if the budget, quality, and schedule showed perfect performance, the overall score for the project would be in the yellow zone.

The process submetric was derived from a checklist of activities that should be done on all projects:

- Involving the customer in creating the project plan;
- Holding weekly project review meetings;
- Entering progress data on a weekly basis using the ACOE project management software;

- Inviting key contractors and partners to project review meetings early on; and
- Keeping the project plan up to date as changes occur.

Measuring Churn

Two other clients (Northrop Grumman Newport News Shipbuilding and U.S. Navy Aircraft Carrier Maintenance Team One) came up with another leading indicator that they now include in their project management analytic: churn. *Churn* is defined as changes to key project parameters (such as scope, deliverables, budget, and schedule). What both organizations had found through research is that poor project planning led to excessive churn, which led to poor performance on project outcomes like cost and schedule. Hence, churn was a good leading metric to include in the analytic.

Some amount of churn is normal and expected, because it is impossible to estimate all the work that will be needed to maintain a vessel as big as an aircraft carrier. However, experienced project managers were able to define reasonable red, yellow, and green ranges for churn, based on past projects. This was also a measure that was easy to track because every time there was a change to a project, the information had to be updated in the project planning records.

Another example that illustrates the churn metric on a smaller scale involves a neighbor of mine who had his house torn down a year ago and is building a new one on the same lot. The move-in date has been changed many times and the scope of the project has changed as well. Some of the changes were a result of alterations requested by my neighbor, but others were caused by the contractor's poor planning, poor-quality work, or failure to meet building codes. The churn metric on this construction project would clearly be in the red zone. If my neighbor had a process metric, that would probably be red as well.

Benefits of Measuring Process and Churn

By making process or churn part of your project management analytic, you will have a more balanced measure of project performance. To roll each individual project up into the overall performance metric, you need to decide which projects get counted and roll up the boss's scorecard. One client measures only the top five most important and costly projects each year in his project management analytic. In contrast, the Norfolk Naval Shipyard counts all projects, but it assigns them a weight based on their size (measured in labor-days) and importance to the navy. This way, the major-dollar projects and other important projects do much more to drive the overall project management analytic than do the smaller ones. However, the commanding officer still wants to know if a small project is in trouble, so even though a small one might not move the overall analytic into the yellow or red, it would certainly turn the little warning light on the analytic red. This is the cue for the commanding officer to drill down into project-level data to locate which one is showing poor performance.

MEASURING RISK ON PROJECTS

A sixth dimension that you might consider adding to your project management index is risk. Changes are made all the time as projects progress, and sometimes project personnel wisely choose to do something that might add to the scope (churn) and cause a deadline to be missed (schedule) because the additional work prevents future problems. This concept is important to a group I work with in the Los Angeles Fire Department (LAFD). They have a division called Supply and Maintenance (S&M) that does maintenance and repair work on the fire department's trucks, cars, ambulances, and fire engines. Manager Mark Clark explained to me that managing risk is an important part of the mechanics' job. They have to make decisions on replacing parts or doing additional work on a vehicle if it means reducing the risk that the vehicle will fail in the field. Sometimes this might make a customer mad because his truck was not done when promised due to the extra work. However, making these decisions is a big part of the day-to-day work of managing maintenance and repair projects. The LAFD S&M division liked the idea of a project management index that summarized all the work going on in the shop and was not really concerned with churn or process. What the division was concerned with was risk, believing that that factor needed to be measured as part of the index to offset the lagging indicators on quality, cost, and schedule. There is more information on measuring risk in Chapter 5.

VARIATIONS

I've seen all sorts of variations in creating indices to track project performance. In fact, just about every client develops their own metric tailored to the types of projects they do and what type of project data they have available. One really great idea one client came up with was to assign a differential weight to each of the submeasures in the project management index, which were budget, quality, and schedule. One client that repairs jets for airlines negotiates on the weights of these factors with the customer on each job. For example, one airline might decide to put a low weight on budget and a high weight on schedule, and is willing to pay the repair company overtime to get its plane back in service quickly. On this project, the repair company might establish weights of 50 percent on schedule and 25 percent each on quality and budget. Another client is having financial trouble and is willing to have the repair company take its time getting the plane fixed, as long as the company does it as cheaply as possible. For this client, the weights might be 60 percent on budget or cost and 20 percent on the remaining factors. The point is, the boss can view one high-level analytic that tells her about overall project performance so she can drive the right priorities from employees who are linked to what is important to the customers. When this was first discussed, the customers typically said all three factors (budget, quality, and schedule) were equal in importance. However, after more discussion they admitted that often one of the three was more important and deserved a higher weight than the others. The weights were not done by client, but by aircraft. A single airline could have one aircraft in the shop where schedule was the number one priority and another aircraft where quality was the most important.

The good thing about this approach is that it forces the customer to define its priories up front, and it tells the project team which of the three factors (budget, quality of deliverables, or schedule) is most important. At the end of each project, customers fill out a report card grading the vendor on how it performed for each factor. The grades are then multiplied by the weights to arrive at a total project score. Each project score is then given a weight in the overall analytic based on the dollar value of the project and the dollar value of the account. This brings up another variation that usually makes sense: assigning differential weights to each of the projects in the index. To keep it simple let's say the CEO's dashboard included a project management index with four projects that feed into the index. Project no. 1 is implementation of a new ERP system, a multiyear, multimillion-dollar effort that is given 50 percent weight in the index. Project no. 2 is implementing a new succession planning process for executives, given a weight of only 15 percent; project no. 3 is opening a new warehouse in St. Louis, Missouri, given a weight of 20 percent; and project no. 4 is creating a new marketing campaign for a renewed old product that has always been a solid revenue generator (15 percent). The assignment of a weight is not just based on the dollar cost of the project but how important it is to the organization's success. Succession planning might get a much higher weight if most of the executives are in their sixties and no replacements have been groomed.

FORMULA AND FREQUENCY

Most organizations do track projects, but rarely do they roll up project data into an index for senior leaders. The following is a description for creating a project management index that allows executives to assess the health of key projects on a regular basis without having to review detailed data and hundreds of charts:

Step 1: Select projects to include in the project management analytic (three to eight is best unless your entire organization is made up of projects).

Step 2: Assign percentage weights to each individual project based on cost, time, risk, and criticality for organizational success.

Step 3: Decide on factors to include in the project management index:

- Costs
- Schedule and milestones
- Quality and customer satisfaction
- Risk
- Churn
- Process

Step 4: Assign percentage weights to each one of the factors selected. This can be done overall for all projects or done differently for each project as in the aircraft repair company example.

Step 5: Develop numerical targets or ranges (e.g., +/−10 percent).

Step 6: Assess performance against targets.

Step 7: Compute individual project performance, multiply by percentage weight of each project, and combine into the index.

Generally this is a monthly metric, but it could be tracked daily and weekly as well, depending on the number and types of projects. A recent homebuilder client had milestones completed every day, so the CEO monitored key project statistics daily.

TARGETS AND BENCHMARKS

Absolute targets do not make sense for many of these project management measures. Most of these measures have a target where in the middle is the green zone, with two yellow zones and two red zones. For example, when looking at budget, if you underspend your budget by a big margin, this is a red flag, possibly indicating that you padded the original budget or that not enough progress is being made. The same is true with quality to a lesser extent. If you do more than the customer is willing to pay for in terms of quality, that is a problem, just as defects or rework are a problem. If you decide to include churn as one of your PMI metrics, targets for churn also work this way. Having zero churn is probably red, and having too much of it is bad as well. The key to setting good targets for all of the project management index submetrics is to gather enough of your own history to have stable baselines and benchmark others that do similar projects to see what they have for targets.

BENEFITS OF DATA

There are some huge benefits of having one high-level composite metric that tells leaders about their key projects:

- More integrity in the data by having actual numbers to review rather than listening to words describing the status of projects.

- No time spent reviewing projects where everything is going fine.
- Up to 75 percent reduction of time spent in project review meetings.
- Real-time project performance data that can be reviewed at any time without waiting for a meeting.
- Ability to drive the right priorities by weighting submetrics.
- Ability to integrate customer priorities with project priorities.
- Assessment of future factors such as risk, churn, and process so the analytic is a mixture of past (percent, quality, schedule) and future.
- Ability to add or delete projects as old ones get completed and new ones begin.
- Ability to have different submetrics and weights for each project.
- Avoidance of reviewing each individual project by having data stacked in layers from the highest-level analytic to individual project data.
- Forcing of a more disciplined approach to planning and managing important projects because of quantifiable tracking of performance in real time.

CHAPTER **4**

The Enterprise Excellence Index

 WHY AN ORGANIZATION MIGHT TRACK THIS

Questions Answered

- Are employees supportive of the enterprise excellence initiatives we are implementing?
- Are people learning the concepts of these programs?

Why Is This Information Important?

Organizations waste millions of dollars each year on programs and practices that don't work, frustrate employees, and infuriate customers. It doesn't matter whether your job is in business, government, health care, or education: everyone will have experienced at least some of these programs. The mystery is how every one of these practices sometimes produces great results for a handful of organizations and fails for the rest. This chapter will provide useful tips on spotting bad programs and practices and for eliminating the waste and making other initiatives successful.

WHY TRASH ALL THESE SACRED COWS?

Well, first of all, it is fun to challenge sacred cows. In fact, according to authors Drs. Robert Kriegel and David Brandt, "Sacred cows make the best burgers."[1] Coming down on something most people are already down on is easy and ruffles very few feathers. Attacking the things people believe in, support, and are emotionally attached to gets a good reaction, however. Sure, you do get people mad, and they may attack you in response for trashing the program their company sells or is enamored with. However, at least you get a reaction and may cause people to think. If nothing else, it might encourage them to improve their programs and practices to make them more successful.

One of the most important skills to learn in life is to become a critical thinker—in other words, to be able to critically evaluate information, assess its truthfulness and accuracy, and decide whether you need to take action or use it in your life. We are bombarded with advertising messages at home and at work. People are constantly trying to sell us a product, service, or idea. Even those of us who pride ourselves on having good internal BS detectors are scammed every now and then. One of my doctors frequently tries to prescribe tests I don't want or need.

We all claim to want the truth, but what we really want is hope. We want to believe that that new exercise machine purchased after watching a late-night infomercial will really give us six-pack abs. We really want to believe that a new president is going to fix our country, or a new CEO is going to fix our company. We all really want to believe that the financial planner we hired will invest our money wisely so we will be able to retire. Whether you are smart or not so smart, we all are human beings, and we all fall for some product, service, or program that does not really live up to its promises. Many of my friends are accountants, and they all say that doctors are pretty much the worst group of people when it comes to finances. As a group, I would guess that most doctors are a lot smarter than your average citizen, so it is puzzling that they are so bad with money. On the other hand, most of my accountant friends are not too handy with power tools. Even routine maintenance like painting a room, changing a light switch, or waxing a car can present a formidable challenge to those who might be more comfortable with balance sheets and computing alternative minimum taxes.

We are all bad at something, just as we all have areas of expertise. We are most prone to buying nonsense if it comes from an area where we have little or no expertise. Try selling CRM software to a group of sales managers and they may buy it, because most don't know anything about software. Try selling it to IT specialists, and you might have a lot of hard questions to answer. Try selling a new CT scanner to a group of radiologists and there will be a very different sort of questions than those that come from the hospital administrators and procurement people.

Smart business people are no different than talented plumbers, smart doctors, brilliant artists, or intelligent engineers; we are all susceptible to buying a line of bull from someone adept at selling it. The thing that sells most business people more than anything else is fear of losing out to the competition. Want to sell to Pepsi? Tell them that Coke is already a customer. Want to sell to Mayo Clinic? Tell them Cedars-Sinai and Cleveland Clinic are already using your program. Getting endorsements from a few brand-name clients goes a long way to selling your program or practice to others. We all tend to trust our peers in the business as well. Most professionals belong to associations and groups where they interact with their peers in other organizations. If most of the sales vice presidents at the conference are raving about a particular sales training program, you are more likely to try it yourself. If everyone at the Conference Board meeting is talking about how one-question customer surveys have saved them money and improved customer satisfaction, you will probably start doing them as well. This herd mentality starts early when some kid in third grade has the cool shoes or toy and continues on through the rest of our lives.

TYPES OF ORGANIZATIONS WHERE THIS METRIC IS APPROPRIATE

This measure is worth considering for any large organization: hospitals, universities, public school systems, manufacturers, service companies, military, and government. No one is immune from the lure of these programs that are mostly peddled by consultants with books and training programs and impressive credentials. As organizations grow they become harder to manage, and results that were easy to achieve in their earlier years become more elusive. Large organizations also become sales targets for consultants and salespeople because they have both the resources and the perceived needs. If yours is an organization that never buys any of these management programs or develops your own, there is no need for this metric on your scorecard. However, those organizations are quite rare, and even if you are not implementing one of these programs today, you no doubt will in the future. These enterprise excellence initiatives are not just management programs with three letters either. They are often associated with expensive new software. I recall working with a big insurance company in Minneapolis that had contracted with Ross Perot's former company to redesign all of their operational processes and implement new software to improve efficiency and reduce costs. This was about a three-year project and there were a lot of Perot consultants there for months on end, racking up those billable hours. If I were CEO of this company, I would want a way to track whether this initiative was going well, other than by looking at the monthly bills I got from the consultants and milestones completed on their project plan.

HOW DOES THIS IMPACT PERFORMANCE?

The most direct way these programs impact performance is that they increase your costs considerably. Most of these programs cost at least a few hundred thousand dollars, and it is not uncommon for organizations to spend millions on them. The biggest cost is not the checks you write to the consultants or software company, but the disruption caused to the organization. Often the entire place is in turmoil with all the extra meetings, training programs, committees and teams, and having to put other projects on hold. One way to get an accurate measure of this is to use the distraction index described in Chapter 19. At least this will tell you how many hours per week are spent on improvement programs. Computing the cost is a simple matter of multiplying employee hours by the average compensation. These programs also have a big impact on employee engagement. For every three people who think these programs add value and are important, there are seven who think they are a waste of time and regret having to take time away from job tasks to participate. For some employees, these programs are interesting and participation provides them with feelings of hope that the organization is really becoming a better place to work and one that produces better results. For others, just the opposite feelings occur. If successful, these programs can actually improve many aspects of performance. Cycle times will improve, costs will go down, productivity will increase, customer satisfaction will go up, profits will increase, and your stock value might actually go up. A big reason you need this metric is to see if any of these promised results actually do occur, along with measures of success along the way.

Another big cost of management programs is a loss of senior management credibility. If people view many of these programs as being a waste of time, and if time reveals that results do not improve, the judgment of senior management may be questioned, with people wondering how they could have fallen for these snake-oil-salesman consultants. The risks are high for all of these programs, but so are the potential rewards.

COST AND EFFORT TO MEASURE

The amount of effort needed to track the effectiveness of the enterprise excellence index is minimal compared to the cost of the programs, but the overall cost would fall in the medium range. You will need to agree on an overall approach for all programs, and then decide how to assign weights and track the performance of each individual program. You may employ the assistance of the consultants who are helping you develop and implement the program, but that might be like hiring the fox to watch the henhouse. A good place to start with outcome metrics is to go back to the presentation that sold you on the program in the first place. Chances are there are a lot of promised results in that PowerPoint deck and examples of results achieved by others. One consulting firm just made a pitch to one of my clients, offering a money-back guarantee if its program did not result in at least a 25 percent increase in customer satisfaction. Of course the program will cost $200,000 the first year, and there are some pretty stringent requirements that must be met in order to invoke the guarantee. There is also nothing mentioned about longer-term impact. If the consultant is promising cost savings, that should be one of the metrics; if the consultant is promising that customer or patient satisfaction will improve, that should be one of the metrics.

Coming up with good outcome metrics should not be hard. The more challenging measures will be the input and process measures. You may also have a political challenge trying to show any hard outcomes linked to programs that are softer and more philosophical in nature, like learning organization (Peter Senge ideas) or teaching everyone the habits of successful people. When I suggested to a military client I worked with that we should try to measure the impact of the millions of dollars it spent teaching everyone these seven magic habits of success, I was met with rejection: "We just have to accept on faith that this program will make us better."

HOW DO I MEASURE IT?

Your first task is to identify the initiatives that are currently being implemented in your organization and establish a weight for each one, depending on its importance and the resources needed for implementation. One aerospace organization had two major initiatives and two minor ones being implemented, so the company set the weights as follows:

**Example Enterprise Excellence Analytic
(Aerospace Company)**

Lean Six Sigma	Activity-Based Management	Knowledge Management	ISO
35%	15%	30%	20%

Activity-based management and ISO were both initiatives that had been going on for a number of years, and the company was more in the maintenance mode with these programs. However, major resources were being dumped into both Lean Six Sigma (a combination of Lean and Six Sigma) and knowledge management, so it was important to put a high weight on those. Those two initiatives were also deemed important because they were of interest to senior management due to the potential bottom-line payoff.

A hospital wanted to have a metric on the CEO's scorecard that told him how well the various initiatives were going. They had a vision of winning a Baldrige Award and achieving Magnet status, and were also working to maintain Joint Commission certification, which is now done by surprise audit. There was a great deal of overlap in the standards and results assessed in all three of these initiatives, but the CEO wanted to look at them separately and collectively, so this was the type of situation where an analytic metric makes perfect sense. The enterprise excellence analytic we constructed looked like the one in the following table. The process of getting the organization aligned with the Baldrige criteria is given the most weight because the Baldrige model is very comprehensive and covers all hospital processes and results. Improving alignment with Baldrige will also help meet the standards for the Joint Commission and Nursing Magnet.

Example Enterprise Excellence Analytic (Hospital)

Joint Commission	Baldrige	Nursing Magnet
25%	50%	25%

Once you have identified the improvement initiatives and assigned a weight to each one based on its importance, the next task is to figure out how to measure whether the programs are successful. As with any process, there are four categories of metrics that should go into the enterprise excellence analytic: inputs, processes, outputs, and outcomes. Some examples of each of these four types of measures for currently popular improvement initiatives are shown in the next section.

KNOWLEDGE MANAGEMENT METRICS

A big challenge for many organizations today is to document and pass on important knowledge to others so they can benefit from it. A long time ago this was a challenge as well, so they invented books, which still remain the major way that most knowledge is documented and passed on to others. Today we also have electronic databases that provide us with access not only to books, but papers, research, videos, and online diagnostics. In a study done by the American Productivity and Quality Center, many companies that are implementing knowledge management (KM) systems have no way to measure their effectiveness. They point to traditional lagging measures like growth and profits, but it would be a real stretch to suggest that a company's growth is mostly due to their knowledge management program. Organizations that are spending thousands or even millions on KM need to have a metric on executives' scorecards that tell them whether the program is adding value. "How's it going?" data is not sufficient for any effort this large and expensive.

An effective knowledge management analytic should be composed of four types of data:

1. **Awareness or input measures**. Employee awareness of what types of knowledge need to be documented, KM tools and system, benchmarking data from KM systems in other companies, forms and processes for documenting knowledge.

2. **Behavior or process measures**. Attendance at KM training, participation in KM activities such as committees or teams, making presentations, leading knowledge sharing sessions, creating KM databases, documenting knowledge, researching best practices, building a KM web site or database.

3. **Output measures**. Measures of the quality, accuracy, completeness, and timeliness of KM outputs like best practices documentation, decision-making aids, white papers, presentations, and training materials.

4. **Outcome measures**. Adoption of best practices by others, awards and recognition for KM system, impact of new knowledge on key outcome measures or organizational performance, such as new product sales, productivity, growth, profits, cost reduction, or quality improvement.

A navy client of mine searched for the best practices when it came to KM metrics and found that most of the activity measures that various companies tracked did not correlate to any meaningful outcomes. These companies were counting the number of databases that were built, web site hits on those databases, presentations made, and knowledge sharing meetings held. There was lots of activity, but no real evidence that any of these things improved performance in the company. The KM metric they were most impressed with was the approach being used by Ford Motor Company. Ford's approach was to measure only outputs and outcomes. They had been down the road of measuring activity and found that all this did was reward people for what could be wasteful effort. What Ford measures for is KM program is how many ideas were developed in one part of the company that are then adopted and implemented in other parts of the company. Ford also measures how the implementation of these approaches and ideas has paid off in bottom-line outcome measures.

Navy Carrier Team One loved the Ford approach, but it was concerned with a metric that was strictly rearview mirror or lagging. This was even a more important concern, since they were just getting started with KM and it would take a while for outcomes to materialize. They came up with a KM analytic that is shown next. You can see that the KM vitality index (or analytic) is made up of two tier two metrics: KSN (knowledge sharing network) commitment (40 percent) and proven practice replication (60 percent). The proven practice replication metric is the lagging measure that they derived from Ford's metric. The KSN commitment metric is the leading indicator of activity and looks at how engaged various parts of the organization are in knowledge management practices. A low level of engagement indicates an organization that sends a few low-level people to the knowledge sharing meetings and those individuals rarely contribute anything or complete any assignments given to them. A high level of engagement is shown when an organization not only has a large number of high-level talented individuals participate, but it is also actively engaged in leadership roles and completing important assignments.

Example Knowledge Management Analytic (Navy Carrier Team One)

KSN Commitment	Proven Practice Replication
40%	60%

Knowledge Sharing Network, Vitality Analytic

Participation	Engagement
25%	75%

LEAN OR SIX SIGMA METRICS

Both Lean and Six Sigma have helped many organizations improve the efficiency of their work processes. Building a metric or analytic that tells senior management how well the programs are working is very similar to the approach I described for creating a KM metric. An analytic for any performance improvement initiative needs to include the four basic categories of metrics already mentioned: input, process, output, and outcome. A Six Sigma or Lean analytic should also evolve with time as your organization more fully deploys the program. Early on the weight on the submetrics should be on inputs and processes, and later evolve toward a greater focus on outputs and outcomes. Some possible metrics to consider in each category are:

- **Input metrics.** Number of people trained and level of training (e.g., green belt, black belt, etc.), processes identified for study and/or improvement, number of teams formed, direction and goals from senior management, resources received, process documentation, performance data.

- **Process metrics.** Number of team meetings held, level of engagement of team members, processes documented, benchmarking studies completed, processes analyzed using proper approach, research and studies conducted using proper methods, use of systematic processes while doing projects, proper documentation of progress, involvement of process stakeholders and owners, knowledge sharing activities with other organizations.

- **Output metrics.** Number of process maps created, research study quality and thoroughness, integrity of process data, sufficient trend data collected, thoroughness of analyses completed, milestones completed on time, budget performance on improvement projects, stakeholder feedback, presentations made, clarity and thoroughness of documentation on improved processes, linkages of Six Sigma or Lean initiatives to company goals and objectives.

- **Outcome metrics.** Cost reductions, cycle time improvements, improvements in safety, waste or scrap reduction, quality or yield improvement, improved margins or profits, increases in employee satisfaction, awards and recognition for team projects, increased resources for Lean or Six Sigma efforts, deployment of Lean or Six Sigma in daily operation of the organization, increased support of effort by employees and management.

Six Sigma and Lean should both have a positive effect on many scorecard metrics in an organization. The test of whether you are measuring the right things in your Lean or Six Sigma analytic is the link to other scorecard metrics. If the Lean gauge is always green and the key measures of company performance like productivity and profitability are consistently red, you probably have the wrong metrics in your Lean or Six Sigma analytic. This metric ought to be a leading indicator or predictor of many measures of organizational success. On the other hand, if company profits increase, you can't just point to your Six Sigma effort as the major reason for that increase.

This same sort of breakdown of four types of metrics could be used for an initiative such as a major new software program, a leadership development program, or any other initiative that costs a lot of money and is supposed to improve organizational performance.

FORMULA AND FREQUENCY

In order to create an enterprise excellence analytic, you have to make sure that senior leaders agree on what is meant by this term and get their views on what to include and not include in this metric. By following the steps outlined next, you can create a customized analytic that suits your own organization.

Step 1 is to create a list of the various enterprise excellence initiatives going on in the organization. A good place to start is to look at all the meetings, teams, and training programs that are going on to make sure you have a complete list of programs. Try to limit the list to the top two to six initiatives or programs that are of concern to senior management.

Step 2 is to assign a percentage weight to each one based on the following factors:

- Cost
- Number and percentage of employees involved

- Time to implement
- Potential return on investment (ROI)
- Urgency

Step 3 is to develop input, process, output, and outcome metrics for each of the two to six initiatives that you want to include in this index. Try to develop four to six key factors that can be measured in each of the four categories and eliminate those metrics that can only be tracked once or twice a year.

Step 4 is to assign weights to each of the four factors based on the life-cycle phase the initiatives are in. A suggested weighting is as follows. The following example is a good straw man that shows how one client assigned weights for a metric to assess a knowledge management program.

If I were constructing a KM analytic for a company just getting started with the program, I would put 70 or more percent of the weight on the input and process measures, since the outputs and outcomes will be few or none in the initial year or two. As the company began to more fully deploy a comprehensive KM system, the weights of the individual metrics in the analytic should evolve to focus more on outcomes and outputs. The following example depicts the changing weights of the individual submetrics:

	KM Analytic Year 1	KM Analytic Year 3	KM Analytic Year 5
Inputs	30%	20%	10%
Processes	40%	30%	20%
Outputs	20%	30%	40%
Outcomes	10%	20%	30%

Step 5 is to assign individual percentage weights to each of the submetrics in each of the four dimensions. Weights should be based on validity of the metric, data integrity, and links of input and process measures to output and outcome measures.

VARIATIONS

One variation I have seen is simply to survey employees and ask them about the value and usefulness of these enterprise excellence programs. You don't need to survey all of them; you could do a sample or even hold some focus groups to get more detailed data on what people think of these programs. Of course, the problem with this data is that it is just people's opinions and often the programs that are interesting and easy get much higher ratings than those that are challenging but produce real results. Surveys also tend to produce the "emperor's new clothes" syndrome, wherein people see value because that is what they have been taught to expect.

Another variation is to skip the input and process metrics, which have a high risk of being false success indicators, and just focus on the outputs and outcomes. This sort of data tends to have much more credibility with management, and ultimately these are the only real measures that matter. The big problem with this approach is that you may be several years and several million dollars into a program before finding out that it does not work.

TARGETS AND BENCHMARKS

Individualized targets need to be set for the enterprise excellence metrics you have selected. However, a good place to start when coming up with targets is the promises made by the vendor who sold you the program. They may promise 30 percent cost reduction, 300 percent ROI, 25 percent improvement in customer satisfaction, or other things. These are good targets to use for defining the "green" level of performance for your own outcome metrics. You might also get some comparative data from other organizations that have implemented similar programs to help develop targets for the input and process metrics.

BENEFITS OF DATA

The benefits of having hard data on each of your enterprise excellence initiatives are huge. Evaluating these expensive and disruptive efforts by relying on anecdotal "How's it going?" data or activity measures like teams and training sessions completed is the height of foolishness, yet quite common. The advantages of having valid measures of these programs are:

- Being able to hold program vendors to promises made during the sales process.
- Pointing out benefits to your board or other stakeholders.
- Showing the effectiveness of the programs to employees, which should help garner their further support.
- Stopping programs early on that are not producing anything besides increased costs and disruptions.
- Having objective data on initiatives that can be reviewed each month to see if progress is being made.
- Adjusting resources and priorities to focus more on programs that are producing results and less on those that are not.

NOTE

1. Robert Kriegel and David Brandt, *Sacred Cows Make the Best Burgers: Developing Change-Ready People and Organizations* (New York: Warner Books, 1996).

CHAPTER **5**

The Risk Index

WHY AN ORGANIZATION MIGHT TRACK THIS

Questions Answered

- Are we prepared for natural and man-made disasters like floods, hurricanes, earthquakes, fires, and acts of war or terrorism?
- Are we taking appropriate and intelligent risks with R&D and innovating new processes?
- Are we managing risks associated with our supply chain?
- Are there risks of major lawsuits from our policies, practices, products, or services?
- Are we managing financial risk properly?
- Are we managing risk associated with legal and regulatory compliance?

Why Is This Information Important?

Life is risky, business is risky; we all take risks every day when getting up in the morning and deciding to go to work. We do what we can, and most of us try to feel safe doing things we have to do to survive and support our families. Yet few individuals or organizations have a good measure of the risks they face on a daily basis. About the only type of risk that does get quantified and assessed is investment risk.

Brokerage and financial management firms tend to have pretty good risk metrics for assessing their own portfolios and those of clients. Insurance companies also usually have pretty good risk metrics that look at the likelihood that they will have to pay a claim. It is shocking when big insurance companies like AIG almost go out of business because of taking too many risks. It appears that greed overpowers fear and risk in most cases. Measuring the risk of your portfolio of investments is certainly important, but the worst that could happen is you could lose some money. Some other risks have much more serious consequences and are harder to assess and prepare for.

Managing risk requires good risk metrics, and there is no perfect way to predict the future or assess our level of readiness, but it can be measured and managed better than it is in many organizations today. Risk is good, just like greed is good, but too much of either can get an organization in big trouble. Measuring risk is important so that organizations can improve. By measuring risk, organizations can apply the right levels of resources to minimize bad risks and encourage good risks like developing new products.

TYPES OF ORGANIZATIONS WHERE THIS METRIC IS APPROPRIATE

Any large organization needs to measure risk. Even government organizations need to measure certain types of risks. Certainly military organizations need to measure risk, as do health care providers; high-risk industries like pharmaceuticals, airlines, energy companies, hospitals, and other organizations that provide critical goods and services.

HOW DOES THIS IMPACT PERFORMANCE?

Disasters of any type can put companies out of business. Both Pfizer and Merck have had to pay millions in damages due to side effects of their drugs. Both companies survived, but a big lawsuit or fine like this can ruin a company. Lawsuits relating to human resource violations can also be devastating. Discrimination lawsuits have also resulted in payment of huge damages. Natural disasters like floods, hurricanes, and earthquakes can destroy facilities, data, equipment, and employees. Many companies in the New York City area took weeks to recover from Hurricane Sandy, and New Orleans has not completely recovered from the flooding years ago during Katrina.

Financial disasters can also be devastating. Too many high-risk mortgages and bad investments put many mortgage companies out of business in the last few years. Big banks and insurance companies like

AIG, Bank of America, and others had to be bailed out by the government to avoid bankruptcy.

Not taking risks can also be hurtful to an organization. Many big companies only reward risk taking when it is successful, and there is a culture of playing it safe. The majority of companies are not innovators but copycats. They wait for others to come up with the innovations and take the risks and then knock off the innovators' products and services. Often by the time the copycat product or service gets to the market, the opportunity for sales may have dried up. Think of the companies that came up with knockoff versions of the iPhone or iPod. Taking intelligent risks is a huge part of the recipe for success for many organizations.

COST AND EFFORT TO MEASURE

The amount of effort and cost required to create a good risk analytic is medium. Most organizations have some financial risk metrics in place that can be used, as well as compliance metrics. However, most of their metrics are simply counts of plans, events, or training attendance. In other words, the metrics do not really provide an accurate view of the level of risk the organization is facing. Most organizations do not have decent risk metrics for:

- Supply chain risk
- Human resources risk
- Emergency preparedness and natural disasters risk
- Intellectual capital risk
- Competitive risk
- Product or service liability risk
- Legal risk
- Customer risk

This is where the cost and effort come in. Coming up with good metrics for these various factors will take time and possibly the expertise of outside consultants. Some risk assessments can be done for free or for relatively low cost, such as the Ready Rating system sponsored by the Red Cross that assesses emergency preparedness.

HOW DO I MEASURE IT?

Step 1 is to do an inventory of available data relating to risk and emergency preparedness to see what metrics you currently have. You might want to evaluate each one of those metrics based on the accuracy of the metric and the integrity of the data. For example, counting the number of fire drills conducted or attendance at emergency preparedness training are easy and objective metrics with good integrity, but they don't really tell you anything about how well the organization is prepared for risks. People could take way too long to get out of the building during a drill, and sleep or do other work through the training, so just counting these activities does not tell you much.

Once you have identified all the metrics on which you currently have data, and assessed the usefulness of these data, **Step 2** is to decide on the types of risks you want to include in your risk analytic. One client brainstormed about eight different types of risks like those in the previous bulleted list and had a team assess each dimension on a scale of 1 to 10 for probability and seriousness. A factor like supply chain risk may get a high score in both probability and seriousness if the organization relies on one supplier for a key raw material used to make their product and the supplier has had some quality problems in the past. Some of the major types of risks to consider include:

- **Supply chain risk**. Many organizations are heavily dependent upon suppliers to manufacture, deliver, sell, and service their products. Many hospitals rely on groups of doctors to treat patients, drug companies to supply medications, equipment manufacturers to provide good-quality equipment, and service suppliers to provide food service, laundry, cleaning, billing, and other services. Hospitals are probably more reliant on suppliers than even most manufacturing companies. Factors that go into assessing supplier risks are the number of suppliers for needed goods and services, supplier performance, availability of alternative suppliers, and dependence on suppliers. Some companies have been working with the same suppliers for so long that it would be a huge risk to switch to someone new who does not know their company and needs.

- **Human resources risk**. Some companies are very dependent upon key people who help develop new products or services, manage the business, keep clients and customers happy, manage production, and market the brand. The loss of a few key people can be devastating to a company. Refer to Chapter 16 on the human capital index for a way to identify your most valuable employees. Then you need to assess the risk of losing each one. Losses may come from death or health problems, early retirement, or someone who decides to go work for a competitor. Most valuable people are contacted by headhunters all the time, and there is always a risk of losing them in spite of the power of your "golden handcuffs."

- **Emergency preparedness and natural disasters**. In this era of global warming–related weather disasters, pandemics, terrorism, and war, it has become more important for organizations to be well prepared for the many emergencies that can occur.

- **Intellectual capital risk**. This is related to human resources risk if someone walks out the door with intimate knowledge of your organization and its products and goes to work for a competitor. However, there are intellectual capital risks that may come from others hacking into your data, which has happened to many organizations in the last few years, or intellectual capital being stolen by a supplier or competitor. Industrial espionage still occurs and is tougher to prevent these days. People are also more mobile now and do not tend to stay at one company for their entire career. Even if it is not intentional, most people can't help but apply knowledge learned at one job to their new job and employer. If you have a lot of proprietary products, services, or practices, this might be a type of risk for you to consider tracking.

- **Competitive risk**. Many organizations fight for market share with existing and emerging competitors. The biggest threats often come from unknown and small competitors that seem to come out of nowhere and steal your market share. Sears did not see Walmart coming until it was too late, and neither did Borders see the threat of electronic books to the bookstore business.

While GM and Toyota are watching Hyundai, Hyundai is watching emerging Indian and Chinese car manufacturers. Competitive risks might also relate to mergers and acquisitions. Perhaps one of your main competitors is a small company that gets bought by a huge corporation and then has the money and clout to squash you. There could also be a risk that your company gets bought, which changes your ability to be agile and customer-focused because of all the new bureaucracy you have to cut through to get stuff done.

- **Product and service liability**. If you are in the medical devices, food, or pharmaceutical business you better have some top-notch lawyers on staff to fight all the liability lawsuits you're likely to encounter. Hospitals and doctors also face huge risks from lawsuits for medical errors and mistakes made. So far I don't think many financial advisors or brokers have been sued for bad advice, but it is a possibility. Each product and service carries its own risks and possible side effects and needs to be balanced with the desire for revenue and profits.

- **Legal risk**. All organizations are subject to the same laws regarding employees, hiring, promotions, safety, financial compliance, and other factors. Some companies are better prepared than others and do a lot more to prevent possible lawsuits. Your history may also figure into the likelihood that you will have future legal problems.

- **Customer risk**. In the early days of my consulting practice I had two big corporate clients who bought about half of my billable days each month for seven or eight years. It was great to have a stable revenue stream and two clients that I really got to know well. It was also a huge risk. When they both decided they didn't need me anymore the same year, there went half my business, and because I was so busy with them, I had not spent much time marketing to others. Putting all your eggs in one basket is a huge risk, even if it is an attractive basket. Many organizations, such as automakers, face customer risks because their customers are getting older and no longer buying cars.

Rolls-Royce experienced this: most owners of their cars were in their sixties or older. Young people viewed Rolls-Royce as an "old man's car" until BMW bought the company and created the Phantom, favored by young music stars and entrepreneurs. Sales went from a few hundred cars a year to several thousand, and Rolls-Royce has also expanded its appeal to other countries besides the United Kingdom and the United States. China now has one of the most successful Rolls dealerships in the world. Moscow is not far behind. With the release of the Ghost in 2011 and Wraith in 2013, Rolls-Royce now has a broad array of models that appeal to different demographics. Another type of customer risk is that your customer could go out of business or have financial problems. When I worked with NORDAM, an aircraft repair company, it was always at risk for a customer to file bankruptcy, which is fairly common in the airline business.

After deciding on the factors to include in your risk index, you have to decide how to measure your performance. The types of metrics I usually see when measuring any kind of risk tend to be the same:

- **Knowledge**. A big factor that impacts how well organizations respond to crises is their level of knowledge. Knowing what to do before and after an emergency can sometimes make a life-or-death difference. In California, the news media tries to do its part in educating us about what to do in an earthquake. In spite of these efforts, there is still a lot of confusion. Should you stand in a doorway, run outside, stay in your bed and cover your head, crawl underneath a heavy table? Many of us are not sure. Knowledge of what managers or competitors are up to is also a major factor in preventing risks. Knowledge can be measured via a test, but it should not be measured by training attendance or eyeballs. Many people attend the training, read the brochure, look at the poster in the hallway, and soon forget the whole thing.

- **Preparedness**. Preparedness is assessed via audits, drill performance, simulations, plans, and processes. The Red Cross

Ready Rating assessment is a comprehensive survey on a wide variety of topics relating to emergency preparedness. What's good about it is the low cost; what's bad about it is that it is a survey. Surveys are not the most reliable way of assessing many of these factors. Having an audit combined with a survey is probably going to provide a more accurate assessment.

- **Risk scoring of products and services**. A good measure of the potential liabilities associated with your products and services is to do a portfolio review once a quarter or so and do a risk assessment on each of them. The products or services might be given a weight depending on the revenue and profit that comes from them, and each one could be given a potential liability score based on the number of potential problems, the seriousness of those problems, and the probability that they will occur. For a prescription drug like Lipitor or Crestor, we might give either drug a high weight because of the revenue in sales and profits generated, and a high (bad) score for the number of potential side effects, but a low score based on the seriousness of the side effects—for example, muscle soreness (1) versus death (10)—and a low score based on the number of people affected in studies. By doing this assessment of each of the products and services in your portfolio you can come up with an overall risk number and try to keep it in the safe or green zone.

- **Customer risk scoring**. Another factor that might be scored at least quarterly is your portfolio of customers. A baby food manufacturer I worked with is a private label producer for Walmart. Walmart is a very successful and stable company, but they are also known for not being loyal to suppliers if a better deal comes along. Having one customer like this ought to put this company's customer risk gauge in the red zone. The types of factors that would get assessed in a customer risk evaluation are the percentage of business that comes from the supplier, the degree to which they are profitable, the financial health of the customer, and the number and variety of customer types and markets you sell to. Companies like BMW lessen their risk by having customers who range from billionaires who buy a Rolls-Royce Phantom convertible for $450,000 to students who drive a Mini Cooper that their parents paid $20,000 for. Having a diverse portfolio of customers and products that meet their needs dramatically lessens a company's risk.

- **Competitor risk scoring**. Assessing competitors is all about sizing up the degree to which they are a threat today and tomorrow. I am shocked at how many Fortune 100 companies do not have good competitive databases that are updated all the time with the most current data. They seem to stumble on competitor intelligence and have it stored in many different locations and databases. In order to get a handle on competitive risk, think about assessing each competitor on factors such as new products they have in the pipeline, relationships with important customers, partnerships with other firms such as distributors, retailers, or suppliers, financial health, and projected growth.

- **Human resources risk**. I observed a good approach for quantifying this at one of my clients. It was focused on the top 100 people in the company, a mix of executives and technical professionals. Each one already had a human capital score (see Chapter 16) based on competencies, traits, accomplishments, and relationships, and they also were assigned a risk score of 0 to 100 (higher means greater likelihood of leaving). The risk score was based on health (see Chapter 20, wellness index), personal situation (age, married, divorced, kids at home, family in area, estimated net worth), opportunities for advancement, marketability outside (would this person be sought after by competitors or others?), and price of divorce—what it would cost for them to leave. These factors were used to score the relative risk of each person leaving, and a risk mitigation plan was put into place to help ensure that they lowered the risk of losing key people. Compliance with the risk mitigation plan also was figured into the overall risk score for each person. The aggregate gauge was a combination of the value of the person to the company along with the risk of losing them. What they didn't account for is how happy or disgruntled the person is. This is the main risk factor. I have several investment banker neighbors who are really mad at their firms, disgruntled with the way the industry is going, and who have enough money to never have to work again. These guys are high-risk and very valuable to their firms.

■ **Risky behaviors**. Another type of metric to consider for your risk analytic is employee behavior. Coming up with new product or service ideas is a desirable behavior you could track. Having an affair with your subordinate is an undesirable risky behavior, as is getting kickbacks from suppliers, such as Super Bowl tickets, invitations to golf outings, and other similar privileges. Organizations I have worked with also track failures as an indication of risk taking. If no one is taking any risks, there are no failures and no lessons to be learned. If there are too many colossal failures, they are taking too many risks and the consequences could be devastating.

VARIATIONS

I have laid out a fairly complicated and comprehensive way of measuring the various types of risks an organization may encounter and an assessment of how well prepared they are to handle them. For a small to medium-size organization or one that is in a very low-risk business, an annual risk assessment that looks at your insurance, regulatory compliance, and emergency preparedness might be enough. However, keep in mind that all organizations experience risk, and the smaller you are, the harder it is to recover from emergencies or disasters. Even with an organization as small as mine (one guy working out of the spare bedroom), I need to track my level of risk. I was almost out of business when I lost my two biggest clients in the same year and had nothing in the pipeline. A small business might just try to diversify its portfolio of products and services, customers, and revenue streams.

FORMULA AND FREQUENCY

As a straw man to start with, consider the following factors and weights:

Emergency preparedness/natural disasters	15%
Knowledge	5%
Plans	5%
Drill performance	5%
Customer portfolio risks	10%
Diversity	5%
Customer stability	5%
Product and service liabilities (risk × revenue)	20%
Human resource risk	15%
Supply chain risk	10%
Competitor risk	10%
Legal risk	10%
Innovation/risky behavior	10%

BENEFITS OF DATA

Most organizations I work with measure risk via annual audits, failures, counting butts in seats in training, and counting activities like fire drills conducted or databases backed up. In short, most organizations really don't have much information on their level of risk. Data is spread throughout many different databases and is often based on verbal reports rather than quantifiable numbers. Organizations have really good daily measure of things like cash flow, costs, and revenue but have little and/or unreliable data on risk. The analytic proposed here will require a fair amount of work to construct, but I find that a lot of organizations have available at least half of the information for what I am proposing somewhere in the company.

The benefit of getting real daily, weekly, and monthly feedback on the level of risk is that it can be managed. Imagine how easy it would be to measure your health if every risky or healthy action provided you with feedback on whether it added or deleted minutes from your life span. We would spend a lot more time eating our vegetables and running than we would sitting at the bar pounding margaritas and devouring a steak burrito. With good and frequent risk metrics, organizations can make better, and more timely, informed decisions about actions to maximize revenue and growth while minimizing the risk of failure.

CHAPTER 6

The Opportunity Management Index

 WHY AN ORGANIZATION MIGHT TRACK THIS

Questions Answered

- How many leads or suspects have we identified and what is the quality of each lead?
- How many suspects or leads turn into qualified leads?
- What is the strategic value of each opportunity we have identified?
- How many qualified leads have we converted to prospective customers?
- How many prospective customers turn into actual customers?
- How do we assess the quality of new customers to determine their value to the organization?

Why Is This Information Important?

Managing the sales or opportunity management process in an organization is a big cost to an organization and is a process that is often managed with anecdotal data. Salespeople are almost always optimists and every prospect is a potential huge customer. For leaders, it is really tough to get an accurate picture of how best to invest resources into opportunities and which ones to take a pass on. Sales calls, travel expenses, and proposals can all add up to big money that could lead to huge losses unless the outreach and business development process is accurately measured and managed. Forecasting is a very inexact process, and even the best salespeople are wrong more often than right when developing a forecast. That deal that they thought was never going to happen is the one that comes through, and the sure thing just does not materialize. The opportunity management index helps to track both the quality and quantity of suspects, leads, and prospects along the entire pipeline, so that accurate decisions can be made about moving forward and making additional investments or dropping the prospect.

Forecasting future sales and customer loyalty is an extremely important part of strategic planning for most organizations. It impacts hiring, recruiting, budgeting, facilities, information technology, and cash flow. I've sat in numerous weekly sales meetings where the boss goes around the table and asks each salesperson to report on their prospects and hopes of getting more business from existing accounts. The information presented is always slanted toward the positive: "I feel certain we are going to be able to close the deal this month, Bill." The only real data presented that is quantified is number of prospects, proposals, and so forth. Most of the information is words, not numbers. Ideally the words should be used to explain the numbers, not replace them.

TYPES OF ORGANIZATIONS WHERE THIS METRIC IS APPROPRIATE

Certainly all organizations that sell to other businesses or government organizations need this metric. Selling to large organizations is complex and there are multiple levels of potential customers who care about different things. Businesses that sell to consumers might also need this metric to manage the process of selling to retailers or distributers. Trying to get a big company like Target or Costco to carry your product can be an enormous amount of work. I have worked with several government organizations that developed an opportunity management index. The Cold Regions Research and Engineering Laboratory (CRREL) in Hanover, New Hampshire, gets a big portion of its work from the Army Corps of Engineers. However, that is not their only client. They do work for the National Science Foundation, universities, other foundations, and companies. Deputy Director Dr. Lance Hansen and his boss, Director Dr. Bert Davis, were concerned with measuring and managing the pipeline of future work. Scientists and engineers spent money and time going to meetings, conferences, and workshops and participating in committees for professional associations. Everyone intuitively believed that this sort of outreach was good for building future business. Meeting new people and collecting their business cards could lead to future work for the laboratory, or it could not. Many of the scientists could describe examples of meeting someone at a conference five years or more ago, exchanging cards, and five years later that individual became a good client with an interesting project. While that was surely true, there were many other people they met and exchanged e-mails and even papers with who never became paying clients. In order to measure and manage this process more systematically, CRREL decided to develop an index that tracked the same sorts of things for-profit companies track: contacts, prospects, qualified leads, demonstrations, proposals, and awards of new projects.

HOW DOES THIS IMPACT PERFORMANCE?

Trying to fill your pipeline with quality prospects and possible new customers is a never-ending task. Nothing lasts forever, and that relationship you have with a key client may someday end abruptly. I lost my two biggest clients in the same year after eight years of working together. We parted friends; one company just had a change in direction, and the other felt that I had trained them so well that they no longer needed my help. That's the goal of any good consultant, to work yourself out of a job. However, while I was busy racking up those billable days each month for years, I had not been doing much marketing and had nothing in the pipeline when the business dried up with my two biggest clients. No matter how good business is right now, it is important to keep up the marketing efforts and focus on building a backlog of possible new business. I am just one guy, so it is challenging to balance marketing with billable work and with product development like writing books and articles. This balance is much easier to achieve in companies that have armies of full-time people to do marketing, sales, and account management. However, even in organizations with large sales staffs, the metrics they track are often flawed or drive the wrong behavior.

We all know that you get what you measure, so if you incentivize sales dollars, salespeople will focus on bringing in as many as they can. I recall working with IBM in New York City, which at the time was changing the way they measured and incentivized their sales force. Paying salespeople for sales dollars was causing them to sell hardware (high price) versus software (high margin). Paying them for the dollar value of the sale also caused them to sometimes recommend extras that customers later found out they didn't need. Remember when Sears Automotive Centers got in trouble for doing this? IBM was changing the measurement of their salespeople from revenue to profit margin and customer satisfaction. This did a lot to drive different behavior from the sales force, which was to IBM's benefit. Salespeople were now pushing high-margin software and services and never recommending anything that the customer did not really need. Customer satisfaction went up, as did profit margins.

Being able to do more accurate forecasting is another way a good opportunity management index can help an organization improve performance. Having reliable estimates of future business allows an organization to plan for future resources such as raw materials, employees, facilities, equipment, and capacity. Having solid data on future business also has a big impact on spending. Organizations these days have to be selective about whom they decide to pursue as potential customers. A lot of money and time can be wasted going after business that will never materialize. I used to respond to posted government requests for quotations (RFQs) and requests for proposals (RFPs), and never got one of them. I learned over the years that most of these things are already locked in with a preferred or incumbent supplier and that the organization is just going through the motions with the RFP when it already knows who it wants to do the work. Some consultants actually help write the RFP so that no one can meet the requirements except them. Being on the inside and doing this is a good place to be—an outsider does not stand a chance and can go broke writing proposals that have zero chance of resulting in work.

Having an accurate measure of the number and quality of leads and prospects can dramatically improve an organization's ability not only to land more business, but also to land the right kind of business. It can also help to back away from opportunities that may end up as big liabilities or prevent you from bringing in customers or accounts that are not profitable and cause much distress for your people. When my client decided to tell GM it was not going to sell to GM anymore, everyone breathed a sigh of relief.

COST AND EFFORT TO MEASURE

The cost and effort to develop an opportunity management index for most organizations is quite low. Most medium to large organizations have CRM and sales software that is used to document and track progress with opportunities. Much of the data from this software will end up in the index. In an organization like CRREL that I mentioned earlier, this measure was a lot of work to establish. The research organization had never measured prospecting or pipeline before, except with "How's it going?" data. Systems had to be developed for tracking and recording contacts, qualifying leads, and keeping track of follow-up activities. Staff had to be trained to use the new tools, and the organization had to establish a new level of discipline for a process that had never been measured or managed before. This took some time and effort. The cost was minimal, however. No new software or tools were required.

Most organizations with a dedicated sales force will find that creating an opportunity management index is only a slight change from the metrics they are probably already tracking. One challenge is getting salespeople to consistently evaluate the quality of their leads and prospects and the amount of authority they have in making buying decisions.

HOW DO I MEASURE IT?

There are three types of variables that typically go into the opportunity management index:

1. **Quantity**. Simply counting the number of contacts, leads, prospects, proposals, and so on is an important part of the metric.
2. **Quality**. Prospects, leads, and potential customers are not all equal in size or other desirability factors such as potential for profit, growth, and match with the organization's capabilities.

3. **Probability**. These factors influence the chances that a contact will move through the sales pipeline and go from a name and e-mail address to a paying client or customer.

Most companies have their own vocabulary for what they call possible opportunities as they move through their pipeline. In most cases, there are at least five categories of opportunities:

1. **Contacts**. These are names, business cards, e-mail addresses of individuals from prospective customer organizations, or just the name of a company that could become a potential client or customer. This is the crudest type of opportunity, which could come from someone looking at your web site, requesting more information, encountering someone at a meeting or conference, attending a webinar or trade show booth, and so on. With contacts, the only real measure is number, since there has been no screening yet to see if there is any potential for them to turn into customers. Some companies call these "suspects," as in a crime where everyone is a possible suspect at first.

2. **Prospects**. These are contacts that have moved from just being a name on a business card to having at least the minimal qualifications to be a potential customer. Most companies have a set of screening questions to use in converting contacts into prospects. An approach used by several clients is to have 10 questions for moving a contact into a prospect, with each one worth 10 percent. Each prospect starts out as a 1 and gets a multiplier added for how many of the 10 questions receive a yes answer. So if you have three contacts that get the following scores, it looks like this:

   #1 × 4 yes answers = 4

   #2 × 1 yes answers = 2

   #3 × 9 yes answers = 27

   Another option is to start out with a contact being worth 1.0 and subtract points for each no answer. Therefore a 1.0 contact could become a 0.3 prospect if they can only answer yes to three of the 10 questions. The scoring should take into consideration both the quality of the prospect and the probability of getting future business.

3. **Opportunities**. These are legitimate potential projects, sales, orders, or work with a prospect that has been identified. Just counting these opportunities is kind of meaningless because they range in size and desirability of the customer. When I worked with Ericsson's police radio business in Lynchburg, Virginia (now Harris Corporation's RF Communications Division), we developed a metric called OSV, or opportunity strategic value, for scoring opportunities. The assessment was based on the degree to which the opportunity fit with the company's strengths, strategy, and capacity, as well as other factors such as the brand-name recognition of the potential customer (e.g., the Miami Police Department versus the Lynchburg, Virginia, Police Department), the potential size of the sale, the extent to which the customer's requirements could be met, the location (easy to get to and close versus remote and far away). Each opportunity was given an OSV score of 0 to 100 points. Only those opportunities that received at least 60 points received approval and funding for further effort. Opportunities with scores of 80 and above got a bigger budget and received a team of the best people to move it to the next level. The OSV score made a dramatic change in the prospecting activities of the salespeople. Now they were out looking for high-quality prospects, not just anyone. This new approach to measuring opportunities also dramatically impacted the company's award/loss ratio and profitability. Along with the number of opportunities and the quality of those opportunities (OSV), it is also important to look at the probability of success, which is another factor used to determine if the opportunity is assigned resources and allowed to move forward.

4. **Proposals and pitches**. The next phase in the opportunity pipeline is to move an opportunity to becoming a prospective customer or client. This set of metrics involves counting the number of bids, proposals, or pitches for new business with a clear scope identified. This might be a competitive bidding situation or one where the potential customer is just talking with your organization. Again, the three measures are the number of bids or proposals that are active, the OSV or quality of the opportunity, and the probability of winning the business. At the point where you are

preparing a proposal or having a meeting with the prospective customer to scope out a project or define their requirements, you typically have more information that can be used to modify the OSV or quality score. For example, I recently encountered an opportunity that I initially scoped out as a two- to three-day project involving a one-day workshop followed by a two-day meeting. When asked to prepare a scope of work and proposal, I learned that it was more like a 150-day project and that they needed three consultants. I also learned that they had a set amount of money in their budget and that this was a pilot for their parent organization that might also want to do something similar. The OSV score rose from a low number to a very high number. The sad news is that the probability went from about 90 percent at the initial opportunity identification phase down to about 25 percent when they informed me that they had to issue an RFQ because of the size of the project.

5. **Awards and orders**. Three things can happen with a proposal or pitch for new business: (1) business is awarded to your organization; (2) business is awarded to a competitor; or (3) business is not awarded or the project is canceled. Most organizations only divide wins by proposals or pitches, and then when they look at losses they do further analysis to identify whether they lost to a competitor or the project went on hold or got canceled. What really matters is the percentage of awards and the quality of those awards. The quality is a further revision to the OSV metric discussed earlier. The actual award may be more or less attractive than when you proposed it. For example, there may be a requirement to provide discounted pricing, or the actual order is less than you proposed, or you have to work with some other company and share the new business. In other words, there are all sorts of things that can happen (good and bad) between the time you submit a bid or estimate or proposal and when the final contract is issued.

Two other metrics that are typically included in the opportunity management index are the movement from one part of the pipeline to the next and forecast accuracy. Movement is calculated by tracking the percentage of contacts that turn into prospects, prospects into opportunities, and so on. In other words, what percentage keep moving forward through the pipeline and what percentage fall out, either by your choice or their choice? Forecast accuracy is also an important overall measure to ensure that salespeople are accurate in their probability metrics.

FORMULA AND FREQUENCY

A generic opportunity management index focuses on counting the number of contacts and how each contact moves through a pipeline to either become more valuable or be discarded as an opportunity not worth expending further resources to pursue:

Number of contacts	10%
Prospects	15%
Number of prospects × screening score	10%
Percent of contacts turning into prospects	5%
Opportunities	20%
Number of opportunities × OSV score	15%
Percent of prospects turning into opportunities	5%
Proposals and pitches	25%
Number of proposals or pitches × OSV score	20%
Percent of opportunities turned into proposals	5%
Award/loss ratio	25%
Forecast Aaccuracy	50%

You can tailor these percentage weights to whatever suits your organization, but you want this to be mostly a leading indicator, not a lagging one. As this was designed previously, 70 percent of the weight is on the leading measures, so you can do a better job of measuring and managing opportunities. Depending on your business, some companies track these measures every day. At the very least, you should collect data once a month and update all of your metrics.

VARIATIONS

One simple variation that I often see is just to track the number of contacts, prospects, and so on, and the percentage that move from one level to the next in your pipeline. My friend's son works for Zillow, the real estate site, and is dialing for dollars all day long trying to talk real estate agents into having their name and picture on listings. He knows that he has to make 100 phone calls (contacts) to get 10 prospects to get two opportunities to get one sale. By tracking these various statistics, his boss can make sure that all the salespeople are making enough calls and moving enough forward through the sales pipeline. With a sale like this, quality does not really matter. However, it may matter, because not all real estate agents pay the same. An agent in Beverly Hills or New York City might pay Zillow $400 a month, and one in Fargo, North Dakota, might may $50 a month for the same service. For any organization that sells to businesses, quality is probably more important than quantity. Even with consumers, quality might be important. Bank of America is a lot more interested in acquiring a customer with a $2 million portfolio than my friend's son who spends all of the $3,000 a month he earns and has no savings.

TARGETS AND BENCHMARKS

Targets for the individual metrics in your opportunity management index need to be tailored for your industry and organization. By having enough data on conversions from contact to prospect, and so forth, you can set scientific targets for the early-on metrics. For example, if you know it takes 100 contacts to end up with one sale, you can set your targets based on that. Where it gets tricky is that one really good-quality contact may be more valuable than 100 random business cards you pick up at conferences. My old boss used to encourage us to gather 25 new business cards every time we went to a conference. Half of those cards were either from other consultants or people looking for a job. A very small minority were from prospective clients.

BENEFITS OF DATA

Managing the sales or business acquisition function is fraught with difficulties. Unlike many aspects of organizational performance other than perhaps innovation, sales is part art and part science. We all know salespeople who don't follow any of the standard processes and techniques and are wildly successful. One my favorite colleagues over the years worked as a consultant for Franklin Covey, and we did quite a bit of work together over many years. Jim was one of the top salespeople in the company, but he was a little bit different than the other consultants and account managers. First of all, he drank (even in front of clients at lunch), smoked, swore a lot, dressed like a slob, and was a bit of a curmudgeon. He did not care for the company account managers in their $200 haircuts and $2,000 suits. Yet he sold more than any of his more polished peers because he was supersmart, completely honest with his clients, spoke in plain language versus the typical consultant double-talk, and always gave his clients solid advice, even if it meant buying someone else's product or service. Jim also did not like to be managed and resented his boss trying to oversee his activity. "Just tell me how you are going to measure me, what my targets are, and I will exceed them." He did just that when his boss left him alone. The benefit of measuring the sales and opportunity management process the way I propose in this chapter is that it acknowledges that there are lots of ways to qualify a prospective customer, build their trust, and turn them from a prospect into a client or customer.

Some of the direct benefits clients have experienced using this metric are:

- Identification of the best and worst salespeople.
- Increased revenue from quality customers.
- Improved efficiency of the sales prospecting processes.
- Improved quality of customers, leading to greater profitability.
- Cost savings from not investing in poor-quality opportunities.

CHAPTER **7**

The External Factors Index

WHY AN ORGANIZATION MIGHT TRACK THIS

Questions Answered

- What economic factors such as the markets, real estate, interest rates, or other factors are having a major impact on our organization?
- What are our competitors up to and how might this impact us?
- What kind of threats or challenges will we face in the next few months?
- How are customer needs and priorities changing?
- Are there any emerging trends that we need to capitalize on?
- Is the political situation at the federal, state, and local level for us or against us?
- How are we handling negative events that have occurred in areas of the world where we do business or operate?

Why Is This Information Important?

Leaders are bombarded with information every day on what is going on in the world. You might read the *Wall Street Journal* each morning as my investment banker neighbor does while riding his exercise bike. You might listen to news radio on the way to work in the car or read another paper while on the train. You probably get news items sent to your work computer alerting you to factors such as market performance, politics, or world events. Other facts about the economy, competitors, or market research might be brought to your attention in meetings or in the hallway. The bottom line is that we are exposed to almost constant information about what is going on in the world. The problem is that we are overloaded with too much information, some of it relevant and accurate, and some neither. Another problem is the information tends to come as words and phrases, not quantifiable data.

It's hard to understand how some organizations seem to be ahead of the curve when it comes to external factors, while others seem oblivious to them. How could Borders miss the electronic book trend and the trend of using bookstores for browsing and socializing but not buying books? All executives needed to do was spend some time in their stores to see people looking through books, going to have a coffee, and ordering those same books on Amazon for less money and no sales tax. Best Buy finally realizes that people use its stores as showrooms but buy products online, where they are almost always cheaper. Best Buy will match the prices of any store, but that is not the competition; it is web sites where things are almost always cheaper. How could pharmaceutical companies not see the rising cost of health care and think that Medicare and insurance companies would continue to pay premium prices for their drugs when cheaper alternatives were available?

All of these external factors and trends seem painfully obvious to us enlightened outsiders, so how is it that brilliant executives miss them? Part of the reason is that this information might get missed among all the other stuff we get bombarded with daily. In order to avoid this, some organizations track and trend external factors data on a daily basis for executives to monitor and use in their analysis and decision making. For a bank, the metric might include interest rates that change on a daily basis and other factors such as the Dow Jones index. For a home improvement retailer, external metrics might be new housing starts, housing sales, prices, and foreclosures. All of these factors might impact the future business of the retailer and could easily be quantified for daily review.

What is going on in the world can have a direct bearing on your own strategy. A health care client of mine had a business unit that was 100 percent funded by the state of California. My client was one of the pioneers in opening adult day care centers mostly aimed at senior citizens. The program—customers were picked up by company buses each day, given a nice lunch, kept busy all day with games and crafts, and returned home in the evening—was a huge success. As word of this program spread, the company opened more of these centers to deal with the demand. Then during 2011 the state of California was trying to get out of debt and had to start slashing state programs. This was one program that was under consideration for elimination. The client had people in Sacramento monitoring activities and reporting to the CEO every time there was news on which way things were leaning. By the time the final decision was made to completely eliminate funding for adult day care centers in California, my client had already implemented its contingency plan to repurpose the facilities and redeploy most of the staff to other parts of the business.

TYPES OF ORGANIZATIONS WHERE THIS METRIC IS APPROPRIATE

Any large organization should consider putting this gauge on its scorecard or collection of metrics that it reviews to assess its performance. If you are a real estate company, you probably want to have an external analytic that includes:

- Housing prices
- Interest rates
- Availability of mortgages
- Inventory
- Average days on the market

A local real estate publication in Manhattan Beach, California, summarizes all these factors into an index every week and indicates whether the market is favored toward buyers or sellers. These external factors exert a major influence on people deciding to put their home on the market, make an offer on a new home, or decide on pricing. An external index for an aircraft repair company I worked with included the following factors:

- Airline financial health
- Flight miles
- Number of operational aircraft
- Average age of aircraft

Most of this company's work was interior work and body work like replacing windows or repainting the craft. Mergers also drove a lot of work their way. The new merger of American and US Airways will require a lot of paint jobs to be done on old US Airways planes. A package delivery service like FedEx or UPS might track fuel costs and sales of major customers like Amazon.com. A municipal water district in Santa Clara County, California, tracked rainfall, reservoir depth, average temperature, and water usage in its index. Obviously the county could not do anything about any of these factors (other than perhaps rationing to cut water usage), but these measures were critical for planning and managing the district. So if you are a government organization, a business, a health care provider, a school, a charity, or a military organization, you probably need to have an external index somewhere on the collection of metrics you track. Even a small organization can track some of these factors using data that is widely available without spending any money.

HOW DOES THIS IMPACT PERFORMANCE?

External factors can put you out of business very quickly if you don't monitor them and develop a strategy for addressing them. One of my friends was too busy making big money to see the high-risk no-documents mortgage business come crashing down. His once successful company is now gone, along with hundreds of others. Their own metrics were looking really healthy until the crash hit. His company was small and survived longer than the giants like Countrywide, but the end was the same. Failing to monitor external factors can also cause you to miss huge opportunities. A scorecard software company I worked with was one of the first to allow users to monitor company performance on their BlackBerries and iPhones. Now everyone else has this capability, but being the first is a big thing. By monitoring external data, you can make real-time decisions about pricing, inventory, new product introductions, investments, and a wide variety of other topics.

At the Inter-American Development Bank in Washington, D.C., we talked about creating an external metric that looked at economic, political, and Mother Nature factors in each of the Latin American and Caribbean countries where they do business. Earthquake in Haiti, gauge in that region goes red. Food crisis in the entire world, the economic portion of the gauge goes red for all countries. Political coup in Venezuela or big surge in crime in Mexico, the gauges for those countries go red.

I was so glad to see *Argo* win the Oscar for best picture. There might have been a good opportunity to have an external gauge that assessed the sentiment of Iran toward America and the rest of the Western world before the embassy got stormed. If the politicians and the CIA had a quantifiable gauge that they could track on a daily basis, they might have taken action a lot sooner and Ben Affleck's character might not have had the narrow escape story that made for such great cinema.

COST AND EFFORT TO MEASURE

The cost to create and track an external factors analytic is low. Most of this data currently exists in public sources and can be easily accessed and put into your index. Quantifiable metrics like interest rates, housing starts, airline flight miles, customer industry financial trends, production figures, weather, and other similar factors are easy to gather and assign weight to in your index. Where this could cost you some money is in a situation where you have to take qualitative data and turn it into quantifiable data. For example, I worked with the Washington office of Raytheon to develop metrics that tracked the success of their lobbying efforts. We developed an external factors analytic that looked at the degree to which things in Washington were going for or against Raytheon getting more business and keeping what they had. Certainly world events played a role. Wars, conflicts, and new weapons from unfriendly countries were events that encouraged the government to spend more on defense. The economy and level of debt of the country was certainly a factor as well. The most interesting and complicated part of the analytic is where they stood with key power brokers in Washington: congressmen, senators, and others who could influence defense spending were each identified, assigned a weight based on their level of power or influence, and assigned a rating of positive or negative 1 to 10 depending on the extent to which they supported Raytheon products with their words and actions (e.g., voting, speaking, making calls, etc.) and were in favor of buying new and existing company products. The level of support of each politician was reassessed each month, because some they had thought were very supportive changed their tune. This measure ended up costing a bit to design and implement, but it gave the company a fairly objective way of tracking the success or failure of its lobbying efforts and predicting how the external political environment might impact future sales and pipeline.

HOW DO I MEASURE IT?

Step 1 is to decide on the broad categories of data that will be included in your analytic. Some of the factors to think about and consider include: political factors, economic factors, competitive factors, customer industry factors, consumer trends, technology trends, regulatory factors, and weather or Mother Nature factors. I recommend selecting three or four of these factors so as not to overcomplicate the index. Once you have selected the three or four dimensions that have a huge impact on your success or failure and strategies, then **Step 2** is to assign a percentage weight to each factor based on its power to influence your business. For example, for Raytheon or another aerospace company like Northrop, political factors, world events, and the economy are probably the big three. Future spending is probably more determined by political factors, so that might get a 50 percent weight, whereas the remaining two dimensions get 25 percent each. For a bank, economic metrics like interest rates and economic stability would probably get a 50 percent weight. For a technology company, what's going on with competitors might get the highest weight as companies try to be the first to market with some new technology.

Step 3 is to brainstorm possible metrics in each of the categories. Try to think of 20 to 30 possible metrics in each category, including ones that currently do not exist. This is best done with a team of four to eight people with experience monitoring external trends and data.

Step 4 is to narrow down the list of possible metrics to one to four per category that represent the measures that have the most impact on your organization. For example, for a drug company, a key external metric might be the number of people with chronic pain who have not found a satisfactory solution for treating their pain. For a bank or credit card company, there are 50 or more economic indicators that we might track, but interest rates probably will always make the short list. For the company I mentioned that repairs aircraft, the age of the fleets is a key indicator that predicts the amount of work needed in the future. Once you have narrowed down your list to one to four metrics per category, each of those metrics has to be assigned an importance weight, which is **Step 5**. The individual metrics that get the highest weights are the ones that are both the most important and with the highest data integrity—in other words, metrics that are tracked by outside companies using reliable data collection strategies, as opposed to subjective metrics that are measured by people who may have a bias.

VARIATIONS

Of course, there are simpler variations that may be enough for smaller, less complicated organizations. In my little business of one guy, external metrics that I track include: citations of my work by others, book sales, and queries (e-mails or phone calls). All three of these external metrics are sales pipeline metrics for me that are external factors. They are also things I can track without spending any money.

An external factor tracked by Purina that is very objective is the number of families with pets, as well as the number of cats and dogs per family. When the economy went south, that was bad news for those in the pet business. Shelters saw an increase in animals being brought in because people couldn't afford another mouth to feed, and sales of new pets from breeders and shelters were also down. Another external factor measured is the trend toward smaller dogs. As people move to big cities, they want smaller dogs because they don't have the room for a big Labrador or German shepherd. Both these trends are external factors that are very important for the pet food industry. A food company might have a simple external analytic that looks at consumer sentiment about their product. Those companies that produce high-fructose corn syrup or beef are fighting a trend of declining interest in these products. Ad campaigns trying to convince us that corn syrup is the same as sugar are a hard swallow for many consumers. If you are in the business of selling pomegranates or Brussels sprouts, business is good, and these products are selling like crazy because of their health benefits. A leading external indicator for many food companies might be whether you are mentioned on *The Dr. Oz Show* and what he says about your product. The cashier at Trader Joe's the other day told me that Dr. Oz was singing the praises of their organic popcorn with olive oil and they have been out of it for weeks because people came in after the show aired and cleaned the store out. A negative review can have just the opposite effect.

FORMULA AND FREQUENCY

This is one metric that really has to be tailored to your organization and industry. All industries and organization types are influenced by a handful of specific factors that they can't control or sometimes even influence (like weather or the world economy). You need to determine what those factors are for you and build this metric. A metal products manufacturer I worked with tracked the price of raw steel, energy costs, and production figures from the three biggest industries that bought their products. Each of these factors was weighted 33 percent. A government organization I work with that helps disadvantaged people find jobs tracks funding for their programs (state, federal, grants, donations), unemployment, and the city economy, which includes things like job growth and new businesses.

Whatever metrics you settle on, make sure the data is from reliable sources and that the measures can be tracked daily. When I worked with Owens Corning, they relied on the Dodge Report, where all new construction projects were listed, along with specifications on the building size and use. This was one of their key external metrics for identifying opportunities for sales.

TARGETS AND BENCHMARKS

This is one type of metric where you don't need to set targets, because these measures tend to be things you can't do anything about. You don't set a goal or target for raising interest rates, unless you are one of these big financial firms that actually manipulated those numbers and got caught for it. Even though you don't set targets for these measures, you still want to define red, yellow, and green levels. These levels, when applied to the data, can help you determine if there is a need to take action based on external factors. For example, if a key politician has abruptly reversed his support of your programs and products, then this turns the gauge red; likewise if there is a big price increase for a key ingredient or raw material used in your product.

BENEFITS OF DATA

Keep in mind that most of what is in this analytic is not brand-new information. It is a way to summarize all the facts and figures that can have a major impact on your organization and how you make decisions. Think of this as a weather gauge for a pilot. Pilots can't control the weather, but they certainly monitor it to determine how and where they fly the plane. The idea of gathering all of this information regarding financial metrics, economics, politics, and world events and summarizing it in a single analytic might seem foolish, but analytics come with warning lights. That way, even if your overall measure is showing green, the warning light indicates that there is some individual external metric that you need to drill into to get more information. One client linked news stories to individual submetrics so leaders could get all the facts behind the red submetric. Essentially what this metric does is screen through all the news we are bombarded with on a daily basis and sort it into data that impact the organization in a good or bad way.

The benefits of having this information at your desk every morning, or on your iPad that you look at on the way to work on the train, are huge. By the time you arrive at the office, you have been alerted to external events and statistics. You can then get together with your team and decide how to address these factors. Having this data can help:

- Increase the speed of responses taken to positive and negative events or trends in external factors.
- React more quickly to external factors than your competitors.
- Jump on emerging trends.
- Nip problems in the bud before they escalate.
- Adjust goals and targets to match the current situation.
- Quickly change or abort strategies that are not working in the current environment.
- Investigate alternative suppliers when prices rise too quickly.
- Develop a counterstrategy against competitors.

A common objection to creating this analytic is that leaders already have this information, which they have gleaned from reading the newspaper, listening to Bloomberg or CNN, and from talking with others. While this is true, much of that news is irrelevant to your organization. This metric only includes the key factors that have a major impact on your success or failure and, in combination with measures of your own performance, allow for faster and more accurate decision making.

CHAPTER **8**

The Sustainability Index

WHY AN ORGANIZATION MIGHT TRACK THIS

Questions Answered

- What is our carbon footprint?
- Are we recycling and minimizing use of resources like energy and water?
- Are our products produced or services delivered in such a way as to minimize pollution and trash?
- Is sustainability part of our culture and values?
- Do outsiders view us as an environmentally responsible organization?

Why Is This Information Important?

Every few years it gets more complicated to run an organization. It used to be if you had a solid financial result, that was enough to be considered successful. About 30 years ago, new types of metrics started creeping in that were used to assess different aspects of organizational health. Product quality metrics became big in the 1980s, followed quickly by measures of customer satisfaction. Next, organizations realized that much of their work was done by employees, so measures of factors such as employee satisfaction and engagement, safety, and even employee health became part of the corporate dashboard. Other measures of supply chain management, processes, and even ethics began to find their way onto what Harvard Business School professors Robert Kaplan and David Norton came to call the Balanced Scorecard.

In the last five years or so, another dimension of the health of an enterprise is sustainability, or the degree to which the organization is environmentally responsible. This kind of thing was originally only considered important by a few tree-hugging companies run by hippies, but it has now become a mainstream concern. It may surprise you to learn that one of the leading companies in measuring and managing sustainability is Walmart! Although I'm sure predictably sustainability-oriented companies like Patagonia or Whole Foods have good sustainability metrics, Walmart is clearly one of the leaders of this effort to measure and focus on sustainability as a key performance factor. The challenge is that sustainability often costs money, and there is no indication that Walmart will be paying vendors more for their sustainable products and practices. By balancing a focus on price, value, and sustainability, Walmart will be putting pressure on its 60,000 vendors to have products and processes that are less demanding on the environment.

Sustainability is important to many consumers. Europe has been ahead of the United States in this sentiment, but more and more consumers today are concerned about the sustainability records of the companies whose products and services they purchase. Even airlines are talking about sustainability these days. Many are finding ways to conserve fuel, such as purchasing more fuel-efficient aircraft such as the new Airbus 300 and recycling trash. If sustainability is something your customers care about, then there is a solid reason to focus on it, measure it, and improve your performance.

TYPES OF ORGANIZATIONS WHERE THIS METRIC IS APPROPRIATE

Any large organization that sells products or services to consumers is certainly concerned with sustainability. Consumers in most countries care about this aspect of an organization's performance, and with price and quality being equal will often choose to give their business to the company that has a good sustainability record. Of course, there are certain businesses where being green is even more important, such as oil, natural gas, chemicals, food (particularly meat), transportation, and manufacturing. Some businesses consume huge amounts of energy and water (e.g., steel or aluminum manufacturing), and others are in a business where sustainability is critical, such as garbage and waste management. Small businesses or health care organizations may think this metric is not important for them, but even the smallest of organizations can do their part to improve in this area. It may not be worth the time and trouble to formally track performance in this area if you are an organization with less than 10 employees, however.

HOW DOES THIS IMPACT PERFORMANCE?

Sustainability has a big impact on a number of different performance measures for an organization. One clear link is to cost. Being green often costs more money. Constructing LEED-certified buildings is often more expensive than standard construction. Using paper rather than plastic bags costs retailers more money. However, many efforts to improve sustainability end up saving money. My friend in Costa Rica cut his monthly electric bill in half by installing solar panels on his home there. Of course, the return on investment will require seven or more years to pay off, but he is still saving money in the long run. Another way sustainability impacts performance is employee engagement. If employees care about this as one of their personal values and practice good sustainability habits at home, they are likely to be less engaged at work if their employer has bad marks in this area. Thus bad performance on sustainability may lead to decreases in employee morale and engagement, and increases in turnover. A poor track record and image in this area may have a big impact on your ability to attract top talent, as well as impact consumer spending, thus hurting your profits and growth. In short, sustainability can have a big impact on your brand and image, as well as all sorts of financial performance measures.

COST AND EFFORT TO MEASURE

I would rate the cost and difficulty of creating and tracking sustainability as medium. Some things like water and energy usage are probably already tracked and will take no additional effort to measure. Others like carbon footprint, trash recycling, and sustainability performance of suppliers will probably require some effort. Walmart is presently only measuring suppliers and vendors on sustainability programs or efforts versus more objective measures such as waste reduction and use of recyclable packaging materials. However, they plan to move from process to outcome measures as vendors have had time to implement their sustainability programs. A poor track record in this area of performance will eventually mean that you are no longer able to sell your product to Walmart.

HOW DO I MEASURE IT?

Corporate Knights, a Toronto-Based research and investment firm, has created a sustainability index to assess corporations across the world. Based on this index, the company lists the Global 100 Most Sustainable Corporations. What I don't like about this index is that it muddles things up with many factors that have nothing to do with sustainability. In fact, only 32 percent of the measures have to do with sustainability. The remaining 68 percent are measures of taxes paid, ratio of executive to employee compensation, R&D investment, and all sorts of other financial measures that assess the overall financial health of an enterprise. To further dilute the index, measures such as employee turnover, diversity, and safety and pension fund status are also included. Given that sustainability is only worth about a third of the weight, it is possible that an organization could be listed in its top 100 and have a mediocre level of sustainability performance that is boosted by stellar financial or human resources results. The four key measures that make up the 32 percent of the index that does focus on sustainability are:

1. Energy productivity
2. Carbon productivity
3. Water productivity
4. Waste productivity

This might be a good place to start in creating your own sustainability index. At least these four factors could be benchmarked against others if they are being measured the same way. I would assign an importance weight to these four factors differently, depending on the nature of your business. For example, a beef business probably uses huge amounts of water, and a transportation business uses huge amounts of gas and oil.

The Santa Clara Valley Water District in San Jose, California, protects and manages all of the reservoirs and watersheds in Santa Clara County and is the wholesaler of drinking water to all of the many cities and communities in the heavily populated Silicon Valley area of the state. The district has a Green Index on the scorecard of the CEO as well as many of the senior leaders. This area of performance is considered so important that it was part of their three-part vision statement "Getting Greener, Leaner, and Cleaner" under former CEO Stan Wilson. The Green Index was divided into internal metrics and external metrics. Internal metrics included factors such as use of solar energy to power their headquarters building, use of carpooling by employees, and recycling of paper and plastics. External metrics focused on the creeks, reservoirs, and other bodies of water in the county. Metrics were gathered on water quality, bacteria, and the health of fish, game, and plants that depend on this water. By measuring and reporting on this Green Index monthly and putting it on the scorecards of many managers of the district they were able to improve performance and went on to win the Silver-level California Award for Performance Excellence, which has the same criteria and standards as the Baldrige Award.

The first thing you need to understand when constructing a measure of this dimension of performance is that sustainability cannot be accurately measured by a couple of simple statistics. As with financial performance, customer satisfaction, or any other important performance dimension, success is measured using a suite of metrics that roll up into summary indices. A common architecture used by my clients includes three categories of sustainability metrics in the index:

1. **Process metrics**. These include variables such as use of energy, water, and other resources, employee behavior measures such as recycling and use of public transportation, facility metrics, LEED buildings, etc.

2. **Partner metrics**. These include measures of supplier and vendor performance, percentage of partnerships with environmentally responsible companies, and green audit scores

3. **Product and output metrics**. These include use of minimal packaging, environmentally friendly raw materials, and product and service safeness for the environment (e.g., fuel-efficient cars, jets, and trucks, biodegradable products, no bad chemicals such as BPAs, pesticides, etc.)

The relative weight of each of the three categories of measures in your sustainability index depends on your organization. For a company like Target or Kroger that sells products manufactured by many vendors, the partner portion of the index might be given a 50–60 percent weight. Similarly, a chemical company I worked with spends 66 cents out of every dollar of expense on outside suppliers, so the partner dimension would get a heavy weight. A service company might put the heaviest weight on processes and its own service (product) if it relies very little on outside suppliers and partners.

Another factor to think about is to make sure to include a balance of leading and lagging metrics in your sustainability index. A lagging measure might be something like gallons of fuel saved or number of suppliers with good green audit scores. Leading or "cholesterol" metrics might include money invested in alternative energy technologies, education of employees or customers, perceptions and beliefs about sustainability issues, processes, use of technology that saves resources, and policies that promote improved environmental performance. The key to determining the validity of your leading measures is that they correlate to the lagging ones. Beware of superstitious leading indicators that sound good but do not really link to improved outcomes.

Part of having a good sustainability scorecard is tracking measures that can be easily compared with others. Each metric in an index needs to have a target or objective to become meaningful. Most companies set values for green, yellow, and red levels of performance. As I mentioned, Walmart is one of the pioneering companies in the area of sustainability measurement, but its initial measure of its vendors is simply a self-report questionnaire that Walmart fills out. The plan is to gradually roll out more sophisticated and comprehensive sustainability over time. Eventually, we may have a more standardized set of metrics that can be used to compare all companies. That day is probably many years off, however, since we don't even have a standard set of financial metrics that all organizations use. In the meantime, try to pick at least a few of the measures in your sustainability index that can be compared to others. This will make it easier to set reasonable targets and to compare your own performance to others.

VARIATIONS

Environmental consultant Emma Stewart, PhD, suggests that while environmental metrics have evolved by leaps and bounds in the last

20 years, there has been a move from tracking discreet numbers like pounds of trash or gallons of water used to ratios or formulas that consider outputs such as energy cost per ton of steel produced. However, even with a number of these ratios, it becomes difficult for executives to get an overall assessment of sustainability without combining a number of these ratios into an index. While it would be great if there were a single index that all industries used, or even if there were one for each industry type, no such standardization exists. What this means is that it is up to you to craft your own sustainability index or use one that has been developed by others. Stewart suggests in a September 2008 blog post that the current challenge is not data availability but suitability, or tailoring to what makes sense for your industry and organization.[1]

A variation that many of my clients have included in their sustainability index is a measure of *external image* and *internal values* relating to sustainability. What the investment community and consumers think of your firm's record in this area is a big factor. Many would not think of Walmart as a company known for sustainability, yet they are clearly working to change this image. Many are not aware either that Walmart sells more organic food than any other retailer. Whole Foods would probably come to mind first or second on both measures, because it may have done a better job than Walmart of incorporating sustainability as part of its brand right from the start. Some organizations have sustainability as one of their core values and hire for that as well as promote it as part of their overall strategy for success. If you hire people who don't really care about sustainability, you might be able to change their behavior at work, but what they do outside of work is important, too. Google made headlines by offering $5,000 incentives to employees who purchased a Toyota Prius. My sister-in-law Meredith was among the first to take advantage of this offer, and Google's parking lot is still filled with these cars, even though the offer is no longer on the table. This move encouraged employees to buy a gas-saving car, but it also helped Google's image when all the news stories broke about how the company gave employees cash toward the purchase. This one program probably did much to move the needle on the brand image portion of Google's sustainability index.

FORMULA AND FREQUENCY

As a straw man index to use to begin the customization process, you might start with a formula like the following:

Process metrics	40%
Energy productivity	10%
Carbon productivity	10%
Water productivity	10%
Waste productivity	10%
Partner metrics	20%
Process performance (see above)	10%
Outcomes	10%
Outcome metrics	25%
Product attributes	15%
Service attributes	10%
Brand and culture metrics	15%
External image—sustainability	10%
Internal culture—sustainability	5%

Typically the process measures are tracked daily, especially if these factors represent big line items on your balance sheet. Airlines track fuel costs daily, and manufacturing plants track energy costs every day. The partner metrics should be tracked at least once a month, but some may be daily as well. Outcome metrics might also be tracked daily. For example, a grocery store might measure the percentage of plastic versus paper bags used on a daily basis. Trader Joe's gets a daily measure of how often customers bring their own reusable bags by having them enter their name in a drawing every visit to win a free bag of groceries. Brand and internal culture measures probably only need to be tracked quarterly, since these factors tend to move more slowly. However, one client tracks these factors monthly by watching internal and external communication regarding sustainability efforts.

The formula should be viewed as just a starting point for discussion, and the weights and individual measures would need to be tailored. For example, a beef processor would put a heavy weight on water consumption to productivity, whereas a bank might not even measure this factor in its sustainability index.

TARGETS AND BENCHMARKS

The targets you set for the metrics in this index and for the overall index are highly specialized and should be based on your own past performance, capability constraints, industry averages, benchmarks and industry best, and other related measures. For example, a goal of reducing construction costs for new facilities might impact your measure of the percent of LEED-certified buildings.

BENEFITS OF DATA

Some measures of sustainability, like external image, are harder to track than straightforward metrics like energy usage, which can be pulled right off utility bills. The cost and effort to collect data on this factor has to be weighed against the organization's desire to get better at it. For a company like Walmart I'm sure there is a strong business case for putting a lot of effort into measuring and improving performance on sustainability. The benefits of data on sustainability are many. More and more organizations are being evaluated on other factors than financial results. That investment advisor firms grade companies on sustainability and that there are mutual funds of only companies with good sustainability and social responsibility performance indicates the importance of this as a measure of your overall success. As the population of the earth continues to grow and resources get scarcer, only those organizations with good sustainability performance will succeed in the world market.

NOTE

1. Emma Stewart, "Building Better Sustainability Metrics," *HBR Blog Network*, September 2, 2008, http://blogs.hbr.org/leadinggreen/2008/09/building-better-sustainability-metrics.html.

PART TWO

Customer and Stakeholder Analytics

CHAPTER **9**

The Outcomes
Index

 WHY AN ORGANIZATION MIGHT TRACK THIS

Questions Answered

- Do our programs actually produce valuable outcomes for customers and stakeholders?
- Can we see a direct link between our processes and activities and outcomes?
- Which outcomes have improved and which ones have not?
- Have changes in our approaches or processes led to better outcomes or reduced costs?
- Did our product or program work with other efforts to contribute to broader outcomes?
- Are there any negative side effects caused by our product or program that could be worse than the problem being addressed?

Why Is This Information Important?

The United States has one of the highest health care costs in the world, and our quality is ranked in the fiftieth percentile worldwide. We continue to dump more money into education but many high schools still have a 25 percent dropout rate, and graduating students can't read or do math at a ninth-grade level. The government spends millions on a program like "Just Say No to Drugs" that has failed to decrease drug use. In today's world of restricted funding for government programs, each activity, initiative, and program is being questioned as to its value to society and taxpayers. Since everyone now has to have health insurance and pay something for the services they receive, government, organizations like Medicare, and insurance companies are looking to avoid paying for brand-name drugs and expensive surgeries, making it harder for pharmaceutical companies and health care providers to make millions or billions as they used to.

Any organization that has a product or service that is supposed to produce an outcome is expected to demonstrate results. I worked with Long Beach Unified School District (the second largest in California), and they had big grants from both the Dell Foundation and the Broad Foundation. Both charities are very generous in their support of education, but the grants had to result in improved education outcomes or the money would stop flowing. When the teachers' union refused to accept the idea that there would be positive and negative consequences for teachers based on the performance of their students, the grants were not renewed. The foundations understood that for performance to improve you need goals, measures, feedback, and consequences.

The Community Development Department in the City of Los Angeles is a shining star among city departments. Through the use of measurement, feedback, and accountability, the Community Development Department was able to dramatically reduce its costs while increasing the number of disadvantaged people they placed into jobs. Its performance was so impressive that the Community Development Department and many of its con-tracted WorkSource Centers won the prestigious California Award for Performance Excellence.

In health care there is a set of 75 metrics used to evaluate organizational performance, called Healthcare Effectiveness Data and Information Set, or HEDIS. But while many of these metrics are good process measures, very few look at health outcomes. The same is true of many education evaluations that focus more on classroom behavior of teachers (process) and curricula (inputs) than on outcomes like student success. Long Beach Unified School District does not measure how many graduates enroll in college, get a job, or go to jail. In fact, the school district doesn't measure any outcomes other than the percentage who graduate, and even that is a gamed statistic by counting the percentage of 12th graders who graduate versus the percentage of 10th graders who graduate high school. Outcome metrics in health care, education, and many government programs are a joke.

The other problem I see with outcome metrics is a lack of shared accountability. The government likes to hold one agency or department accountable for one outcome so blame or credit is easy to assign. So who do you blame for the high unemployment of the last few years? Clearly jobs and full employment are important outcomes for a healthy economy, but who is held accountable for that metric? The Commerce Department, Treasury, the Federal Reserve, the SEC, Congress, the Senate? When I worked with the Federal Highway Administration, one of the key outcome metrics it was held accountable for was highway fatalities. Even though it doesn't set or enforce laws, the administration got the blame if fatalities increased. The major causes of traffic fatalities are speeding and driving under the influence. Texting or talking on the phone is probably right up there these days as well. The point is that there are multiple federal, state, city, and county organizations that might have some accountability for traffic fatalities. Certainly local police departments, as well as state police, would have some accountability. What I have not seen is a bunch of government departments getting together to collectively decide what outcomes they should be accountable for and who owns what percentage of the accountability. Instead what happens is that if performance is good or improves, they all stand up and take credit, and if it is bad or declining, they blame others.

TYPES OF ORGANIZATIONS WHERE THIS METRIC IS APPROPRIATE

This metric is appropriate for any city, state, county, or federal government organization that is tasked with providing some sort of outcome for taxpayers or other stakeholders. Some government organizations are easier to measure than others. The IRS has outcomes that are measured in dollars every month. An agency like the Department of Energy may have a tougher challenge coming up with outcomes, but this department was originally formed to eliminate the United States' dependence on external sources of energy. I don't think that outcome has been achieved and I think the trend is going in the wrong direction. The Energy Department's current mission statement is much vaguer and harder to tell whether it has been achieved:

> The mission of the Energy Department is to ensure America's security and prosperity by addressing its energy, environmental and nuclear challenges through transformative science and technology solutions.

It would be tough to come up with some good outcome metrics for prosperity and security, but one of them might be how much of income the average American spends on gasoline, electricity, and natural gas.

Not only do government organizations need to measure outcomes, but so do organizations that sell to government, like defense companies, or are paid by the government, such as health care providers, as well as schools and government programs. Even profit-making manufacturers and service companies might measure outcomes if the product is designed to save people time or money, or somehow improve the quality of their lives.

HOW DOES THIS IMPACT PERFORMANCE?

What is scary is that a lack of demonstrable outcomes sometimes does not impact performance in government organizations. If an organization fails to achieve its mission, it continues to exist, get funded, and maybe even get more money. Luckily, there are some rewards for organizations that do achieve positive outcomes. *U.S. News and World Report* and other organizations rank hospitals based on key outcome metrics like mortality, and this seems to be having an impact. More people check into the good hospitals, so their financial health improves, they can hire better staff and buy better equipment, and health care improves even more. Two recent examples are Henry Ford Hospital in Michigan, which recently won the Baldrige Award, and Southcentral Foundation, a community health care provider in Anchorage, Alaska, that also won a Baldrige Award. Both organizations not only demonstrated improved health outcomes, but also lower costs. Demonstrating improved outcomes might also help ensure that you get your share of the budget when things get tight and make you much less of a target when leaders are looking for programs and places to cut. Most leaders are loath to cut programs that are clearly producing measurable outcomes, particularly those that are important to politicians and taxpayers. So one of the reasons to have a good outcome index is that you demonstrate a genuine desire to improve your performance. A secondary reason may be side benefits like recognition and rankings, awards, ability to hire better staff, avoidance of budget cuts, and promotions for managers and others.

Another important way this affects performance is that the data allows you to detect processes, programs, and initiatives that do not produce outcomes or cost more than the value they produce. Outcomes always need to be compared with costs. Some countries have much better services for their citizens than we have in the United States. People also pay much more in taxes. If you think it is bad here, go to Holland or some other European countries like Denmark. Being able to demonstrate improved outcomes at lower costs is really what gets attention and recognition.

COST AND EFFORT TO MEASURE

The cost to develop and implement a system for tracking outcomes ranges from low to high, depending on the type of organization you're in. If you are a health care provider, I am sure you already track key outcomes like successful surgeries, mortality, patients discharged, infections, and other factors. If you are in education, you have a lot of work ahead of you. School systems track test scores of academic achievement, but this is not really an outcome metric. An outcome metric is something like the percentage of graduates who get accepted to college and what colleges they get accepted to, or the percentage of graduates who are able to find a decent job. Our local Manhattan Beach school system is one of the best in the state and tracks many of these key outcome metrics. Harvard Business School tracks what percentage of its MBAs are running big corporations or holding high-level government jobs.

Where the cost will come is in collecting the data rather than designing the metrics. Getting access to data that may be in other databases is sometimes a challenge. If the Just Say No to Drugs program wanted to really track their effectiveness they could keep track of how many people are arrested for possession of drugs, how many are in rehab, how many are in jail, how many dealers are arrested, and how much pot is being dispensed in states like Colorado and Oregon and California. In other words, getting data on drug use would require accessing many different databases, which would take lots of effort and probably cost a bit of money.

HOW DO I MEASURE IT?

Step 1 in developing an outcome index is to decide on the broad categories of outcomes that will be measured. A good reference point is to go back to your mission statement. If Disney's mission is to make people happy, then happiness should be the key output the company measures, and it certainly does measure it and does a great job of managing it. The Community Development Department I work with in the City of Los Angeles strives to provide its clients with independence and the improved self-respect that come with having a decent job. Therefore key outcomes might look at independence, self-respect, and employment. These might be the broad categories of outcomes that the City of Los Angeles measures. For some organizations that have a very broad mission like the World Bank or the Inter-American Development Bank, broad categories of outcomes might include factors such as:

- Economic outcomes
- Health outcomes
- Education outcomes
- Transportation and access outcomes

Step 2 is to develop four to six outcome metrics within each of the categories. Unlike most of the HEDIS metrics for health care, outcome measures are just that. Screening people for diabetes is not an outcome metric. Reducing the incidence is an outcome metric. Graduating students is an outcome, but so is preparing them for work or higher education, so a measure for high school would be the percentage of students who are employed or enrolled in college. When you are selecting outcome metrics, don't ask whether you can control the outcomes, but ask whether your organization can influence them. A school district might not be able to control the number of kids who are in gangs, but it can certainly influence it. The Long Beach schools did not want to measure the health of the students even though it feeds them sometimes two meals a day and provides them with exercise. Student health is clearly a metric that a school can influence and could be considered an outcome.

Other than the degree to which you can influence the outcome, you need to think about the integrity of the data. If it is an objective measure tracked using reliable methods by an unbiased source, then the metric should probably make your short list. It is often helpful to create a list of eight to 10 outputs for each area and then narrow them down to the two to four best ones. Where this gets complicated is an organization like a hospital that has lots of health outcomes. The most basic outcome is that people recover from whatever is wrong with them and don't develop additional problems (like infections) from being in the hospital. A hospital administrator or a CEO should be able to look at one overall health outcomes index and get an assessment of how the organization is performing at its healing mission. Yes, there will be lots of sub-metrics that break down the data into various categories by process, illness, or procedure performed. For example, delivering healthy babies is one of the more positive outcomes for a hospital. Hospitals also have to deal with cancer, death, accidents, and not so pleasant outcomes as well, so the idea behind this metric might be to sort the outcomes into a positive and a negative category.

Step 3 is to assign weight to each of the outcomes. Metrics assigned a high percentage should be those with the strongest link to the organization's mission, the greatest integrity, and the greatest degrees of influence and control. For example, for a university, a measure of graduates finding jobs in their field of study would be a really important outcome metric, as would getting accepted into graduate school. Less important outcomes might be student and parent satisfaction with their education.

FORMULA AND FREQUENCY

An example of an outcome index for a community development department in county or city government might be:

Jobs	40%
Number of new jobs	10%
Number of people employed	20%
Promotions	5%
Turnover	5%
Economic development	40%
Number of new businesses started	15%
Slums and blight eliminated	15%
	(square footage)
Turnover of new businesses	10%
Youth	20%
Percent graduating high school	10%
Percent completing vocational training	10%

The exact formula that you use will be up to you, and there is no right answer. However, what you don't want to do is take 50 to 100 metrics and roll them all into an index. Data should be stacked in a pyramid with the outcome index being the peak of the pyramid that breaks down into three to six dimensions, which break down into four to six metrics, which might break down into four to six submetrics.

VARIATIONS

One variation is just to have a couple of outputs and not create an index or analytic metric comprising lots of different measures. This might work if you are a simple organization with a single product or service. An airline, for example, is a pretty simple business, and it might just measure the percentage of passengers who are transported on time to their desired destination. One outcome metric certainly makes it simple. However, an airline has other outputs like bags and cargo delivered on schedule. Cargo and bags undamaged is another important outcome. Most organizations are sufficiently complex that they have multiple outcomes for multiple services and products, and each needs to be measured and combined so that management does not have to review 50 charts to see how the organization is performing on its core mission.

Another variation is to combine process, output, and outcome metrics into a single index. For example, a hospital or medical clinic might take all of the 75 or so HEDIS metrics and combine them into a single index. Most of the HEDIS metrics are input or process metrics. I think this is indeed possible, but it is not recommended. It is better to keep process and outcome metrics separate, even though there should be a link. Washing hands after each patient is probably a good process measure for preventing infections, but infections are an outcome that should be tracked separately. It is possible to be diligent about hand washing and still spread infections by other means, like those ties doctors still wear.

TARGETS AND BENCHMARKS

Outcome metrics are probably the easiest to get averages, benchmarks, and all sorts of comparative data. Regulators often track performance of various organizations, as do professional associations and trade groups. Each individual outcome metric needs to have a unique target set based upon customer and stakeholder requirements, industry averages, your own capacity and history, resource constraints, and benchmarks. As with most composite indices, "green" is usually defined as 80–100 percent compliant or greater. This may vary greatly depending on the industry and metric. A rating of 80 percent safe landings or 80 percent successful surgeries would probably not be good standards. With many outcome metrics we are looking for Six Sigma (less than three defects per million), or very close to perfection. On the other hand, a school system that had 80 percent of its graduates go on to college would probably be doing a great job.

BENEFITS OF DATA

There are huge benefits to having one aggregate index that can be viewed every day that tells leaders how the organization is performing on its key outcomes besides the financial ones. Having one overall metric also minimizes the chances of leaders micromanaging or obsessing about minor outcomes rather than focusing on the big ones. A CEO I worked with obsessed about getting ranked in the bottom 25 percent of a survey of customers, when those customers only represented about 10 percent of his business. Staking the outcome data in layers by importance and dimension allows leaders to drill down as necessary into the detail when there are problems but most of the time stay focused on the 30,000-foot view of the organization. Having good outcome data like this can also be helpful when it comes time to present to your board, donors, finders, the community, and other key stakeholders. Being able to demonstrate the value you provide to society, the taxpayer, or whoever your customers and stakeholders are is a huge advantage that many of your peers may not have.

CHAPTER **10**

The Customer Engagement Index

Questions Answered

- Do we have customers with desirable characteristics?
- What is their level of relationship with our products, services, people, and company?
- What is the probability that customers will be loyal?
- Do we have any customers we would be better off without?
- Are we executing plans to manage the relationships with our customers?
- Do our CRM plans help or hurt relationships with customers?

Why Is This Information Important?

Organizations spend a fortune on advertising and marketing to attract new customers. They think nothing of dropping a couple of hundred thousand for a trade show booth or a couple of million for a Super Bowl commercial, but spend as little as they can to keep the customers they already have happy. Store employees are bothered when you ask for help, and they know nothing about the products they are selling.

135

Measuring and managing a relationship with a customer is a delicate process, and following a script and employing a one-size-fits-all approach pretty much guarantees that you will alienate a large portion of your customer base. Being able to measure the level of engagement of each of your customers is important. Each new transaction, order, or experience with someone from your company is an opportunity to improve or degrade the relationship. One big problem can ruin a long history of someone being a loyal customer, and that person probably won't fill out a survey before leaving and never coming back.

Measuring and managing a relationship with a customer is important to most organizations today. Most of us cannot survive by counting on a new stream of customers every day. Even places like Disneyland try to build relationships with customers. For some people, a visit to Disneyland is a once-in-a-lifetime event, and some parents rank it right up there with a root canal. However, for thousands of others, a visit to Disney is like going to heaven. Disney sells thousands of season passes to local Californians, many of whom go to the park every day! Can you imagine what a great job they must do to get people to come to Disneyland every day and spend money? When I did some work with Domino's Pizza, I learned that their most loyal customers order from Domino's at least four times a week! That is a loyal and engaged customer. So how do places like Marriott, Domino's, and Disney pull this off? By carefully measuring the relationship they have with their customers every day and by delivering a consistently good product and service. They don't achieve it by teaching everyone to recite customer service scripts that are supposed to make us feel they care: "Your call is important to us, please continue to hold," or "I understand how you feel; that must be very frustrating." If my call is important, then answer it! If you understand how frustrated I am, solve my problem!

TYPES OF ORGANIZATIONS WHERE THIS METRIC IS APPROPRIATE

This measure is appropriate for any medium to large business that can't just observe to get a good feeling on the level of customer engagement. It is harder to measure customer engagement when you have millions of customers and sell your product through stores or distributors. However, with the advent of big data, it is now possible to summarize millions of data points from millions of customers to get an assessment of customer engagement. This type of measurement is much easier and less costly if you have a dozen or so big business customers. If you have two or three customers you probably don't need this metric, because you know where you stand on a daily basis with them since you talk with them every day. You also probably don't need this measure if you see customers once or twice and hopefully never again. A surgeon who does hip replacements is not looking for a customer for life. If the surgeon does a great job, she sees the patient after surgery, maybe checks in a few months later, and then does not see them again. If your organization is built on selling a product or service that is good for life and you never need to sell them anything else, there is no reason to measure and manage the relationship you have with them. However, this is only true for a small minority of organizations. Even organizations with a captive audience of customers, like the Department of Motor Vehicles or the IRS, seem to care about managing the relationship they have with their customers or citizens.

HOW DOES THIS IMPACT PERFORMANCE?

The relationships you have with customers directly impact your revenue, profit, costs, and even your stock price. Losing a major account could cause your stock to decline in value. Losing a big customer could not only result in a loss of revenue from that customer, but also inhibit new business from future customers who might talk with that lost customer. Losing a customer is often devastating to an organization. Even if it is not, managing relationships is critical. Even if you are a consumer products company, or a service firm with literally millions of customers, one consumer can impact your entire business. In the past, big companies like banks, airlines, carmakers, and retailers did not bother themselves much with individual consumers and did not try to track and manage relationships with them. However, with the advent of new software and big data, this is now possible, and organizations that do it have a huge edge over their competitors.

Measuring and managing relationships with customers also has a big impact on your costs and your account management and sales processes. Detecting small problems and getting them corrected is the secret to managing a relationship with a customer. This means frequent measurement and follow-up actions to see if the problem has been resolved and the relationship is still positive. Marriott is a master at this. It knows the lifetime value of a customer and that 20 years of a highly engaged customer can turn sour with one bad hotel experience. Understanding the value of a customer relationship helps customer-facing personnel make the right decisions regarding spending a few bucks or doing something extra to make a customer happy.

Customer engagement also directly links to employee engagement. Happy, engaged employees tend to provide better service to their customers, but the reverse is also true. It's pretty hard to be happy and engaged in your job if most customers are angry and seem to hate your company. Often the anger is caused by factors outside of the employees' control, like stupid policies, poor-quality products, software and hardware that is too slow, inaccurate databases, and under-resourced call centers. In short, customer engagement can have a big impact on most measures of an organization's success. The ironic thing is that the vast majority of organizations do not have good measures of this factor.

COST AND EFFORT TO MEASURE

The cost and effort to construct a good customer engagement index are both high. Of course, the value is also high. Taking a halfhearted approach to this metric does not make sense, and you are better off not tracking anything than taking shortcuts like relying on surveys as your only measure. The cost will be in both determining the factors to measure and collecting the data. If you sell to consumers, the cost could be much higher than if you have 20 to 30 business customers that account for 80 percent of your revenue.

In some cases, you might have to buy the data. Grocery stores keep track of the purchases of each customer through the use of their discount cards. Big stores like Safeway and Kroger deal with millions of customers who make millions of purchases. Getting at that data could be extremely useful for a consumer products company. However, it won't be free. The retailers know the value of this information and will charge for it. However, it might be worth the money. Imagine if you sell Tide detergent and you buy a big jug of it every couple of weeks either at Kroger, Walmart, or Target, depending on where you are shopping that week. The value of that customer to Procter & Gamble is huge, because he may also buy Crest toothpaste and lots of other P&G products. So let's say that consumer joins Sam's Club or Costco for the first time and decides to try that store's private-label laundry detergent, which is a lot cheaper than Tide. He takes it home, tries it out for a few weeks, and the laundry comes out really clean—just as good as or better than with Tide. So he keeps buying it and does not go back to Tide. On the next visit to Costco he decides to try Kirkland toothpaste and Kirkland vodka instead of the Crest and Absolut he usually buys. Once again, if the experience is positive, then it's more sales lost for P&G and the maker of Absolut. Being able to track stuff like this could be hugely beneficial to P&G and other consumer products companies. A customer who has tried a competitor's product once or twice is usually not sold right away. Imagine if you knew when a customer tried a competing product for the first time and you could send her a coupon for 25 percent off or some enticement to keep her buying your product? By the time she has finished the jug of laundry detergent or bottle of vodka, the consumer might realize that it is not quite as good as the name brand, and a coupon for a big discount could be just the ticket for luring her back.

HOW DO I MEASURE IT?

Before talking about how to measure customer engagement, I need to spend a little time talking about how *not* to measure it. Three measures to avoid except as minor submetrics are:

1. Net promoter score
2. Loyalty
3. Complaints

Net Promoter Score: The One-Question Survey

The most typical way of measuring customer satisfaction is via a survey. To combat the fact that surveys have a very poor response rate, a new technique is to ask just one question: "On a scale of 1 to 10, would you recommend our company's products or services?" The idea is that customers will be much more likely to answer one question and provide feedback to your organization. These one-question surveys do tend to get a better response rate than longer ones, but the majority of customers still ignore them. The results are turned into a Net Promoter Score, another practice that many have adopted. The approach proposes that customers who give you 8, 9, or 10 ratings are your "promoters" and talk about you in a positive way to others. Those in the 4–7 range are on the fence and could easily be lured away by a competitor, and the customers who give you 1–3 ratings are already very unhappy and may tell others about how bad your product or service is. The appeal of this approach is its simplicity. Executives now can focus on a single measure of customer satisfaction: Net Promoter Score.

The biggest problem with one-question surveys, or a Net Promoter Score, is that the data is not actionable. If you find out that 20 percent of your customers give you a 1–3 rating, you have no idea why or what to do about it. Relying on a single-question survey as your only or main measure of customer satisfaction or engagement is also a huge mistake. An article by the Gallup company called "A Popular Idea That's Dead Wrong" talks about the folly of relying on a Net Promoter Score as your primary measure of customer satisfaction.[1] Of course, Gallup wants to sell you a longer and more expensive survey.

Don't Confuse Loyalty with Satisfaction

The fact that your customers stick around does not necessarily mean they are happy with your products or services. Loyalty is often driven by laziness, risk aversion, habit, and a lack of better choices. Most of us hate paying our cable or satellite bill for television and have looked around at alternatives, but they are all around the same price and have the same channels, and we may be stuck in a contract, so it is easier just to stay where we are. Predicting future customer buying behavior and loyalty is a tricky business. A customer who consistently rates you a 10 on your Net Promoter Score survey may be gone tomorrow because someone came along with an attractive offer, or she just got bored and wanted to try something new. Leading companies like FedEx and others have found that a daily metric that tracks the occurrence of errors that frustrate customers can be a simple and easy way of measuring and predicting when a customer might leave and never come back.

Most Unhappy Customers Don't Complain

Measuring customer engagement by tracking complaints can provide misleading data. I read that only one-tenth to one-hundredth of unhappy customers bother to complain. Some people have learned that if they complain they get free stuff. My mom is always writing some kind of complaint letter to someone, and this behavior is often rewarded with free stuff. Most of us don't bother complaining, but we display our dissatisfaction by never going back. Losing a customer is actually a pretty accurate measure of their dissatisfaction, but it comes a little too late.

WHAT FACTORS SHOULD BE INCLUDED IN A CUSTOMER ENGAGEMENT INDEX?

There are a number of different dimensions that tell you about the degree to which a customer is engaged with your firm and its products and services:

- Product and service quality problems and their severity (see Chapter 13 on the customer rage index)
- Share of wallet and level of engagement
- Personal relationships and politics
- Price of divorce (cost of finding a new supplier)
- Quality and value of alternatives
- Current satisfaction levels

Product and Service Quality

A big factor that impacts the relationship you have with customers is the quality and value of your products and services. People may love the account executive they deal with, but if the product quality starts to slip, so too does the relationship. It is a good idea to include internal quality control metrics in the customer relationship index, like on-time delivery, order and billing accuracy, defects, and other related measures. One simple way of tracking these factors is to take the customer rage index described in Chapter 13 and insert it as a submetric in this analytic. I often see this done where organizations will have an index that they look at separately as well as it being part of a larger measure. Having consistently good-quality products and services does not necessarily deepen the relationship, but not having them can certainly degrade it quickly.

Share of Wallet and Engagement Level

This second dimension is a big deal because it is a measure of the degree to which your products and services are part of the organization or individual's life or operation. My friend Roy is a consultant and contractor with a number of clients, but his main client is the research and development arm of the Army Corps of Engineers. Roy works with the director and other members of the management team to help develop strategic plans and performance measures and to improve processes. Roy is viewed as a valued member of the senior management team even though he is a contractor. He has worked with the Army Corps of Engineers for many years, helped it solve many problems and challenges, and is an integral part of the organization. This client is highly engaged with Roy.

My wife and I are highly engaged with Purina. Purina is one of the best companies I have worked with in 30 years. I buy many Purina products for our two Persian cats, including prescription food and probiotics, and we have pet insurance through PurinaCare. We watch the company's television commercials, and my wife is often on its web sites, which provide really helpful advice to pet owners. To us, Purina is not just a company that makes cat food, it is a trusted partner and client.

We have a high level of engagement with Trader Joe's as well. When we were thinking of moving to Austin, Texas, one of the negatives was no Trader Joe's. I know, it is just a grocery store, but we love Trader Joe's and spend a lot of money there every week. Trader Joe's has about 80 percent of our grocery dollars each month, so it has a big share of wallet. Imagine how useful it would be to have a measure of the degree to which your products or services are an integral part of your customers' lives. This is the real measure of engagement or relationship, and it cannot be measured with a survey. The measure looks at the number of ways in which your company is connected with a customer. Banks can easily track what they call "share of wallet" by looking at the different products you have and the percentage of your net worth that is with them. For example, with a big company like Citibank I can have:

- Credit cards
- Mortgage
- Checking account
- Savings account
- Retirement account
- Brokerage account
- Safe deposit box
- Line of credit

Having all my financial services handled by Citibank makes me a highly engaged customer and much more valuable to Citibank than if I just had one of their "products." Collecting data on share of wallet is much easier for a bank than it would be for a retail store or consumer products company. Trader Joe's probably does not know if I go to Vons to buy some things. However, if Trader Joe's saw that the average amount of my spending at its stores was cut in half, it would be pretty easy to figure out that I have started shopping elsewhere.

How people spend their money is probably the strongest measure of engagement. If you start out as a third-tier backup supplier and work your way up to primary supplier with the largest share of the business, that is a great measure of the level of engagement of your customer. Growth and declines in business and diversity of your products or services purchased is a really important hard measure of engagement.

Personal Relationships and Politics

Relationships between firms are really relationships with people. If you sell to millions of consumers you can't measure personal relationships and you don't really have them with consumers. However, many big consumer products firms have relationships with their retail partners, like dealers do with car manufacturers. A factor in customer engagement is the connections you have with customers and who you are connected with. I recall a client who repairs aircraft having a close friendship with then CEO of Continental Airlines Gordon Bethune. Did this impact the relationship between the two firms? You would be naïve to not think so. These two guys were friends outside of work and had a business relationship that lasted over 25 years. Employees of Continental also had some friends and former coworkers at the supplier firm, so relationships went deeper than just the two CEOs. Walmart seems to understand this, so they rotate buyers every two years so they cannot become close to vendors and suppliers. This makes trust hard for the vendor, since as soon as they develop a trusting relationship with the Walmart buyer, a new one gets appointed. Personal relationships can be quantified by the level of the person you have a relationships with (i.e., CEO = 10, worker = 1) and the length and depth of the relationship (1 = business only, 10 = close personal friends for 20-plus years).

Price of Divorce and Cost of Switching Suppliers

Part of what makes two firms or a consumer and a firm stay together as partners is the price and effort required to switch suppliers. Most firms have trusted suppliers they have been working with for years and tend to stay with them even if their performance is not perfect because it would be too hard to switch. There is also something to be said about the devil you know versus the one you don't know. Many people stay with their bank, insurance company, and mechanic because it is too hard to find a new one. Finding a new bank and switching all your accounts is a pain, and who's to say the new bank is really any better than the one you have? Often businesses stay with suppliers because of lethargy, but a supplier that really knows your business and needs is very valuable. The higher the cost of switching suppliers, the more likely an organization is to stay with the ones they have. This is true for individual consumers as well as for big companies.

Quality and Value of Alternatives

A related factor is whether more attractive alternatives are available. You can switch your wireless provider from AT&T to Verizon, or try one of the smaller companies, but chances are you will have to sign a contract and you will pay about the same. You can switch from Colgate toothpaste to Crest, but not save any money there either, and you'll probably find that either product gets your teeth clean. Many organizations stay with an existing supplier because they perceive that the alternatives will be the same price and quality or close. When an alternative comes along that is cheaper, of better quality, or a better value, organizations and individuals may not be loyal. A few years ago every company and business person had a BlackBerry and most people really liked the product. BlackBerry pretty much had the business market locked up until the iPhone came along. At first many people had a BlackBerry for business and an iPhone for their personal device. That seemed like kind of a waste, and most found they preferred the iPhone. Some even convinced their companies to adopt the iPhone instead of the BlackBerry. Even though BlackBerry/Research in Motion had excellent relationships with their corporate clients, the pressure to switch to the iPhone was strong and many did so.

Current Satisfaction Levels

A big factor in assessing the strength of your engagement with customers is their current satisfaction level with your product, service, and firm. As you know from reading other chapters, I am not a big fan of surveys, for reasons already expressed. However, you do need a way of gauging customers' opinions and perceptions. As explained earlier, Net Promoter Score is a one-question survey that might be one of the submetrics here in the customer engagement index. Another alternative is a face-to-face meeting and report card. Younger Brothers Construction in Phoenix uses this technique. Jim Younger visits each of his 15 to 20 homebuilder customers a couple of times a year and asks the president of the customer company to give his company a report card on four or five factors like quality, value, flexibility, and service. The cool thing about this as a data collection method is that Jim takes the time to visit customers himself, and when someone gives less than an A grade, that person can talk about reasons for the grade and what can be done to get a better rating next time. It becomes a dialogue and his customers love that he takes the time to have these meetings. If he just sent out a survey, it would be ignored. If you are doing any kind of survey you can use that data as one of your sub-metrics here. Other methods such as focus groups using automated rating devices like those on TV game shows, follow-up visits, and recommendations can also be ways of measuring satisfaction levels.

VARIATIONS

One common variation is to measure customer engagement by tracking action items completed in the CRM (customer relationship management) plan. This sounds good in theory. If your account exes do everything they are supposed to do to build a stronger relationship with customers, the engagement score should go up. This is not always the case, however. I recall a client who loved to take customers out for golf, expensive lunches, and spectator sporting events. Some of the clients loved these outings and took advantage of every one they could. Other clients were offended by the offers, seeing it as an unethical way to bribe them, and they would rather be at work or home with their families than out at a Red Wings game with a bunch of drunk customers. Customer relationship management is important, but the strategy has to be tailored to each customer, making it tougher to use events or activities as valid measures.

Another measure I often see is loyalty, or length of the relationship. I mentioned earlier that loyalty can just mean laziness or a lack of better choices, but having a customer for a long time is sure to be worth something.

One client calls this entire analytic the Matrimonial Index, and rates customers on a 1–10 scale, with 10 signaling "married and will use our product even if there is a less expensive alternative" and 1 signaling "we are a backup supplier only and customer is married to another suppli-er." What makes the metric even more strategic is they don't set a goal of being married to all their customers. For some customers they are looking to pull away and eventually divorce them, whereas they are working on building a marriage with other more attractive customers. Everyone understands this index, and they reassess the attractiveness of each of their customers once a quarter because things change.

FORMULA AND FREQUENCY

The specific design of your customer engagement index will vary a lot depending on whether you sell to business (B2B) or to consumers (B2C). Personal relationships and even share of business may be impossible and impractical to measure. A straw man formula for a B2B company is shown below. Note that a B2C company would leave a few of these dimensions out of the formula.

Product or service quality	20%
Share of wallet and engagement level	30%
Personal relationships	10%
Price of divorce and cost to switch suppliers	10%
Quality and value of alternatives	10%
Satisfaction levels	20%

BENEFITS OF DATA

The benefits of having this data at your disposal are enormous. First of all, you will be able to adopt a much more scientific and refined approach to sales and customer relationship management. Another big benefit is that you might decide to pull away and even drop some of your customers. You will also have a way to track the return on investment from your CRM activities. Most companies do all sorts of things for customers with nothing other than anecdotal data on how it impacted their engagement. Using this metric in combination with attractiveness metrics such as customer lifetime value allows an organization to directly link customer engagement to profits. The organization I mentioned that created the Matrimonial Index made dramatic improvements in revenue, profit, and market share using this metric to drive the activities of their marketing and sales departments.

NOTE

1. John H. Heming, "A Popular Idea That's Dead Wrong," *Gallup Business Journal*, December 14, 2006, http://businessjournal.gallup.com/content/25822/popular-idea-thats-dead-wrong.aspx.

CHAPTER **11**

The Social
Network Index

 WHY AN ORGANIZATION MIGHT TRACK THIS

Questions Answered

- What are consumers saying about our products and services?
- Are customers satisfied with our products and services?
- How many customers did we make mad today and how mad did they get?
- Has any customer experienced outstanding service today?
- Are there any customer contact employees who need to be recognized for doing a great job?
- How influential are the customers we made angry or happy today?
- What are business customers saying about doing business with our organization?
- How likely is it that customers will be loyal?
- What operational or product problems occurred today that we need to address now?

Why Is This Information Important?

Just about every type of organization today has acknowledged that they have customers, and that customer satisfaction is something that is important to track and manage. Everyone from your lawn guy to your kids' teachers wants to know if you are satisfied with their service. This really is a good thing, and most of us are delighted to see that even places like the Department of Motor Vehicles (DMV) and the IRS seem

149

to want our feedback so they can try to improve. In the case of the DMV in California, it really did seem to have improved, since it is now possible to make an appointment online and to dramatically shorten the amount of time you would have spent at the DMV compared to a few years ago. The bad news about this increased concern with taking care of customers is that the methods used to measure our satisfaction have become no less invasive or sophisticated, and now everyone you deal with at work and home wants your feedback via some survey.

Back in the 1970s, the car companies and a few other industries started hiring firms like J.D. Power to do customer surveys. A car is a pretty big purchase, and many of us took the time to complete the 50- to 100-question surveys that asked all sorts of questions about the car itself, the sales process, and any service experience we had at the dealership. These surveys became so important that car manufacturers began using them to rate dealers and give preferential inventory to the best-performing dealers. Rather than improve service, which could get expensive, crafty dealers figured out how to cheat on the surveys by offering incentives to customers like free floor mats or detailing service for a positive rating. If pilots started offering free drinks for positive airline surveys, flying might get to be more fun.

In today's world, managing performance means collecting real-time performance data, monitoring it using your smartphone or other mobile device, analyzing problems, and making decisions to solve problems and prevent them from growing. In the not too distant past, organizations measured financial and operational performance daily, but other important dimensions such as customer satisfaction and employee satisfaction were measured with annual surveys. Problems could go undetected for many months, and by the time we discovered a disgruntled customer, he or she was long gone and had spread negative feedback about our product or service to anyone who would listen. Managing any dimension of performance with annual data is a common and colossally stupid approach. Relying on a survey as your only measure of customer or employee satisfaction is also shortsighted. Even a great survey only gets a 20 percent return rate, and thus organizations make decisions based on 20 percent of their customers' feedback, which is likely to either be glowingly positive or really bad.

Social media data can be viewed as a friend or enemy. Having customers comment on your business and having their comments read by hundreds of others is scary. One bad restaurant review on Yelp can drive away a lot of prospective customers. A bad rating on Angie's List can hurt your plumbing business. Being able to track daily feedback on how customers really feel about your products and services is something organizations have been trying to figure out for decades. All sorts of things have been done to try to get customers to provide more feedback. Sadly, most of these ideas have failed. Social media has provided the solution to this long-standing problem.

NET PROMOTER SCORE: THE NEW AND IMPROVED SURVEY METHOD

Most of us consumers are surveyed to death, and we delete the majority of e-mail surveys we receive, hang up on the phone surveyor, or throw away surveys that come in the mail in an important-looking envelope. To combat this, a consultant from Bain & Company developed a brilliant solution: a one-question survey. The survey asks you to rate the product or service on a 1–10 scale as to whether you would recommend it. Simple, eh? Predictably, more people respond to these one-question surveys than to longer ones. There are four major downsides, however. First, it is still a survey of someone's opinion, and happiness with a product or service does not necessarily mean I will buy it again. I would rate the Kia I had as a rental car as a 10 out of 10, but I would never buy one and give up my classic British car. I might rate my flight on United as a 3 out of 10, but I would fly United again because I want to earn my 1K status again to get free upgrades. Second, I don't want to take up my time to give your business feedback when I am already mad or even if you did an okay job—I have better things to do with my time. Third, most people don't respond to any survey unless they are really mad or really happy, so survey scores may not reflect the entire group of customers. Fourth, if you get a low score on a one-question survey, you have no idea why, unless you follow up with more questions, aggravating a disgruntled customer even more. Therefore the data from these one-question surveys is not actionable. There is no way to tell from a one-question survey why people are happy or angry about your product or service.

TYPES OF ORGANIZATIONS WHERE THIS METRIC IS APPROPRIATE

Any organization that sells products or services to consumers needs to think about using the social network index. Even though you may rely on others to sell and service your products, you need this index on your dashboard. What this means is that any organization that manufactures products or provides services to consumers needs to track this. Stores, restaurants, toothpaste manufacturers, car companies, package delivery companies, online retailers, and hundreds of other types of organizations need real-time data on what consumers are saying about them. What about business-to-business? There a lot of big companies that do not sell directly to consumers. Cargill, the largest privately owned company in the world, sells almost exclusively to industry. It produces and sells food products, everything from flour to corn to meat. It sells raw materials such as tanker cars of corn syrup to Coca-Cola and also sell eggs to McDonald's for its Egg McMuffins. When a consumer drinks a Coke and scarfs down a couple of Sausage McMuffins with that Coke, the consumer often has no idea he or she is consuming Cargill products. However, it might be interesting to see what consumers are saying about the products made with your ingredients. It is also pretty important to hear what Coca-Cola and McDonald's are saying about your products. Businesspeople use social media to communicate as well, and they are consumers also.

In short, just about any size or type of organization needs to have this metric. Schools, hospitals, government organizations, and others that tend to have more of a captive audience of customers should be monitoring what people are saying about their experience with your organization. The beauty of this metric is that you don't have to spend hundreds of thousands or be a big corporation to track and use this analytic. The data is available, sometimes free of charge.

Another useful approach to measuring customer satisfaction without surveys is to monitor what customers are saying about your business on sites like Twitter and Yelp. Yelp is a site that started in San Francisco but has migrated to other cities; it gives consumers a way to review businesses using 1 to 5 stars and provide detailed comments on their experience. A small business that cannot afford surveys or simply doesn't want to do them can monitor its reviews and use average rating as an overall metric. The reviews often provide a wealth of useful details on what people liked and did not like. The sad thing for many small businesses is that a few angry consumers can post things that may or may not be true about your business. Twitter or Facebook might be a better bet, but there is no overall numerical rating system like Yelp's 5 stars, so it is harder to get quantifiable data. Yes, the words and comments are interesting, but it is tougher to sort and categorize them into useful summaries. There is software available to help you make sense out of all the tweets. Online surveillance of social networking sites has become the latest tool in the arsenal of techniques for measuring and predicting customer buying behavior. According to an article in *USA Today*, Indiana University has developed techniques for capturing daily tweets, analyzing them with mood measurement tools, rating the mood of the tweets as positive or negative and calm versus anxious, and then quantifying the data in summary form.[1] So many people use Twitter and other social networking sites to comment on their experiences that this is a wealth of data that might be used to measure customer satisfaction without having to do surveys.

Data from tweets is viewed as unstructured data that is harder to quantify and hence less useful than ratings of 1 to 10 on survey questions, or even counting numbers of delayed flights, lost packages, or power outages. However, firms that have figured out how to tap into this data, quantify it, and use it for performance assessment and decision making are often leading their competitors. Several investment firms are even using data from daily tweets to make buy or sell decisions and beat the market. Thomson Reuters's news analytics service measures how positive or negative a news story is about your firm and, combined with circulation information, it can use this data to predict actions such as a drop in stock price. Market Psych is a company that is selling data feeds from its proprietary mood measurement software to investment firms.

HOW DOES THIS IMPACT PERFORMANCE?

The impact of this analytic on all other measures of an organization's performance cannot be underestimated. In the past, companies could easily ignore disgruntled customers or placate them with a small gift or apology. Hotels always use the ubiquitous fruit basket as the standard apology for any error or problem. I like Marriott's new approach much better. When the valet was loading my luggage in the back of the car at the JW Marriott in Palm Desert, he knocked the suitcase into a glass vase my wife had back there and broke it. She had purchased it a few days before and we had forgotten about it. The valet was appropriately horrified and offered to refund the close to $100 for valet parking that the Marriott was charging for our three-day stay. Since the vase was $6.99, we thought that was a fair deal, so we gladly accepted his offer and waited while he credited my card for the parking fees. We left the Marriott feeling good rather than being mad about the vase. My wife immediately announced this to the world on Facebook as we drove away, no doubt causing a few of her friends to place inexpensive breakable objects in their trunks during their next visit to the Marriott. The impact of this valet's quick action is that my wife and I are probably more likely to stay at this Marriott again, and I am more likely to seek out Marriott properties during my many nights on the road for business. So the action of the valet not only helped ensure my future business, but this episode was broadcast all over Facebook to my wife's friends and contacts, further enhancing Marriott's reputation for excellent customer service.

Being able to monitor good and bad qualitative data like this is invaluable to organizations. Not only can you learn whether a customer is happy or angry, but you can learn exactly what made them feel this way. The best part about this type of data is that it does not require you to ask anything of the customer. For some reason people hate doing surveys, but they love posting their opinions on Facebook or Twitter. I think I know why. When you fill out a survey, there is zero reward and zero feedback. Even if you do get feedback it is almost always delayed. Psychology 101 teaches us that behavior must receive immediate reinforcement or reward if it is to be repeated. There is no reward for filling out a survey. If you have negative ratings, there is often a negative consequence—more questions or someone calling you to ask about the reasons for your low ratings. Posting comments on social media often results in immediate feedback and positive reinforcement. Friends and contacts read your comments, and often provide their own comments about what you wrote. Write a comment about the new restaurant you went to last night being horrible, and several friends might respond that they loved it or agree with your perceptions. Whether people agree, like, or dislike your comments, you are getting feedback. Most of us like to be listened to, and we really like it when others laugh at what we say or agree with it. Social media provides a lot of immediate positive reinforcement for the behavior of posting our comments about a product or service. There is zero feedback and no positive reinforcement provided for filling in a survey other than an e-mail saying, "Thank you," which just doesn't do much for most of us.

As the way we communicate with one another continues to evolve, social media is quickly becoming the dominant force in customer buzz. According to a January 23, 2013, news release from CFI Group in Ann Arbor, Michigan, people shared their experiences regarding a business with others 47 percent of the time within the 2012 CFI sample, up from 45 percent of the time in 2011.[2] Of those people who shared, a full 91 percent of them used social media in some form to do their sharing. Facebook dominated the social media channels, representing 33 percent of the "sharing volume." What this data tells us is that almost half of consumers regularly comment on businesses they frequent, and that almost all of them use social media as the method of proving this feedback. What they don't do is fill out surveys!

COST AND EFFORT TO MEASURE

The cost of using social media data to measure customer satisfaction can range from zero up to hundreds of thousands of dollars. If you own a restaurant with 13 employees and 40 seats, chances are you have to work as the host, busboy, waiter, manager, accountant, and possibly sometimes the chef. There is no way you can afford a company like Gallup or J.D. Power to do your survey, and you don't have the time or expertise to do it yourself. Yet you are very interested in getting feedback from customers. Asking people about their experience as they leave might be one way to get real-time feedback, but many won't want to give you negative feedback to your face, so they may just say it was fine and never come back. Also, data like this is hard to quantify, and you might tend to overreact to one negative customer who might be the type of person who complains about everything. A better way is just to go on a web site like Yelp where consumers post daily feedback about their experiences at stores, restaurants, and other types of businesses. Not only are there numerical ratings that can be viewed as quantifiable metrics, but there are comments to support the ratings as well. This can provide you with a wealth of information and you can ignore comments that may be unfair and just from one person and look for trends and common themes. So by reviewing the data on Yelp on a daily basis you have a way to get real-time quantifiable and qualitative data from your customers without spending any money. The one caution is that not everyone takes the time to go on sites like Yelp to write reviews, and not everyone goes on Twitter, Facebook, or other social media sites to post their comments. So you are not getting feedback from a lot of your customers, but the same is true of surveys, and I would guess that a lot more people use social media to post comments and ratings of a business than those who fill out surveys.

If you are AT&T or Nestlé, you probably are willing to invest some money to measure customer satisfaction, and because you have millions of customers, dealing with all this data requires the help of some professionals. Companies like Verizon can track daily tweets and Facebook posts that mention Verizon and can then detect whether the comment is positive or negative as well as the amount of emotion. If they find that most of the comments are about dropped calls and there is a lot of the negative emotion of frustration, Verizon can zero in on the geographic region where the comments originated and work on solving the problem. While this kind of data is clearly going to cost some big dollars to collect, its value is huge. Being able to pinpoint problems with real-time customer data has immeasurable value for an organization. Being able to identify exceptional service and tie it to individual employees is also useful for employee recognition and for figuring out how this great service occurred so it can be duplicated and deployed to other locations.

HOW DO I MEASURE IT?

One of the first steps in developing a measure of customer satisfaction via social media is to first decide whether you want to count all customers the same. Yes, all customers are important, but for most organizations some customers are much more important than others. This analytic is usually more meaningful if it includes both what people are saying about your products or services and who is saying it. For example, what an important restaurant critic says about your new menu is probably more important than what the average customer says. However, looking at the importance of an individual customer can be deceiving. The relatively unknown country singer whose guitar was broken by careless United baggage handlers became very well known when his ballad and YouTube video "United Breaks Guitars" went viral. The social media commentary of a single customer caused a drop in United's stock price. Individual consumers have an unprecedented level of power these days. Through social media and eventually going on television shows like *Ellen*, a single teenage girl got Pepsi to remove a chemical from Gatorade that caused her health problems.

SORTING OUT THE BEAUTIFUL FROM THE UGLY CUSTOMERS

Lenders have been scoring the relative attractiveness of customers using credit scores for years. We all have some number from 400 to 800 that influences the likelihood we will get credit as well as whether we will get a preferential interest rate. Well, it turns out that we are being rated on more than just our creditworthiness. We are being rated on how influential we are. If you have an account on LinkedIn, Facebook, or Twitter, you are already being rated.

Influence scores range from 0 to 100. On Klout, the dominant company doing these ratings, the typical score is in the teens; a score of 40 would indicate a strong niche following. A score of 100 would indicate you are someone like Oprah or Lady Gaga. Marketers of the influence scores claim that over 2,500 companies are using this data. Audi recently announced that it would be offering promotions based on Klout data. Last year Virgin America offered highly rated influencers in Toronto a free flight to either Los Angeles or San Francisco. The good news from all this is that your level of influence is based on more things than how good-looking, rich, or powerful you are. The bad news is there is now another number we are getting labeled with that will impact how easy or hard life will be for us. A Klout score on its own is not a measure of customer satisfaction or dissatisfaction but a factor that allows you to assign weight to the importance of social media feedback. A 5-star rating and enthusiastic positive comments from a highly influential person are valued at many times more than a similar rating from an unknown person.

The second decision that has to be made is which social media sources you want to include in the index. Based on the study from CFI Group mentioned earlier, Facebook is the most common way for people to voice their opinions about products and services they buy. Yelp is something to consider, because it already includes numerical ratings that can be tracked, but I don't believe that Yelp is used in all cities. Amazon is another place where people can write reviews about things they buy and give numerical ratings. However, this won't work if you are a hospital or a dry cleaner. Each organization has to review the various social media sources where customers might comment on the organization and pick three to five of them to include in your social media index. Once you have selected the sources that are most appropriate for your organization, you need to assign a percentage weight to each one, based on its potential to be viewed by others.

A third decision you need to make is whether you want to quantify the verbatim data or just use ratings. A good part of social media data is not 1- to 5-star ratings but the comments people make. Not including the verbatim comments certainly makes it easier and less expensive to track social media data, but the feedback is not very actionable if you don't review why someone rated you 1 star out of 5. Without any numerical data you will need software to analyze the posts for whether they are positive, negative, or neutral, and to assign a numerical value based on the degree of emotion displayed.

As with many of the analytics described in this book, your approach to constructing this index needs to be customized based on your budget, number of customers, and the type of organization where you work. A small community hospital or restaurant would be expected to have a very different approach than a big corporation with 25,000 employees. The straw man model presented here is for medium to large organizations with thousands of customers and probably at least hundreds of employees:

Numerical ratings	40%
Sites like Yelp, Amazon, Trip Advisor, Zagat, and Angie's List and comments on Twitter, Facebook, and other similar sites	60%

Each individual rating (assumes comments converted to 1–5 rating) is multiplied by the Klout score or some similar measure that evaluates the importance of the reviewer to the organization and its customers. Klout scores range from 0 to 100 points, which is a good scale to use even if you are creating your own metric. Rather than multiply the ratings by the importance of the customer, a more common and probably better approach is to code and analyze the data according to broad categories of customers in bands of 20 or 25 on the 100-point Klout scale. A third and even simpler alternative is just to compute average rating or number of stars like they do on Trip Advisor and other sites. That way each customer review is counted equally and the organization just looks to improve its average rating. Whether the Klout score is a factor in your analytic depends a lot on the type of business you are in. Many industries have identified people they view as thought leaders, or individuals whose opinions are important for the industry's success. For a pharmaceutical company, these might be important doctors and researchers at prestigious universities or clinics. For a film production company, thought leaders might be reviewers and members of the Academy who vote on Academy Awards. For a bank these might be high net worth individuals, as they call them. If your employer is a medium-priced hotel chain, you might just want to count all guests' feedback as being worth the same value and not bother with the idea of a Klout score.

If you decide that the concept of factoring in the importance of the customer providing the feedback is worth including in your social network index, then each individual rating (assumes comments are converted to 1- to 5-star ratings) is multiplied by the Klout score. As mentioned, Klout scores range from 0 to 100 points. You want to set up the metric so a strong positive or negative review by a really important customer has a big impact on your overall performance. Therefore, a few really important people giving you 5 stars and lots of kudos on Facebook can offset bad reviews by 15 unimportant people. Of course, the danger of this is that readers of Facebook posts or Trip Advisor ratings look at the overall number and percentage of positive and negative reviews, and don't really care who did them. If you are a five-star hotel, it might be important for you to know that a billionaire frequent guest was not happy with his or her stay versus a middle-class family who used all their frequent flyer miles to pay for the stay and will probably never come back.

Regardless of how you decide to calculate the social index data and combine it into an analytic, this data should be tracked and reviewed daily in most cases. By reviewing this data every day you can quickly detect small problems, isolate them by location or even staff member or product, and take quick corrective action. If you wait until the end of the week to read the horrible reviews about the rancid walnuts in the arugula salad, you would have served a lot of bad salads and angered a lot of guests who might not come back.

VARIATIONS

The easiest and most common approach to getting started using social network data as a customer satisfaction metric is to simply use average ratings done by customers on sites like Yelp, Amazon, and Trip Advisor. Since this is the same data prospective customers will use when deciding whether to buy your product or visit your establishment for some surgery, this is probably a good metric to track.

Another variation is simply to use the Klout rating as a measure in and of itself. If you are a professor, writer, consultant, doctor, director, investment advisor, advertising executive, or are in any other profession where your image, credibility, and reputation are key, the Klout measure by itself is probably the best social network metric to use. My colleague Bernard Marr reports on this metric in his excellent book, *Key Performance Indicators: The 75 Measures Every Manager Needs to Know*.[3] Like your FICO or credit score, the exact formula for calculating the score is not widely publicized, but it is comprised of three variables:

1. **True reach**. Size of the person's Facebook and Twitter audience who actively listen and react to posts.
2. **Amplification score**. Percent likelihood the person's posts will generate reactions like retweets, comments, or "likes."
3. **Network score**. How influential the engaged audience is on a 1–100 scale.

Marr suggests that his own score is 68 out of 100, whereas Barack Obama's is 88 and Lady Gaga's is 93. I haven't bothered to check mine, but perhaps I should. Another common metric used by researchers and writers is citations—number of times others have cited your work in theirs. I just gave my friend Bernard a few points by citing his book.

TARGETS AND BENCHMARKS

General targets for a social media index would be to receive at least an average of 4 stars out of 5. Many people think twice about buying a product or giving their business to an organization with a rating of 3 or lower. Some will only buy things that are rated at least 4.5 stars. Overall, I would set targets as: 4 stars or above is green, 3 stars is yellow, and 1 or 2 stars is red.

Your targets for a Klout score or something similar like citations should be set based on studying competitors you admire. A benchmark for me is Bernard Marr, with his score of 68, since he is an author and consultant and we are in the same field. Another benchmark for me might be Dr. Robert Kaplan, who has written extensively on activity-based costing and balanced scorecards.

BENEFITS OF DATA

The benefits of getting real-time data from almost half of your customers on a daily basis are enormous, and include:

- Saving money by not having to survey your customers.
- Avoiding making customers angry by sending them surveys.
- Gathering verbatim comments that can be quantified as well as read for details.
- Diagnosing the precise reasons why customers are satisfied or dissatisfied with your products and services.
- Getting early feedback on new products or services before broad-scale introduction.
- Detecting minor problems before they become bigger problems.
- Showing your customers that they matter and that you listen to them by responding to their feedback.

NOTES

1. Adam Shell, "Wall Street Traders Mine Tweets to Get a Trading Edge," *USA Today*, May 4, 2011.
2. "Social Media Best Used for Damage Control by Call Centers," news release, CFI Group, January 23, 2013.
3. Bernard Marr, *Key Performance Indicators: The 75 Metrics Every Manager Needs to Know* (London: FT Publishing, 2012).

CHAPTER **12**

The Service
Excellence Index

 WHY AN ORGANIZATION MIGHT TRACK THIS

Questions Answered

- How easy do we make it for customers to do business with our organization?
- How easy is our web site to navigate and for people to find what they need?
- How do we respond when there is a problem?
- How do we perform on key "moments of truth" that define the caliber of our service?
- Does our service tell customers that we value their business or just the opposite?
- How do we perform on key measures like quality and speed?
- How well trained are our customer-facing personnel to deliver consistently excellent service?
- How well do our systems and tools perform in making it easy for our staff to provide excellent service?

Why Is This Information Important?

People and organizations today have more choices available to them than ever before. We truly have become a global economy and people can buy goods and services from all over the world and have them at their doorstep in a few days. You would think that all this increased competition would mean better service, but that does not seem to be the case. When was the last time you had a really great flight attendant on a

163

flight you were on? When was the last time you got really great service from the DMV or some other government office? When was the last time you had a contractor or repairman who really did his job well and on time at a fair price? A handyman in my area has named his business "I Show Up" because so many of his competitors just don't even show up for work, let alone get the job done right.

Service quality is important because it is so rare today. That means we really notice when we get it, and most of us try to spend our money with organizations that really do a great job. Sure, you can find the same sweater online cheaper than it is at Nordstrom, but you won't get the kind of service you can from Nordstrom. There are cheaper alternatives to Southwest these days on many routes as well, but you won't get that friendly and reliable Southwest service if you try to save money on one of the other low-cost airlines.

In Chapter 13 I talk about the customer rage index as a way of tracking how often your organization infuriates customers. This metric is about how you perform on key measures of service quality. Many of these are more positive in nature and help strengthen the relationship you have with customers.

TYPES OF ORGANIZATIONS WHERE THIS METRIC IS APPROPRIATE

It does not matter whether you sell to consumers (B2C) or to other businesses (B2B), good-quality service is important and needs to be measured. Certainly this metric is appropriate for health care organizations that range from clinics to hospitals to doctors' offices. Good service in health care is about as rare as good service on an airline these days. This measure also applies if you are in any kind of service business—airlines, restaurants, retail stores, online retailers, travel companies, hotels, repair businesses like auto dealerships, banks, credit card companies, insurance companies, and pretty much any city, state, and federal government agency that provides direct services for taxpayers and visitors. Even products like hardware and software usually come with service contracts, and you might have to deal with repair people or customer service call centers to address issues and problems. Universities and schools are in the service business as well and need to measure service excellence.

HOW DOES THIS IMPACT PERFORMANCE?

Most industries today are producing good-quality products. The total quality management (TQM) movement of the 1990s seems to have paid off in many industries. Cars are now very well built, as are most of the things we buy today. Appliances don't seem to last 20 to 30 years like they used to, but most other things have gotten better. What has gotten steadily worse is service. We have learned to accept bad service or are unwilling to pay for it to be better. Call your health insurance company that you pay $1,000 a month to and you get to talk to a machine that makes you repeat everything. Many online retailers like eBay don't even have a published phone number—you have to e-mail them or try to use another method of contact.

Bad service has a huge impact on all sorts of success measures, like revenue, profits, customer loyalty, brand image, and even employee satisfaction. No one wants to work for a company that everyone hates. No one wants a job talking to mad customers all day long. Yet there are a few shining stars showing us that it is possible to offer good service and still make a profit. Discover Card in Chicago has TV commercials out right now showing that if you call 1-800-DISCOVER you will immediately get through to a live person who is both friendly and knowledgeable and sounds like a native English speaker. Wow, what a concept! Discover has always been this way, but I guess it didn't realize what a competitive advantage that was. The company has a really great culture (see Chapter 18) and provides good service in many other ways besides answering the phone. Other examples of good service exist as well: Starbucks, Zappos, UPS, Nordstrom, Southwest Airlines, and Orchard Supply Hardware. Good service is so rare these days that we are almost shocked when we get it. When we do get good service and we get it consistently, those are the organizations that continue to get our business.

COST AND EFFORT TO MEASURE

The cost of developing a good service quality index is going to be high. This is not as simple as developing a survey. One of the most important first steps is to do a thorough job on "voice of the customer" research to define exactly what people want and expect and what their priorities are. One organization that does this exceptionally well is pet food company Purina. In fact, their research methods are viewed as one of their competitive advantages and are a big part of why they are number one in sales and market share in a very competitive and profitable business. Once you have spent the time and money to figure out exactly what people want and don't want, the next step is to develop mechanisms to track compliance with these needs. Sometimes these are operational metrics that you already track, like on-time delivery for package companies or airlines, or fixing the car correctly the first time. Other times they are behavioral measures such as whether you are greeted with eye contact and a smile when you walk into the doctor's office. Behavior measures are often the key to good service, but these are the toughest and most expensive to measure. What is even tougher is getting frontline employees to engage in the right behaviors on a regular basis. Places like Disney and Marriott spend a lot of money on training and supervision to ensure that everyone does the right things to ensure a positive customer experience.

HOW DO I MEASURE IT?

Before talking about how to measure service excellence, I need to start by warning you about how *not* to measure it. The following are some of the more common mistakes to avoid when developing service metrics:

Mistake 1: Surveys. If you are thinking about doing a survey to see how good your service is, go back and read Chapter 11 on the social media index and read ahead to Chapter 13 on the customer rage index for some good alternatives to surveys. Customers are inundated with surveys at work and at home, and the vast majority of us do not bother filling them out even if we are happy or upset. We just go on Yelp or Facebook and provide some feedback that is read by lots of other people.

Mistake 2: Stupid operational metrics. A metric that most call centers track is ASA, or average speed of answer—how quickly they answer the phone. The problem is that the phone is answered by a machine that asks a series of questions to try to route the calls to another machine or someone who cannot solve your problem. Another common service quality metric is cycle time. Doctors' offices measure how long it takes from the time you sign in until you get into the treatment room. What that means is now you are in a little room that is freezing and there are no magazines and you have to wait an additional 20 minutes for a doctor to come in and give you seven minutes of his or her time. Fast-food places measure cycle time as the time from when you yell your order into the drive-through microphone until the time they take your money and give you change. "Please pull over there and wait for your food." Five minutes later you get your food. That part of the cycle is not measured.

Mistake 3: Reciting customer service scripts. Some companies think that good service is just a matter of learning a few snappy phrases that you repeat over and over with each customer: the restaurant manager who walks by and says, "How is everything, folks?" as he keeps walking so he does not hear the answer; the server who says the word "Enjoy" as he or she sets down your plates of food and beats it out of there before you can ask for anything. When I was on the phone with Expedia trying to get the customer service rep to figure out why my reservation was canceled, I must have heard "I am going to put you on hold again; I apologize for the wait" 15 times during a 45-minute call that never did resolve my problem. I recently called HP several times for a computer problem, and I noticed that each call started with, "Yes, that must be very frustrating. How can I help you today?"

Okay, so now that you know what to avoid, how do you measure service excellence? A call center I worked with had one metric for customer service reps (CSRs), which was an index comprised of three submetrics:

1. Accuracy—did the CSR solve the customer's problem?
2. Efficiency—how long was the call?
3. Courtesy—was the CSR polite to the customer?

The three factors were weighted so that solving customers' problems were worth 50 percent of the score, getting them off the phone quickly was worth 30 percent, and courtesy was 20 percent. This encouraged the right behaviors of never getting a customer off the phone or worrying about the "Have a nice day" stuff until you are sure you have solved the problem. While this is a call center, there is something to be learned here in developing a service excellence metric for any type of organization.

Service Quality

The first type of metric to develop for your service excellence index is one that measures the quality and accuracy of whatever transaction is being performed: 10,000-mile service on the car, package shipped to your parents, hotel check-in, annual physical at the doctor, or whatever the service is. The point is to make every attempt to measure service quality without having to survey the customer. A quality call is measured by a supervisor listening in or a lack of callback. A quality car repair is measured by the customer not having to come back. A quality flight is one that lands on time and has no claims for lost or delayed bags. Service quality might also be comprised of several different metrics. For example, your car dealership might have a checklist of things that must be completed before returning a car to a customer: called customer to inform them when car is ready, car washed, complete documentation on repair order and invoice, floor and steering wheel clean, and so on. Service quality in a grocery or retail store might be an accurate receipt. My wife frequently catches mistakes (which are always in the store's favor) as items are scanned by the cashier. In fact, a local news story indicated that this happens quite frequently. A service quality measure for a government organization might be whether Medicare paid your hospital bill, or unemployment sent you a check, or the doctor cured your problem.

Service Efficiency

AltaMed, the largest community health care organization in California, recently partnered with the PhDs at Purina to help conduct "voice of the customer" research. They researched patients of AltaMed as well as patients of competing health care providers like Kaiser

Permanente. One of the findings is that men and women have different priorities for health care service. The number one concern for men is getting in and out of there as quickly as possible. I recall Pfizer telling me that 70 percent of doctor visits in the United States are made by women. Men don't want to go to the doctor in the first place, and when they do go, all they want is to get out of there fast. Women care about efficiency as well, but they care more about the doctor spending time to really diagnose their problem and treat them properly. They also want to get all of their questions and concerns answered. A simple and easy measure of efficiency is cycle time. However, you need to measure the total cycle time from the customer's perspective, not yours. You need to track how long the patient was in the clinic from the time he walks in the door until the time he leaves.

Hotels need to track how long it took to get checked in and into the room from the time the guest walks in the door. This includes time spent waiting in line, walking to the room, and walking back to the front desk because the stupid electronic key does not work. Some hotels are getting smart about this and have put phones by the elevator so you can call the front desk and have them bring a replacement key, rather than making you schlep your luggage all the way back to the desk and wait in line again for another key. This small improvement probably reduces the cycle time of getting guests into their rooms. If you are a call center, you need to measure the total time the person was on the phone, including time spent waiting on hold and listening to the recorded voice telling you, "Your call is important." The DMV in California has dramatically improved efficiency for key processes by letting you renew your registration online, which takes about five minutes and you don't have to leave home, and by letting you make appointments online for in-person visits to the DMV. Both of these changes have dramatically improved efficiency for both customers and DMV personnel.

Besides cycle time, other service efficiency measures might include self-service options. Home Depot might track the percentage of customers who check themselves out using the new scanners that don't require cashiers. I don't know if any of you have tried these things, but they are often not efficient for the customer. Checking out takes a lot longer since you frequently have to scan everything two or three times because the scanner didn't get it the first time, bag your own stuff, do the payment, and so on. However, these automated self-serve checkouts lower costs for Home Depot. Other transactions actually are faster if customers do them themselves. Booking a trip on the Internet is a lot faster than going to a travel agent. Automation is great if it saves customer time but not if it makes life harder. I recently stayed at the Grand Hyatt New York, and it had self-serve check-in kiosks. Swipe your credit card, get a room key. Simple and efficient, and it really does save time. The self-service check-ins at the airport are not quite as reliable, and for some reason I always have to have a person help when the machine won't issue my boarding pass. However, checking in at home and printing my boarding pass saves me about 15 minutes at the airport, so total cycle time to get a boarding pass has been dramatically reduced. Hertz has a new service where you just drop off the car and walk away. An employee checks the car and e-mails you a receipt that you usually receive before you get too far.

Service Courtesy

This one is way down the list on most people's priority list, but it is still important. Dealing with someone who is nice and polite can help differentiate a company—that service advisor at the dealership who always remembers you and asks about your dog or kids; the receptionist at the doctor's office who actually looks up and smiles and greets you by name; the Starbuck's barista who remembers both your name and order and starts working on it as soon as you walk in the door. Little things like this make a big difference. However, many companies choose to focus on courtesy over competence. Most call centers these days are staffed by really nice idiots. They teach people all these comforting phrases, but they don't teach them how to solve your problem. Service courtesy can help make up for inefficiency. Our local Italian restaurant Mama D's always has a long wait. Many people bring their kids, who are hungry and sometimes cranky. The friendly hostess comes out to smile at the people waiting for a table and hands out focaccia bread and crayons and coloring placemats for the kids. The restaurant has even installed several child-size desks on the sidewalk so kids can color or play with some of the provided toys while the family waits for a table. A restaurant I used to go to in Chicago would hand out small glasses of Chianti to people waiting for a table. A smile and a glass of wine or piece of bread can certainly do a lot to offset a wait for a table.

Of the three metrics, service courtesy is the toughest to measure because it usually involves observing and recording behavior. Many organizations use mystery shoppers to measure employee behavior. They can track things like eye contact, smiling, tone of voice, and other factors that might be hard for even a supervisor to track if he has seven people to supervise. Call centers record telephone conversations and listen to a small sample of them and score the CSRs for their courtesy—"This call may be recorded for quality purposes." Another measure related to courtesy is communication. I recall an article in *Fast Company* that said people's anxiety levels go up several notches when the person they are talking to to get a service problem resolved has a foreign accent. Knowing this, a simple metric might be the percentage of your customer contact people who have an accent. Another related measure might be the nationality of your customer contact personnel compared to the nationalities of your customers. A health care client has found that Hispanic patients give Hispanic service providers higher courtesy ratings. Chinese patients give Chinese service providers higher courtesy scores. Matching the demographics of your customer-facing personnel to the demographics of your customers could be something that is measured as part of your courtesy score.

Service Recovery

The fourth type of submetric that goes in your service quality index is one that looks at how well you recover from service problems. When I worked with Sheraton Hotels years ago, the standard response to any guest problem was a fruit basket. Fruit baskets seemed to solve all customer problems in the hotel business, or so the Sheraton thought. How you recover from problems can often make the difference between keeping and losing a customer. I will never return to Expedia based on how it handled my problem that was caused by the company, but I am a lot more likely to return to Marriott after how it has handled problems in the past. Empowering employees to solve guest problems on the spot and spend money to do so is part of what makes Marriott service so great. United Airlines used to have a good system for doing this, but it appears to have stopped it. If you had any kind of problem on your flight, the flight attendant gave you a coupon that you could redeem for 10,000 to 30,000 miles, which is enough for a free ticket! Getting a few of these and an apology more than made up for not being able to recline my seat or listen to the movie. A simple metric for United was counting out how many of these recovery coupons its employees handed out. I am sure Marriott tracks service problems and their resolution. Tracking how many service recovery episodes you have is a simple and objective way of measuring excellence.

FORMULA AND FREQUENCY

Of course the specific metrics under each of these categories need to be tailored to your organization, but the following configuration is a good generic model to start the design of your own service excellence index:

Service quality	35%
Service efficiency or cycle time	35%
Cycle time	25%
Deadline or promised date or time met	10%
Service courtesy	15%
Courtesy	10%
Communication	5%
Service recovery	15%
Number of incidents × severity	

One of the good things about all of these measures is that they are unobtrusive. In other words, you don't have to ask your customers to fill out your surveys to get the data. Quality is measured via internal observations or using operational metrics like checklists or repairs completed correctly. Efficiency is just total cycle time for a transaction from a customer perspective. Courtesy can be measured via supervisors or mystery shoppers, and communication can be tracked the same ways. Call up your call center 20 times throughout the day and see how often you encounter someone with an accent. Combine that with the demographics of your customer-facing personnel versus the demographics of your customers, and you have an easy and important metric.

Most organizations that deal with consumers track the service excellence index every day. Those that have business customers might track it once a week or even once a month.

VARIATIONS

One common variation is to combine the proposed metrics with a customer satisfaction measure gathered via a brief one- to four-question survey. Even though I am not a big fan of surveys when used in combination with other metrics, I think they have their place. Another variation is to have a number of specific quality and efficiency metrics to go into this part of the index. For example, a call center I worked with had a service efficiency measure that included:

- Average speed of answer
- Call length
- Blocked calls (busy)
- Hang-ups
- Callbacks

TARGETS AND BENCHMARKS

Targets for these four individual metrics need to be set based on your own baseline and benchmarks. A big factor in achieving benchmark-level performance is hiring and training. You find that just about every firm that provides excellent service is very careful about each person they hire. Disney claims it hires the smile, and Marriott has identified important traits (things you are born with, not competencies) for every job, and it selects for these traits. You will also find that the best service companies do an amazing amount of training. Disney spends days and days training new cast members (the company's name for its employees), knowing that many won't even stay a year. Zappos offers new employees $2,500 to quit in the first 30 days, and almost no one takes the offer. When you set your targets for service metrics, you need to be realistic about the caliber of your employees, policies, tools (e.g., hardware and software), training, and other resources. Simply measuring service excellence does not help if your organization is unwilling to spend the bucks to make it improve.

BENEFITS OF DATA

Having a composite metric that gives you an indication of how the organization is performing for customers is going to be very useful. Of course, some CEOs don't seem to care that their company's service is bad, so a metric like this is not going to help at all. If your organization does care about service quality and thinks improving it might give you a competitive edge, then this is certainly going to help you do so. Some of the benefits of data generated from the service excellence index include:

- Identification of operational problems that cause dissatisfied customers.
- Identification of exceptional and bad customer-facing employees.
- Finding links between service quality and customer loyalty.
- Saving money on expensive customer surveys that are only filled out by a small minority of customers.
- Recovering from service problems faster and winning back customer goodwill.
- Improving your hiring and training of customer contact personnel.
- Identifying policies and procedures that detract from good service.
- Detecting system problems that slow down service or lead to poor-quality outcomes.

CHAPTER **13**

The Customer Rage Index

WHY AN ORGANIZATION MIGHT TRACK THIS

Questions Answered

- How hard do we make it for customers to do business with our organization?
- How many customers did we make angry today and how angry are they?
- How many customers are close to leaving?
- How many product or service quality problems occurred today?
- How likely is it that customers will post a negative review on social media?
- How many avoidable mistakes did we make today?
- To what extent have customers experienced bad service from our organization?

Why Is This Information Important?

I think it is rather obvious why this is important. Consumers have more power today than at any time in the past. One guy had the power to lower United Airlines' stock price when a YouTube video song he did about United breaking his guitar went viral and was seen by millions. Many of us really pay attention to reviews and consumer feedback before buying a product or service. We have all been disappointed by products that don't work as they promised or services that are poorly performed, so we now check before buying a lot of things. Mad customers often don't bother filling out surveys or even doing an online review. They just don't go back. Or they put up with the mistakes time and time again until they reach a boiling point and take their business elsewhere. By measuring how much you aggravate your customers you not only predict their future loyalty better than any survey can do, but you predict the likelihood that angry customers will tell many others about their past experiences via Facebook, Yelp, or just through casual conversations.

I don't know about you, but I hate customer satisfaction surveys. We are all inundated with them thanks to e-mail. It used to be these things came in the mail (easy to throw out) or by telephone (hang up). Now most of them come via e-mail. I stay in hotels 100-plus nights a year, and no matter how big or small the hotel was, they always manage to send me a survey several days later. Like you, I delete the survey unless I had a really bad experience.

I did waste 15 minutes filling out one I got from a St. Regis Hotel vendor and was madder after filling out the survey than before I started it because there was no place for me to explain the problems I experienced at the property. Plus, I had to spend 15 minutes of my time telling a company to which I just paid a lot of money how it screwed up. What is ironic is that those same customers who won't fill out your survey won't hesitate to post comments about every store or restaurant or airline they interact with on a daily basis. I guess we all want to be heard and have an opinion, but with surveys you get no feedback. When you post a comment on Facebook about some horrible experience you had at Home Depot or Target, others are likely to respond with sympathy and their own horror stories that top yours—immediate and interesting feedback. There is no reward for the behavior of filling out a survey.

Companies know that people are busy and hate filling out lengthy surveys, so two of the latest techniques are to make some vague offer that you might win something if you fill out the survey ("Earn a chance to win 100,000 airline miles") or to make the survey really short. A big trend now is one-question surveys, called a Net Promoter Score. The biggest problem with these brief surveys is still that most people don't fill them out unless they are mad, and if you only ask one question and get a low rating, you don't know what made them mad or what to do about it. Net Promoter Score surveys were really popular for a few years with companies like Verizon and Apple, because executives only had to review one simple statistic to measure customer satisfaction. However, most of the early adopters of Net Promoter Score surveys have moved away from them after realizing that: (1) most people still don't respond, (2) nothing can be done to determine the reasons for high or low ratings, and (3) relying on a single unsophisticated metric for something as important as customer satisfaction is foolish.

PROBLEMS WITH CUSTOMER SURVEYS

The big advantage of surveys is that they are cheap and easy, and anyone with access to Survey Monkey or similar software create one. The biggest problem with surveys is that most people don't respond or fill them out, and those who do tend to be really happy or really unhappy, provided an inaccurate reading of overall satisfaction of all customers. A 30 percent return rate on a survey is considered good, and most don't even get that. Some of the other problems with surveys are:

- Surveys take up valuable customer time.
- Surveys may frustrate unhappy customers even more.
- Surveys rarely generate any kind of follow-up response, making you wonder if anyone even reads them.
- Surveys often fail to include the most important questions, like "Did you get a good night's sleep at our hotel?"
- Surveys may not provide enough detail to diagnose and solve problems.
- Surveys cannot be done frequently or you could aggravate customers more.
- Some corporations like Walmart have policies of not filling out vendor surveys.
- Employees figure out how to cheat—real estate agents have handed out surveys only to customers they knew were happy with the transaction, and car dealers have been caught offering incentives to customers for high ratings on J.D. Power surveys.

One big advantage of surveys is that it is easy to compare your organization to others in your industry as long as everyone uses the same survey. J.D. Power and other firms like Gallup do surveys of customers for most of the companies in a number of industries such as hotels and hospitality, wireless phone service, Internet providers, automobiles, and others. By using one of these widely accepted surveys you can better set targets for your own performance and see how you compare to peers and industry benchmarks. This information tends to be very useful. However, as I have mentioned numerous times throughout this book, you can't manage with a measure that is tracked once a year. And no survey tends to capture 80 percent or more of your customers. Even if you had a survey that 100 percent of customers responded to, it is still a survey of someone's opinions at a given point in time. Further, responding to a survey takes up valuable time of your customers, who probably have other things to do besides help your business improve.

TYPES OF ORGANIZATIONS WHERE THIS METRIC IS APPROPRIATE

All organizations have customers, whether they are businesses, consumers, students, or patients. Similarly, all organizations do things that aggravate and frustrate their customers—people paying you money for a product or service. If your organization has more than 25 employees, you might want to consider this metric. Another factor to think about is whether your customers will fill out your surveys. Many businesses will not bother filling out surveys from their vendors or suppliers, and some even have policies against it. Even if you are doing a survey and getting back 20 to 30 percent of the ones that are distributed, you are still not measuring the satisfaction of the vast majority of your customers. While customer surveys are good for measuring the people who are really satisfied or dissatisfied, those who do not have strong feelings one way or the other are not being measured. Another criterion for selecting this metric is if there are operational factors that can be easily tracked that you know impact customer satisfaction. For example, waiting time in a doctor's office, hold time or hang-ups in a call center, or product returns for quality problems are all things that could be measured every day and are important to customers. An organization that might not want to bother with this metric is one that has a product or service that is so unique and popular that customers will put up with all sorts of aggravation in order to get it. However, no matter how unique and popular your product or service is, someone will undoubtedly rip you off and try to come up with something that is better and cheaper. I love my iPhone and am on my third one, but I did take a look at the new Samsung Galaxy this time, which is a very cool product. So my point is that even if you have a unique product or service now, it won't last, and you might want to measure how easy or hard it is for customers to do business with you.

HOW DOES THIS IMPACT PERFORMANCE?

The two most direct impacts of customer aggravation are loyalty and future revenue. Aggravated customers are not only less likely to be loyal, but they might just decide to spend their money on one of your competitors at the next opportunity. Even a customer who is only slightly aggravated is more likely to be lured away by a competitor and probably won't fill out your surveys to let you know this. What companies don't seem to track or be able to predict is how mad they have made customers. Losing a suitcase and recovering it 24 hours later may be a minor inconvenience for one customer, but it could be enough to make another customer never fly that airline again for the rest of his or her life. My friend Rob and his wife were flying to France for an important business contact's black-tie wedding. The airline lost their suitcase with Rob's tux and his wife's dress. Of course, they were dressed in jeans for the flight, and when they arrived in Paris they had no clothes for the wedding. Purchasing new outfits was not an option because there was not time, stores were closed, and it would have cost thousands that would not have been reimbursed by the airline. The suitcase showed up about 12 hours after the wedding, but it didn't matter at that point. This one event made Rob and his wife so angry at the airline that they will never fly it again. Ten years and several other long trips later, they have maintained their allegiance to Southwest and Virgin. You can bet that they have told this story for years to probably hundreds of people, who have told others, and then it ends up in a book!

One lost customer can result in the loss of thousands in revenue. Think of the impact if my friend Rob happened to be the CEO of a big company with 50,000 employees! CEOs have been known to change policies after such events in a refusal to spend any more company money on vendors that screw up like this. I would guess that the more important a person is, the less likely they are to fill out customer surveys, either. Can't you just imagine the frustrated airline sales executive trying to explain to his boss how one lost suitcase cost them the entire account? Chances are, without the type of data I am proposing in this chapter, the airline executive would have no way of knowing why the company stopped buying tickets.

I am sure that the airline only knows that it lost X number of bags that day and that X percent were recovered. If that number was in its normal range of bags misrouted, it was a good day according to the airline's scorecard. What the airline needs to know is, how many people did it make angry today who have given it money for air transportation, and how angry did it make them? Of course, a small minority of those mad people may decide to fill out their survey or write a complaint letter, but most will not.

Angry customers also have an impact on your brand. With the power of social media these days, consumers can tell thousands or more about your horrible service or shoddy product, which can have measurable impact on your brand image, which will in turn directly impact your revenue and profits.

COST AND EFFORT TO MEASURE

Depending on your approach, the cost and effort required to collect this data is probably medium to high. Of course, the value is also high, as is the integrity of the data since you will be measuring objective variables versus perceptions and opinions. If you deal with consumers as customers and have thousands of them, you may need additional software and hardware to handle the big data that could be generated. However, for now, understand that big data usually means big money. The reason big data might be necessary is that you had to track thousands of transactions for thousands of customers. If your business is a restaurant that serves 100 people a night you need not worry about tracking this, but for a software company with tens of thousands of users and hundreds of corporate customers, you might need to spend some dollars to start keeping track of how many customers are aggravated on a daily basis.

On the other hand, I have had a number of clients start tracking this index with very little cost. Often the factors that go into the customer rage index are already tracked via operational or quality metrics, so it is just a matter of assigning weights and rolling them into an index. There is some upfront cost to pull all this together, but the overall implementation does not require new hardware or software and can be done fairly quickly. The cost and amount of effort totally depend on how many of the factors that go into the index are currently tracked.

HOW DO I MEASURE IT?

It is vitally important for an organization to measure customer satisfaction and to try to predict customer loyalty. It is also important to detect even minor dissatisfaction levels so something can be done to improve the relationship and keep the customer. An important point to remember about this measure is that it is not based on surveys or opinions. Customer perceptions and opinions are gathered up front to construct the index, but the index is comprised of objective factors that aggravate or frustrate customers that can be counted hourly, daily, or at least weekly. The rage or aggravation index is not a survey!

For example, look at FedEx, which was the pioneer in developing a daily metric that tracks how many customers it made mad on a daily basis and how mad it made them. By holding focus groups with customers from a variety of industries and locations, they gathered a long list of things FedEx had done to aggravate them over the years.

Once FedEx narrowed down this list to a reasonable number of problems, it had customers rank-order them from the most maddening to least, assigning 1-to-10 severity ratings. It turns out the 10, or worst thing FedEx could do, was lose a package and never recover it. A minor aggravation rating of a 1 or 2 might be a package that is an hour or two late. Every day, FedEx tracks occurrence of these problems, multiplies the frequency by the severity, and rolls it up into an index that measures customer aggravation levels. It turns out that this index is directly correlated to disloyalty.

Big surprise: If you make customers angry enough, they take their business elsewhere and usually don't bother filling out your survey.

TRACKING AGGRAVATIONS AT DIFFERENT TYPES OF ORGANIZATIONS

Milwaukee airline Midwest Express liked the idea of a daily metric that predicted customer loyalty and already had data on many of the factors that frustrate customers. Other than for a crash, the 10 rating is for an airline customer to use when the airline cancels the last flight of the night when you are on your way home, every hotel room in Chicago is sold out, and you have to sleep at O'Hare until you can get a flight the next morning. A minor aggravation for an airline customer might be having to check his or her carry-on luggage because the bins are full or getting placed on hold for 20 minutes by a reservation agent.

DTE Energy, the electric and gas company in Michigan (formerly Detroit Edison), liked the idea of an aggravation index as well and started tracking power outages, billing errors, and other factors on a daily basis. Discover Card in Chicago adopted this metric for a while as well and tracked call center waiting time, average call length, billing questions, handling of fraud, talking to someone in their call center with a foreign accent, and other factors that many people find aggravating. A big frustration for Discover Card customers was trying to use the card and finding out it was not accepted by the merchant. Although this is a big source of frustration, it is impossible to measure since the clerk or person taking the card will simply ask for a different one. Discover Card closely tracks the number of merchants it has and the number of transactions, but it has no way of tracking how many times the customer tries to use his or her Discover Card and is told it is not accepted. When deciding on the factors that get tracked in your own customer rage index, it is important not only to narrow them down to things that really bug customers but also things on which you can collect data. Amazon or my online vitamin company can track how many times it is out of stock on an item. However, Target might not have a way to measure how many times customers look for their brand of dog food and can't find it.

HOSPITAL RAGE INDEX

Going to the hospital can be a maddening experience, but hospitals can do a lot to lessen the amount of frustration and aggravation they cause patients and their families. Some of the variables that can be tracked daily that might go into this index include:

- Noise, which can be easily measured in decibels
- Wrong food measured against patient requirements
- Changes in patient contact personnel (doctors, nurses, aides)
- Unkept promises measured via schedule changes
- Number of pages of bills sent and degree to which bills are understandable (measured via sample)

- Inaccurate diagnoses
- Infections and other standard Healthcare Effectiveness Data and Information Set (HEDIS) health outcome metrics

I'm sure you can think of others, but this is just an example list of possible factors that might go into a patient aggravation index. Talking to family members and patients might reveal another list of aggravation factors, such as not answering the phone at the nurses' station, getting incomplete updates regarding the patient, limited seating in room and waiting areas, and so on.

ADVANTAGES AND DISADVANTAGES OF THE AGGRAVATION OR RAGE INDEX

The biggest downside of a metric like this is that it does not provide data on overall satisfaction levels or situations where you might have surprised and delighted a customer—it only measures screwups.

However, I think the list of advantages far outweighs the limitations:

- The aggravation index can be tracked and reported on a daily basis, providing real-time performance data.
- Customers do not have to put out any time or effort to give you data on their level of dissatisfaction.
- Most organizations track the things that frustrate customers already, so there is not a lot of cost in implementing this metric.
- The metric is simple enough for all levels of employees to understand.
- The data is actionable—levels of aggravation can be analyzed to determine the specific events or errors that occurred, and action plans can be put in place to improve outcomes.
- Aggravated customers eventually leave, and this measure gives you a way to detect minor problems before this occurs.

CONSTRUCTING THE INDEX

The basic process is to talk with customers to determine the factors that make them angry and to assign a severity weighting to each event or factor based on the degree to which it aggravates them. **Step 1** is to hold a series of focus groups with customers from various market segments and spend about 45 minutes getting them to brainstorm things that your organization or one of your competitors has done to aggravate them or make them angry. The goal is to get them to list at least 50 things without going into stories or details. Write down everything on a whiteboard or flipchart. **Step 2** is to get everyone to select their top 10 biggest aggravations, the things that would make them really think about never doing business with your company again or buying your product. Often you will see that there is a great deal of overlap in the top 10. Then have everyone indicate which one of the 50 or so factors made it to their top 10 list to come up with a group top 10 (**Step 3**). Sometimes there may be some duplication, so these factors can be combined. Once the group top 10 has been identified, **Step 4** is to have everyone rank-order the group top 10 list from worst to least aggravating. It helps to start by identifying the 10, or worst thing. In FedEx it is losing the package and never recovering it. In a restaurant it might be getting seriously ill as a result of the food. In a call center it might be getting disconnected after waiting on hold for 45 minutes on your fourth call for the same problem. Focus group participants work to complete their ranking from the most to least serious. This information is then used later to assign importance weights to each factor from 1 to 10. So 15 lost packages gets multiplied by 10 and equals 150. Twenty-eight damaged packages gets multiplied by 9 and gets a 252, and so forth.

The process is then repeated with other focus groups until you start getting consistent data, and then it is repeated every year or two to see if customer priorities have changed. As quality improves with most things, customer expectations become higher, and what might have been a minor aggravation before is now a big deal. It can work the other way as well. Most of us have such low expectations about air travel these days that we just know that it will be a mostly unpleasant experience. Consequently, it may take something major to really get our blood boiling.

FORMULA AND FREQUENCY

The basic formula is to count the number of events that occurred (e.g., power outages, dropped calls, hold time longer than 30 minutes, canceled flights, etc.) and multiply each event or occurrence by the 1–10 severity factor. By counting both the number of occurrences and events and multiplying each one by a weighting factor, you can gauge how angry or frustrated your customers are on a daily basis. Generally, this measure is tracked daily in most organizations that have adopted it.

VARIATIONS

Some organizations have opted for a more sophisticated analytic that considers three factors:

1. Number of negative events.
2. Severity of each event according to customers.
3. Number of customers impacted and importance of customers to organization.

This tends to make it more compelling data if we know that the power was out for three hours for a big area employer that buys 5 percent of our total power, versus the power going out at night for a few households. The way this works is that the number of negative events gets modified by adding two multipliers. So if we have one canceled flight and it is the last one of the night, that is a frequency of $1 \times$ a weight of 10. The importance of customers (180 passengers with 28 Million Mile Flyers) might be 8. So the one canceled flight gets a total of $10 \times 8 = 80$ points on our analytic.

TARGETS AND BENCHMARKS

Once you have established baseline levels for each of the top 10 negative events, you can begin gathering comparative data and benchmarks to help set targets. You can also use customer input to help set targets. Targets are generally set for each individual negative occurrence, and then you can set a target for the overall index once you get a stable baseline.

BENEFITS OF DATA

The biggest benefit of having data on how many customers you make angry on a daily basis is that you can more accurately predict their loyalty than some survey questions that ask customers about their future loyalty. Another major benefit of this data is that you push responsibility for customer satisfaction and loyalty down through the operational side of your organization. Often people in manufacturing and operations are disconnected from customers and feel no real accountability for their satisfaction. Salespeople or account managers may be responsible for landing new customers, but the product or service delivered is what will determine whether or not they are loyal.

CHAPTER 14

The American Index

 WHY AN ORGANIZATION MIGHT TRACK THIS

Questions Answered

- Are we growing jobs for Americans?
- Are we paying our fair share of taxes?
- Are we favoring U.S. suppliers and partners?
- Are we helping to contribute to a more prosperous economy?
- Are we minimizing the use of materials and supplies manufactured elsewhere?
- Are we supporting businesses in countries that are unfriendly to the United States?
- Are we supporting education and training to help create a more skilled workforce for the future?
- Do our products or services help improve quality of life or degrade it?
- Do we thoroughly research possible negative side effects of our products and services?
- Are we really filling a need?

Why Is This Information Important?

This last recession impacted just about everyone in the country and changed our values and consciousness. When the economy was booming, companies made more and more profits by selling people stuff they didn't need, continually driving down the cost of products by using foreign manufacturers and raw materials produced elsewhere, taking major risks in order to produce major profits, and using technology wherever possible to replace employees. Many companies created a mostly part-time workforce so they would not have to pay benefits and used a lot of contract labor so they could expand and shrink the workforce at whim and save on payroll taxes. Life was good. We were all house rich, there was plenty of work. And then it all came crashing down. There is not a person who was not somehow impacted by the recession that began in 2008 and for some is still going on. Housing prices in places like Las Vegas and Detroit may never recover.

All of this changed the way companies define their success. No one ever really thought about what was good for the country; a business thought about what was good for their shareholders. Now more and more companies are starting to assess their strategies in a new light. The UK bank Barclays made big news at the start of 2013 by announcing that it was closing its Tax Avoidance Unit, which helped corporations on a massive scale to avoid paying taxes. Some think the move was part of damage control to repair the bank's tarnished image for rigging LIBOR (the London Interbank Offered Rate) and paying its executives 2 billion in bonuses. The new Barclays has decided that advising customers on how to avoid paying taxes is unethical and not for the good of the countries in which they do business. Could it be that big banks like Barclays are really sincere about supporting the local economies and countries where they do a lot of business, like the United Kingdom and the United States? Whether it is a public relations stunt or due to a real change in values, the action is real, and the bank has eliminated an extremely profitable unit.

I think we will start to see more of this in the future. Some manufacturing companies are starting to bring back previously outsourced jobs to the United States. As wages have risen in China, Mexico, and other countries, it is no longer as inexpensive to have products manufactured elsewhere. Apple, whose products are pretty much all made in China, has received a lot of backlash for using Foxconn in China to manufacture its products. Foxconn is the subject of an investigative report on suicides by workers because of extreme stress levels.

It amounts to a financial drop in the bucket, but the $100 million Apple is investing to make some Macs in the United States could be priceless for national manufacturing. Apple is just one of several companies—Google is another—that has or plans to import manufacturing jobs back to the United States because of the economic and political advantages of producing them at home. Recently, Apple CEO Tim Cook said the company will produce one of its existing lines of Mac computers in the United States in 2014. He offered no other details. This is a major change for Apple. Steve Jobs told President Barack Obama, "Those jobs aren't coming back," when asked at a dinner in early 2011 whether Apple would consider shifting some manufacturing to the United States from China. It seems that some of those jobs are indeed coming back.

TYPES OF ORGANIZATIONS WHERE THIS
METRIC IS APPROPRIATE

This analytic is worth considering for any large organization that is a for-profit business. If you are a government organization or a nonprofit, this metric probably does not need to be tracked. However, this measure might also be appropriate for a hospital. I worked with a hospital in San Diego that went to the Philippines twice a year to recruit nurses. Hospitals also buy a lot of supplies from overseas manufacturers and may use foreign companies to perform key services like billing and legal document processing. Basically any large nongovernment employer should think about putting this metric on your balance sheet. An important dimension of performance is to balance the short-term desire for profits and growth with the longer-term concerns of supporting your own country and encouraging a healthy economy.

HOW DOES THIS IMPACT PERFORMANCE?

Doing a good job of supporting your country and community can have a big impact on your image with business and consumer customers. It can also have a big impact on potential employees. As the economy improves, people will get more selective in picking a potential employer. Being a company that is supportive of the U.S. economy is a factor important to many job seekers. Of course, your product or service has a lot to do with your image as well. If you manufacture cigarettes or kids' cereals loaded with sugar, creating new jobs for Americans may not offset the harm you are doing to society with your product. Supporting your country is also something that could increase your costs. The major reason companies started outsourcing manufacturing, call centers, and other key functions is that those things can be done overseas for a fraction of the cost. Call center workers in India earn a few thousand dollars a year, whereas American workers doing the same job get that much a month. Another reason that some things are not done here in America is that we lack the capacity or skill. Hospitals cannot find enough American nurses to fill their needs, and schools are not graduating enough nurses. Apple claims there is no manufacturer in the United States that can handle the capacity needed to make millions of its products. Thinking about supporting your country is important but so is making a profit. As with any of the analytics in this book, excelling at one thing may cause problems in another area of performance. Now that wages are down in the United States and up in other countries, manufacturing cars and electronics here in the United States might make financial sense.

When companies choose to outsource jobs or functions to other countries, they often don't think about the side effects of doing so. They look only at the short-term cost savings. I read an article that said that when consumers hear a foreign accent when calling a call center, their stress level automatically goes up a few notches because past experience tells them that the CSR's name is not really Bill, and that you two are going to have problems communicating. Another common problem is encountering a CSR with excellent communication skills who can't solve your problem. This experience may make a customer less loyal to your firm, after he or she sees that you don't care enough about customer service to staff your call center with competent people with good communication skills. Manufacturing overseas sounds good too and usually saves a lot of money in the short term, but there are other costs, such as hiring an agent or representative in the local company to oversee the manufacturer, sending your own people over there, waiting a long time for goods to be shipped, dealing with poor quality, and having the supplier steal your intellectual capital and end up being a competitor. Those are some pretty big costs that often don't get calculated until it is too late.

COST AND EFFORT TO MEASURE

The cost of measuring the factors that go into this analytic is low, and the amount of effort needed to track it is minimal. If you decide to include perception or opinion measures as part of this analytic, it might cost some money to conduct a survey or some focus groups, but the index is probably better if it just includes hard objective metrics like jobs and money spent on domestic versus foreign suppliers. Tracking down the supply chain may also be a bit of a challenge. It could be that you are buying something from a local distributor, but the product is made somewhere other than the United States. Many GM cars are made in Mexico and other countries, just as some Toyotas are manufactured in Georgetown, Kentucky, by American workers.

HOW DO I MEASURE IT?

The first step in creating an American index is to decide on the factors that will be measured. The broad categories of measures and the specific metrics to consider are:

- **Jobs**. Ratio of domestic to foreign employees, growth of domestic employees, ratio of part-time to full-time employees.

- **Wages**. Average compensation, ratio of worker compensation to executive compensation, growth in compensation for workers.

- **Suppliers**. Money and percentage of costs spent with domestic versus foreign suppliers.

- **Image**. Opinions or perceptions of customers, potential customers, community, stakeholders.

- **Taxes**. Total taxes paid versus industry averages and benchmarks.

VARIATIONS

Where this measure gets a little confusing is if you employ a lot of American workers to make a product that does not really help the country. What if you employ 10,000 American workers in factories that make guns or soft drinks? Calculating the type of business you are in probably does not make sense, because I'm sure American gun manufacturers believe that by employing 10,000 people they are doing their part to help the U.S. economy. What you might measure is the percentage of your sales that come from products good for society and the country and products that are bad. For example, a big company like Pepsi sells lots of its sodas but it also sells Dasani water and Gatorade sports drinks. A big company like Nestlé sells Nestlé Crunch candy bars but also sells lots of nutritional products and has a vision of moving the company more into nutrition and wellness:

Nestlé Vision and Values

To be a leading, competitive, Nutrition, Health and Wellness Company delivering improved shareholder value by being a preferred corporate citizen, preferred employer, preferred supplier selling preferred products.

Whether you are selling products or services that are good for your home country is a matter of opinion. Perhaps guns keep down the crime rate, and soft drinks do provide calories and energy, as do candy bars. You might even say a candy bar is nutritious because chocolate contains antioxidants. So as not to muddy up the index, I suggest focusing on tracking objective measures like jobs and use of domestic suppliers.

Other variations might occur if yours is an international firm with employees scattered all over the world. You might be a big employer in the United States and provide lots of good jobs, but you might also have plants and offices in 30 other countries. This is not necessarily bad and should not make your index look negative. The overall purpose of the analytic is to show that your organization is doing what it can to promote U.S. companies, create new jobs, and provide good wages for domestic employees.

FORMULA AND FREQUENCY

A generic straw man American index that you can tailor is as follows:

Jobs	30%
Number of new domestic jobs (growth)	15%
Ratio of foreign to domestic employees	10%
Ratio of full-time to part-time employees	5%
Suppliers and partners	25%
Growth in domestic supplier	15%
Ratio of foreign to domestic supplier	10%
Wages	25%
Average worker wage	10%
Ratio of full-time to part-time employees	10%
Ratio of worker pay to CEO pay	5%
Image	15%
Customers	10%
Public	5%
Taxes	5%

TARGETS AND BENCHMARKS

This is one metric where you really need industry and competitor data. If 20 percent of your furniture is made in the United States by American workers, you will probably stand out as a shining star among your peers in the industry since almost all furniture is manufactured in China, including the high-end brands like Henredon. If you purchase the vast majority of your raw materials for manufacturing pet food from domestic suppliers, you will stand out in your industry as being very pro-America when many of your competitors' raw materials come from foreign countries. If you are growing faster than any other retailer and hiring more Americans than any other company, like Walmart, people might forgive you for selling guns and ammo. Targets for metrics like job growth should also be set based on the local economy where you have facilities. Perhaps you have only had 10 percent job growth in the last year, but the area might have a net job loss of 10 percent so that makes your results look pretty good. In any event, targets need to be set based upon what is going on in the economy, your industry, and the geographic areas where you are located.

BENEFITS OF DATA

If you don't really care about supporting your own country and just care about making as much money as you can, this metric has no value to you. However, even if you don't care, your customers probably do. As much as people love Apple and its wonderful products, horror stories about Foxconn, its Chinese manufacturer, have tarnished Apple's image with many Americans. I'm sure that this is a big part of why Apple has agreed to start manufacturing some of its products in the United States in the future. Toyota has always been very supportive of its native country, Japan, but it was also a pioneer in building U.S. plants employing U.S. workers. America is a big market for Toyota, and it makes people feel better buying a Japanese car if they know it was made by American workers—unless you live in Detroit. It is still considered socially unacceptable to drive a non-American car in Detroit, even though many are made here. The benefits of this data are that you can now set a goal and track your progress toward being more supportive of the country where you live. The other benefit of this index is that you can track whether your being more supportive of the American economy makes a difference to your customers. People may feel bad that the jeans they just purchased for $50 are made in a sweatshop in Indonesia, but it does not stop them from buying the jeans. Promoting American jobs and the American economy is just one of many things a well-run organization needs to aspire to in order to be judged as successful.

CHAPTER 15

The Corporate Citizenship Index

WHY AN ORGANIZATION MIGHT TRACK THIS

Questions Answered

- Do we make sure that no one will be harmed by our products and services?
- Do we have a culture that rewards ethical behavior?
- Does everyone have the same understanding of right and wrong?
- Do we support our key communities and selected charities?
- Are we seeing good results from our social responsibility programs?
- Do consumers and others perceive us as a responsible company that cares about the community?

Why Is This Information Important?

Many organizations today have adopted a philosophy called the "triple bottom line" (TBL) that stands for:

- People
- Profits
- Planet

The "People" dimension addresses how you are doing at satisfying customers and your own staff. The "Profit" dimension is obviously financial results, and the "Planet" dimension is an assessment of how an organization performs on measures of sustainability (see Chapter 8) and supporting their own country and culture (see Chapters 14 and 18). Part of supporting our planet is demonstrating good levels of corporate responsibility or citizenship. This has long been part of the criteria for winning a Baldrige Award, as well as 70 other awards that are based on the Baldrige Award. Being a healthy company is not just about making good profits and having happy customers; it is also about supporting your key communities and managing your business in a socially responsible manner.

Research suggests that it is possible to have good scores in all three Ps. It is not a matter of trading off corporate citizenship for profits or vice versa. Google has been listed among the world's most ethical companies on a number of lists and always makes the top 10 of the best companies to work for from an employee standpoint; shareholders and customers are pretty happy with Google's performance as well. Target is another company that has an excellent reputation for being a good corporate citizen as well as being a top-performing company on many other metrics.

In an article in the *MIT Sloan Management Review*, "Does It Pay to Be Good?," research indicates that consumers will pay more for ethically produced goods, and that companies do not have to be 100 percent ethical to be rewarded with an improved brand image and more business.[1] The research suggests that the opposite is true as well—consumers expect a big discount from companies that produce products in an unethical manner. Previous research was based on surveys asking people if they would pay more for ethically produced goods. Of course, most said they would, but what people say and what they do are actually two different things. The *Sloan* article is about research of actual buying behavior versus stated intentions, which is a much better metric. According to the authors of the article:

> The era of self-interested companies trying to maximize shareholder wealth at any cost appears to have been supplanted by an era of corporate social responsibility, a phrase used by the company's management to consider the impact their decisions will have on their customers, employees, suppliers, and communities as well as their shareholders.[2]

I recently saw T-shirts for sale in a CVS drugstore for one dollar. These were not clearance or closeouts but stacks of new T-shirts in lots of different colors for one dollar. If you buy one of these, you pretty much know you are supporting a company with shady manufacturing practices. It looked like they were selling pretty fast, so I guess sometimes people don't want to think about how something is made, kind of like sausage or hot dogs.

No one is going to argue whether it is important for an organization to demonstrate corporate responsibility, but the challenge is how to measure your performance.

This chapter is about how to develop an index that tells you about your performance on key aspects of ethics, governance, and corporate responsibility.

Another reason corporate responsibility is important is to prevent problems. There are a lot of hungry lawyers out there looking for work, who love cooking up class action suits against pharmaceutical companies or other consumer product firms. To combat this and prevent potential lawsuits and executives from being carted off to jail, it is important to have a comprehensive ethics program in place. For most companies, the only measure of their ethics is that none of their executives have been arrested this year. Being a whistle-blower is a dangerous thing in many organizations, and most just keep their mouths shut and look the other way when they see unethical behavior, especially from top leaders.

Many people in positions of power are tempted to abuse that power, but this aspect of human nature seems to have become worse over the last decade or two. In the last 10 years, we have seen some major corporations disappear, or at least have their executives hauled off to jail, because of ethics problems. Every one of these companies had policies, audits, a code of ethics, and ethics training. Executives monitored the doctored financial results on their corporate dashboards and felt good because the gauges were all green— until the FBI showed up. Today, many companies are busy working to ensure compliance with the new Sarbanes-Oxley regulations that are supposed to make companies more ethical. Yet this is unlikely to do much to control unethical behavior among some organizational leaders. What it will do is make it easier to convict them when they get caught.

TYPES OF ORGANIZATIONS WHERE THIS METRIC IS APPROPRIATE

Any large organization with 1,000 or more employees and at least $10 million in revenue should think about measuring corporate responsibility and ethics. Most medium and large organizations have ethics and corporate responsibility programs and clearly spend money on these things, but few have good metrics to tell them about the success or failure of those efforts. Corporate responsibility also applies to government organizations. Many of them do a wonderful job in this area, and their ethics are without question. I have had the U.S. military as a client for more than 20 years and I don't think I have worked with any other industry or type of organization that is as ethical and concerned about the community as these men and women. Nevertheless, even if ethics and corporate responsibility are part of your DNA, you still probably want to measure your performance to make sure it continues to be good. Hospitals and other health care providers need to measure this since they draw patients and staff from the local community. Most hospitals rely on donors as well, so it is really important that they perceive you as an organization with strong concern for the community and impeccable ethics. No one is going to donate money to an organization that they fear will misuse it.

HOW DOES THIS IMPACT PERFORMANCE?

Like many of the other indices I discuss in this book, this is an area of performance that is as important as financial results and directly links to them. It also links to your survival. Think about Arthur Andersen, one of the biggest and most successful accounting and consulting firms in the world. That company is now gone because of unethical behavior from a few of is people. Gone—out of business. It is shocking that an institution can be brought to an end over ethics. Liability lawsuits have almost put several pharmaceutical companies out of business. Pfizer received a fine of over $1 billion and was told by the judge that the next time, someone is going to jail. Pfizer paid the fine and stayed in business, but many companies could not withstand a loss like this. Merck, another pharmaceutical company, almost failed over a similar situation.

Being a good corporate citizen can also have positive impact on your bottom line. Your brand image is deeply impacted by your efforts in this area and how well you communicate them to your stakeholders. A news story about how executives from one of the nation's largest charities were flying first class and staying in five-star hotels led many people to put their charitable donations elsewhere.

This measure is likely to correlate to the following other measures of an organization's success:

- Recruiting and selection
- Marketing and brand image
- Customer satisfaction
- Customer loyalty and engagement
- Employee engagement and satisfaction

- Revenue
- Profits
- Avoidance of fines and lawsuits
- Competitive advantage

COST AND EFFORT TO MEASURE

Both the cost and difficulty of constructing a corporate responsibility analytic are medium to high. There may be some costs in benchmarking other organizations that are really good at this to see what and how they measure performance in this area. You might have to pay for some consulting help in designing the analytic or getting access to proprietary measures. You might also need to spend some money for an external assessment of your programs, or for surveys. On the other hand, I have worked with organizations that developed good corporate responsibility metrics without spending any external money, using their own staff to design the index and collect the data. I don't think this is a difficult aspect of performance to measure, such as human capital or customer engagement. The types of metrics that go into this index are fairly straightforward and not too expensive to collect.

HOW DO I MEASURE IT?

Becoming an organization that shines in this area is somewhat dependent on your history. If you have a track record of poor performance in this area and that is part of your culture, it will be tough to change, but that is part of why you measure anything—so you can get better. The basic categories of measures to include in your corporate responsibility index are:

- Knowledge
- Perceptions, values, and beliefs
- Policies, procedures, products, and programs
- Decisions and behavior
- Outputs
- Outcomes

Knowledge Metrics

In order to have an ethical organization your own staff has to understand the difference between what you consider right and wrong, and your customers and stakeholders need to know what you stand for and how you operate your organization in such a way that shows corporate responsibility. This section of the index has two parts: inside knowledge and external knowledge. Inside knowledge needs to be measured with a test evaluating whether people know the right things to do and the company's code of ethics. Some things will be easy and everyone will know the right answers without attending any training, but many other things will not be as clear. With one of my associates, Denise Shields, I developed a course for one of our government clients called Shades of Gray. It teaches people the right thing to do in situations where the right answer is not so obvious. The same program was then adapted for the Florida Department of Revenue. The clients used the test at the end of the course to assess the degree to which employees learned the material, and did a follow-up test on a sample of employees several times a year to make sure they retained the knowledge.

In order to measure external knowledge about your ethics and corporate responsibility, you should consider tracking exposure and customer knowledge. Exposure is measured by counting the messages, or "impressions," as advertising people call them, where your message is getting out to the public or your target audience—articles about your organization, news stories, citations in publications, web site hits (your own web site and others) on corporate responsibility information, awards, advertising exposure, and other things that you do to communicate your corporate responsibility to the world. Each communication is assigned a score based on level of exposure. For example, a YouTube video about your volunteerism program that is viewed by 1.2 million people counts for way more than two inches of copy at the back of the business section of your local newspaper that has a total circulation of 40,000. Actually measuring the knowledge the general public has of your company's efforts in this area is tough, but you could query customers and job applicants.

Perceptions, Values, and Beliefs

The second category of measures is an assessment of your employees' perceptions, beliefs, and values regarding ethics and corporate responsibility. This is best measured using focus groups where people are presented with a series of statements that describe how the organization operates regarding ethics and corporate responsibility. The idea here is that people might understand your values and rules about the right thing to do yet still perceive that the company does not follow those values and policies. For example, an organization may have a policy about buying from ethical suppliers but always selects the cheapest supplier regardless of its ethics. That organization may also have a policy about accepting gifts from suppliers but accepts sporting event tickets, trips, and other things on a regular basis and expects suppliers to hire executives' kids when they graduate. The words on the brass plaque regarding a company's values are often quite different from the real values it operates under. This metric is an attempt to expose that hypocrisy. In order to change behavior you have to change both knowledge and perceptions.

Perceptions of consumers regarding your company can be assessed via focus groups or surveys, or if you are a business-to-business organization, you can ask corporate customers to complete an anonymous assessment regarding your culture and corporate responsibility efforts.

Policies, Procedures, Products, and Programs

A big part of excelling in the area of corporate responsibility is having policies and programs that support this versus detract from it or at least make it difficult. For example, I worked with a company that had a policy that all employees must volunteer eight hours per month on community service. The company paid for four of those hours and gave employees half a day off each month, expecting them to match that with four hours of their free time. This policy went a long way toward encouraging high levels of volunteerism, and the organization got lots of positive press about this radical policy. Another company I worked with had a workaholic culture where most people put in 70-hour weeks and then were expected to do community service or charity work on top of the 70 hours, adding an additional layer of stress to people who were already burned out.

Probably the best way of assessing your practices, policies, and programs is an annual assessment done by some outside experts. As you know, I am against annual metrics, but this is only one of many measures that look at corporate responsibility, and most of the others are metrics that can be tracked monthly. Palomar Health in Escondido, California, contracts with the Council for Ethical Organizations to do an annual assessment of its ethics and governance programs. Each year Palomar Health receives an overall score compared to other hospitals and benchmarks, as well as specific feedback on their strengths and weaknesses. They use another company to assess their community support and charitable work. Outsiders are able to compare your programs and policies to industry averages and benchmarks so you can see where you stand. You might also ask employees whether they know the policies and are aware of the community support programs (knowledge), and survey them about their perceptions regarding the policies and programs (perceptions, values, and beliefs).

Another way to measure social responsibility is by assessing your products and services to make sure they are not harmful to the larger society. It would be pretty hard for a cigarette company to claim high marks for social responsibility, since there does not seem to be any good that comes from making and selling cigarettes, other than that the industry provides a lot of jobs. But what about companies that make guns, or sell soft drinks, or cars that go 200 miles an hour? Even if your product is good for health and society, such as coffee (which contains loads of antioxidants), there are ways to produce it in a socially responsible manner. In fact, coffee is the focus of the research discussed in the *MIT Sloan Management Review* article referenced previously. Its research showed that consumers would pay an extra $1.40 a pound for coffee produced via fair trade practices and good farming techniques.

Each of your products and services can be evaluated based on the raw materials used to produce it, the manufacturing methods used, and finally the extent to which your product or service itself is socially responsible. If you look at a big company like Nestlé, which makes everything from Nestlé Crunch bars to baby food, the different products would get different scores.

Programs also need to be assessed as part of the metric. For example, you might have a whistle-blower program, but it is administered by HR and no one trusts it, so nothing is reported. One that is administered by an outside company would probably get a higher score.

Decisions and Behavior

Another type of measure of corporate responsibility is the decisions made by your leaders and the behavior or actions of all of your employees. One company I worked with gives out awards and recognition to employees who demonstrate socially responsible behavior. For example, taking on a leadership role in a community group or association might get recognition, as might coming up with an idea that helps improve the safety of a product. Decisions by management can also be made in support of corporate responsibility or merely in support of making more money. Each major decision made each month is evaluated on the extent to which it is good for society and the local community.

Outputs

Outputs are quantifiable variables that you can count that help the community or society. These are not your own products or services but are other outputs. For example, Purina measures the pounds of dog and cat food it donates to animal shelters. A food manufacturer measures the pounds of food it donates to food pantries. A restaurant might measure the number of meals it donates to a homeless shelter. A computer manufacturer might measure how many computers it donates to schools. A generic output measure that all organizations could track is hours spent working for volunteer or community groups and dollars donated. These figures can be compared against averages and benchmarks in your industry to see how you are doing.

Outcomes

The difference between outputs and outcomes is that outcomes are something of value to a community or society. An outcome might be to make people healthier. For example, my client AltaMed measures the impact of its programs on childhood obesity. If you work with Habitat for Humanity, an outcome might be the number of families for whom your employees helped build a house. The Asian Development Bank tracks outcomes like reduced poverty, increased access to clean water and electricity, and more females graduating school. Outcome measures are tricky, because an outcome can improve and have nothing to do with the help your company provided. Whatever community outcomes you decide to measure, make sure you can attribute them to the efforts of your organization. Outcomes might also be the avoidance of bad things—for example, a reduction in the use of raw materials produced using improper methods or increased access to your product by more people by lowering prices or improving distribution.

FORMULA AND FREQUENCY

Knowledge	10%
Internal knowledge	5%
External and stakeholder knowledge	5%
Perceptions, values, and beliefs	10%
Policies, procedures, products, and programs	25%
Policies and procedures	5%
Programs	5%
Products and services	15%
Decisions and behavior	15%
Leadership decisions	10%
Employee behavior	5%
Outputs	15%
Monetary donations	5%
Volunteer hours	5%
Other outputs	5%
Outcomes	25%
Economic	5%
Health	5%
Safety	5%
Education	5%
Quality of life	5%

VARIATIONS

Many organizations simply set some objectives regarding key outputs like volunteer hours and donations by employees and track those as their only measure of corporate responsibility. Others only measure their image regarding social responsibility and ethics with the general public and key stakeholders like customers. External image is certainly something to think about including in your index. You could be doing a wonderful job in this area, but no one knows about it so you don't get any credit for being a socially responsible organization.

TARGETS AND BENCHMARKS

The targets you set for the individual metrics in this index have a lot to do with your overall philosophy and values regarding corporate responsibility. As mentioned in the *MIT Sloan Management Review* article referenced previously, corporate responsibility can be a strategic advantage and differentiator, particularly in an industry not known for this. All the clothing sold at Whole Foods, for example, is made with organic fabrics and from environmentally responsible farming and manufacturing techniques. I don't think you would find that to be true of the one-dollar T-shirts at CVS. If being regarded as a leader in this area is one of your goals or part of your strategy, you need to set high targets based on other organizations that excel at this like Microsoft, Google, or Dell.

If, on the other hand, you are just looking to be as good as your peer companies in this area, or to get slightly better than current performance, targets can focus on either maintaining current levels of performance or improving in key areas where there is currently poor performance.

BENEFITS OF DATA

The biggest benefit of having data on your performance in this area is that you will be able to assess whether your efforts really make any difference. Many organizations have a completely reactive approach to corporate responsibility. They wait for charities and community groups to ask for money and volunteers; they wait until a negative story appears in the news about their manufacturing practices (like workers committing suicide at Apple manufacturer Foxconn in China). Companies wait until one of their executives is arrested because of ethics problems to decide they need to do a better job measuring ethics. Smart organizations take a proactive approach to community and corporate responsibility. Almost all large organizations spend time, money, and other valuable resources on corporate responsibility, but very few have any measures on how well their efforts are working other than on activities and donations.

Having a corporate responsibility index that gets tracked every month allows an organization to actually manage this dimension of performance in much the same manner as it manages manufacturing, HR, suppliers, and financial performance. Corporate responsibility is becoming more than just a nice thing to do and a way to get some tax savings. For many consumers and businesses, this is one of the major criteria they look at when deciding how and where to spend their money.

NOTES

1. Remi Trudel and June Cotte, "Does It Pay to Be Good?," *MIT Sloan Management Review*, Winter 2009, http://sloanreview.mit.edu/article/does-it-pay-to-be-good.
2. Ibid., 61–62.

PART
THREE

People Analytics

CHAPTER **16**

The Human
Capital Index

 WHY AN ORGANIZATION MIGHT TRACK THIS

Questions Answered

- Do we have the right mix of skills and experiences to get our current work done well?
- Do we have enough people with the right mix of competencies for our current needs?
- Do we have the right numbers of people in each job category and business unit?
- Are we hiring the right people?
- What human capital gaps should be filled via hiring versus developing our existing people?
- Am I overstaffed for some competencies and understaffed for others?
- Are we developing the right knowledge and skills in our staff?
- Do we have a good succession plan for replacing our key leaders and technical professionals?

Why Is This Information Important?

Many organizations today place a much higher value on their human assets or employees than they do on physical assets like real estate, equipment, and even patents. In fact, companies like Microsoft believe that 80 percent of their value is in their people. Having the right people is often critical to an organization's success, yet most organizations have poorly designed metrics to keep track of their human capital. What is so ironic about this is that every single manager can identify the most valuable individual on her staff. She can also identify the person whom she would not be devastated to lose. Almost never do these subjective assessments match up with the human capital scores given to individuals by human resources. In other words, some of the least valuable employees end up with high scores on the human capital index because the wrong variables are measured.

There are many qualities that make an employee valuable to an employer:

- **Technical knowledge and skills.** These are the detailed abilities, skills, and knowledge that are required to perform important work assignments well—for example, the skill to repair an expensive piece of equipment, detailed knowledge about how the military funding process works, or how to diagnose and repair software problems. All jobs require some degree of technical knowledge and skill, even entry-level positions such as working in the mailroom.

- **Interpersonal knowledge and skills, or nontechnical abilities.** These are skills such as the ability to make a convincing presentation, or mediate a conflict, or motivate a workforce, all of which are valuable skills for managers or supervisors. Nontechnical skills are important for nonmanagerial employees as well, such as use of proper grammar, writing skills, creating a good PowerPoint presentation, and the ability to work with a team.

- **Traits.** These are characteristics employees have when they first come through the door and probably inherited or developed at an early age. They are not a measure of specific knowledge and skills. Traits might include intelligence, emotional intelligence, energy level, attention to detail, compassion, creativity, ethics and values, charisma, and analytical ability.

- **Relationships.** Some of your seasoned employees have probably developed trusting relationships with other employees and managers, customers, and vendors or partners. Relationships take years to develop and are the key to getting many things done at work. The relationships an employee has built are often a big part of what makes them valuable to both your organization and your competitors.

- **Accomplishments.** Another big factor that needs to be considered in a human capital measure is what the person has accomplished. For a salesperson this might be his or her sales over the last few years, or awards the person has won. For a research professional this might be new designs or patents. For a customer contact employee this might be his or her productivity or levels of customer satisfaction. For a consultant or engineer, accomplishments might be repeat business from clients, referrals, or extensions on projects. Accomplishments might also include credentials or degrees if these are required and important for success. Being a certified project manager, or having an MBA from Yale, could certainly be considered accomplishments.

- **Position.** The level of a person in an organization is certainly a factor that should figure into the human capital index as well. A chief financial officer who is paid $1.2 million a year would probably be worth a lot more in your index than a customer service rep in your call center who earns $25,000 a year. Position is also important when considering the impact to the organization when you lose a seasoned key executive or professional compared with losing an entry-level person after six weeks.

TYPES OF ORGANIZATIONS WHERE THIS METRIC IS APPROPRIATE

Any organization that has more than 100 employees and that spends at least 25 percent of its costs on salaries and benefits should have this measure and monitor it frequently. If you are a small company with 40 employees, everyone knows one another and managers have intimate knowledge of the strengths and weaknesses of each of their staff. In such a case a measure like this would be a waste of time, because with this small a staff it is possible to know everyone. A client of mine doubled in size over six years from about 900 employees to 2,000. The CEO was employee number three and in the old days knew every one of his employees, and many of them still work there. As the company grew and expanded locations, it became impossible for him to even learn the names of all the employees, not to mention their skills and abilities. He could rely on his managers to at least know all their staff members, but eventually they had too many people as well. Consequently, the organization worked to develop a human capital metric that would reveal areas of strength as well as gaps.

The other criterion for deciding whether you need a human capital metric is the skill level of your employees. One of my clients (Flagship in San Jose) is a janitorial and facilities maintenance firm. Even though they have over 1,000 employees and offices in different cities, most of their employees have rudimentary skills needed to perform cleaning and maintenance tasks. The president and owner,

Dave, has a small team of managers and he knows their strengths and weaknesses well. I think Flagship could probably do just fine without tracking human capital as one of their key metrics. However, even a company like this might find a simple human capital metric useful. It might include head count versus plan, average seniority, absenteeism, and regret turnover. With over 100 employees it is probably useful for Dave and his human resources vice president to know when they are short-staffed or have too much absenteeism, and when the experience level dips too low.

HOW DOES THIS IMPACT PERFORMANCE?

If you had to pick one thing that most correlates to positive outcomes and business results, it's having the right mix of talented people. Even one leader can make a massive difference in an organization's success or failure. Think of Apple when Steve Jobs left or what GE would have become without Jack Welch. The value of a single leader is probably overrated, but a single individual can make a big difference. That brilliant scientist who has more patents than anyone in the company, or that frontline worker who solves every mechanical problem that arises in minutes can both have a huge impact on performance. Similarly, one really bad manager can have a major negative impact on many measures of performance. Even if you have people who are unhappy in their jobs, you can get good performance out of them. I saw a program on PBS recently about Henry Ford, and how once he redesigned jobs so that workers just did the same task over and over, he got more productivity out of them and made higher profits. He had to up workers' pay to keep them from quitting the mind-numbing jobs, but they showed up every day and worked very hard. I can't imagine that the employees were very happy or engaged in a monotonous job like that, but they were skilled and continued to crank out those Fords every day.

Losing a key employee or leader can have a devastating impact on an organization's future performance. However, most organizations do not have human capital metrics that are sophisticated enough to show this. I've reviewed the human capital metrics of many big corporations and large government organizations and almost always find that they opt to measure what is easy to count versus what is important or really a measure of someone's worth. Most organizations have a strong desire to track human capital, but the majority fail when trying to put together a meaningful and accurate analytic.

Mostly Worthless Human Capital Metrics

- **Training hours**. The logic here is that if we continue to invest in training and developing our employees, they will maintain their knowledge and skills at the highest level. But there are some big leaps in logic here. First of all, counting the number of butts sitting in chairs at a training session is not a measure of knowledge and skill acquisition. Rather, it is a measure of how many people sat in how many classrooms for how many hours. In the real world, even that metric is often inaccurate. The training sign-in sheet is usually passed around in the morning. Some people don't come back after lunch because they have already signed in.

  A second problem is that much of what gets called "training" is not training but talking. *Listening to someone talk while he or she shows PowerPoint slides is not training.*

  The third problem with this measure is that it does not include an assessment of whether the content covered in the training is even relevant to the job a person is doing. It is tempting to measure training hours, because the data is so easy to track. However, the type of data being tracked does not really measure the knowledge and skills of employees. In fact, some of the most competent people in organizations don't go to training—they are too busy doing meaningful, productive work.

- **Completion of "individual development plans."** Most large companies and nonprofit organizations have an annual process called individual development planning (IDP), during which an employee sits down with his or her boss and decides what knowledge and skills should be worked on for the following year. This is actually a good idea, but the execution is usually flawed. The product of most IDPs is a list of conferences or workshops the employee wants to attend. If the employee lists four courses and attends all four, the score on the IDP is

100 percent. What this number does not measure is whether the employee really learned a new skill or mastered a new subject or content.

- **Certifications**. Many fields require some form of certification—a piece of paper stating that the person holding it has attained competence in a particular field. For example, you can become a certified public accountant, registered nurse, certified financial planner, or certified welder. The problem with counting these certifications as a measure of competence is that they are not. There are countless incompetent people out there with pieces of paper saying they are certified, but most of these people passed certification tests that measured their ability to memorize rather than their ability to perform. If the certification test actually requires the person to perform job tasks (i.e., fly a plane), it is a good measure of competence, but passing most certification tests requires nothing more than memorizing a bunch of rules, facts, and principles. In other words, the tests assess specific knowledge but not skills. People study for the exams, pass them, and then mostly forget what they learned. Whether they become competent in their field depends a lot on experience, intelligence, and further training and mentoring. Certifications are like training hours—they're easy to count, but they are not very revealing as a metric.

COST AND EFFORT TO MEASURE

The cost of collecting data on human capital metrics is typically low, but much of that determination is based on how much data you have today on your people. If you have fairly comprehensive databases on each of your employees, rolling up the measures into an analytic should not be much of an effort. Where the biggest time and expense usually comes is in designing the analytic in the first place. I worked with a big government R&D laboratory called the Engineer Research & Design Center (ERDC) in Vicksburg, Mississippi, to help them develop a human capital analytic. They had already done a lot of work on their own and decided to call in some outside help to get new ideas and facilitate the design process. Much of the discussion in the design meetings was objectivity of the metrics, the degree to which data would be accurately collected, and the extent to which the measures proposed would be good assessments of an individual's value to the organization.

HOW DO I MEASURE IT?

Sadly, there is no uniform method or formula for tracking human capital or calculating the knowledge and skills of your workforce. All organizations acknowledge its importance, but there has been no agreement among human resource professionals about how to measure it. You would think that professional organizations of HR professionals would have gotten together to agree on this, and I am sure they have tried. The American Society for Training and Development cannot even get all companies to agree to measure training the same way. Coming up with a valid and acceptable metric for human capital is much more of a challenge, so each organization needs to develop a metric that best suits it. That said, it is likely to include a number of different variables for it to be valid. Sadly, just as with health and wellness, there is no single metric or ratio that can be tracked that provides a good measure of the human capital of an organization.

I have helped many organizations develop human capital metrics, and almost always what they end up with is a compromise between what they would like to measure and what is feasible. Not only is measuring human capital extremely difficult, but there is a lot of emotion surrounding it as well, because we are putting numbers onto people based on their value to the organization. It's funny how most of my clients object to the equivalent of a credit score for human capital assigned to each employee, but none have a problem assigning vastly different compensation levels to different jobs. By doing so, you are assigning value based on the worth of the individual and the position. The problem is that high pay does not equate to high value all the time. I'm sure you all know a few highly paid executives or professionals who are idiots, and a few invaluable staff members who are way underpaid.

While I have seen lots of different good and bad approaches to measuring human capital, I can provide you with a description of what the ideal metric would contain, and you can use this as a benchmark to approximate in your own design. Some of the factors I discuss are fairly common; others are not, but they are no less important.

Traits

Companies like Marriott have defined key traits needed for each position in the company. For the job of housekeeper, attention to detail is an important trait. For the job of CFO, analytical ability is an important trait. As I mentioned earlier, traits are not competencies, behaviors, or skills. Traits are things that someone was born with or developed in childhood. For example, one of the traits that audio company Bose hires for is creativity. Many people are not creative. Instead of teaching creativity, Bose selects for it. In other words, they purposely recruit people from professions that require creativity to be successful. Bose hires a lot of musicians, painters, and individuals from other artistic or creative professions because their success in artistic fields is a good demonstration of their creativity. The most common way of assessing traits for new recruits is behavioral interviewing. If, for example, you were trying to determine if someone had the trait of paying attention to detail, you might ask a potential employee how they get ready for work in the morning. There will usually be marked differences in how a detail-oriented person will answer this question and how someone without this trait will answer it. Some traits can actually be measured better than others. Intelligence, analytical abilities, strength, flexibility, emotional intelligence, and other traits can be assessed using validated instruments. Other traits like charisma or leadership will be a lot harder to evaluate. Some traits can also be assessed based on past accomplishments. Looking at an artist's portfolio of work and awards received is a better way to assess creativity than some behavioral interviewing question. Once you have identified the top three to six traits for each job, each person in that job gets assessed on the degree to which they possess high levels of the trait. The most simplistic assessment might be a high, medium, or low score. Assessment of traits is not a yes or no issue but a matter of degree. Other clients have assessed levels of traits in employees on a 1 to 10 scale.

Competencies: Knowledge, Skills, and Abilities

Competencies have to be defined for each job as well. I see lists of competencies defined in many organizations that are actually not competencies or skills, but a mixture of traits, behaviors, and skills. Generally, competencies are collections or groupings of individual skills and knowledge. An example of a broad area of competence required for a sales job might be determining customer needs. A specific skill under that area might be interviewing. Most organizations have competencies sorted into two groupings:

1. **Technical competencies**. These include IT skills like trouble-shooting software problems, diagnosing why a "check engine" light is on, creating a web site, solving a logistics problem, designing an experiment, creating a social network marketing strategy, or landing a 747 in a rainstorm at night. Each job and field has its own set of required technical competencies. Many large organizations assign a level of competency required for each skill for each job. For example, a level 2 (deep knowledge) might be required for the area of mechanical theory for an auto mechanic job, whereas a level 7 (high-level mastery) might be needed for the job of automotive engine designer.

2. **Nontechnical competencies**. Every job requires some technical knowledge and skills and some nontechnical ones. Nontechnical skills and knowledge are not traits, but are specific learned skills such as verbal communication, written communication, presentation skills, leadership skills such as giving constructive feedback, use of generic tools like Excel and PowerPoint, and problem solving. As with technical competencies, it is important to specify the level required for each competency for each job and also to assess the level of competence of each employee in that job. So, for example, if a job requires a competency level of 4 out of 7 (the highest level) for negotiating a contract with a customer, and Bill is rated as a level 2 in competence, there is a gap there. He may be a level 6 on another competency, but the job only requires a level 2, so he gets no extra credit for being better than the requirement. In other words, you

can't make up for skill gaps in important job competencies with strong skills in other areas if they are not needed or important for the job. For example, at the ERDC research lab I mentioned earlier, there are a lot of scientists who are extremely competent at building physical models to do simulation experiments. The problem is that work these days is done with computer simulations, not physical models. So all those physical modeling skills are not as valuable to the organization as they were 10 years ago.

Relationships

All jobs have requirements for traits and competencies, but relationships are not important for all jobs, just most of them. The types of relationships that make someone valuable to an organization are relationships with:

- Peers or other professionals in the field
- Thought leaders or experts
- Customers
- Suppliers and vendors
- Partners
- Other employees

Three dimensions have to be considered here. First of all, the importance of relationships needs to be assigned for each position. Salespeople obviously would have this as an important job requirement, and so would executives, but relationships are important for lots of other job types as well. For example, a client just hired a doctor to head up its clinical quality area who is not only affiliated with a major university but has connections with many others doing research in the field of clinical quality and with leaders of key regulators and professional associations. The doctor was a great hire because of his many competencies but also because of his connections and relationships with key players in the field. The second factor that needs to be assessed is how many relationships the individual has. Both depth and breadth need to be assessed. Finally, the third dimension that needs to be assessed is the level of the individual with whom an employee has a relationship. I recall working with a CEO in an aircraft maintenance and repair company who happened to be close personal friends with the CEO of then Continental Airlines. The two had gone to college together and had worked together for years. This relationship made the CEO even more valuable to the company he ran and helped ensure that they kept Continental's business. After Continental CEO Gordon Bethune retired before United bought the airline, the relationship lost a lot of importance, even though Bethune was still an influential figure in the airline business.

Only a few of my clients have attempted to quantify the level of relationships as a factor that gets assessed as part of a human capital analytic, but not one would consider it unimportant when looking at the value of an employee. For entry-level jobs it probably doesn't matter, but for many higher level jobs it is a big part of what you are paying for when hiring a key manager from a competitor or another similar company. In fact, relationships are often a factor that distinguishes one job candidate from another and are a big factor in determining compensation. A recent pharmaceutical client paid big bucks to lure away the sales vice president from a competitor, in part because of the many relationships she had with important players and thought leaders in the industry. She hit the ground running as well and was extremely productive within a few weeks on the job.

Accomplishments

We all know people who accomplished a whole lot in the first 20 years of their career but just seem to be coasting now. We all know people who are brilliant and talented but haven't done a whole lot in the last five years. Accomplishments are certainly an important part of what makes an employee valuable. I recall working with a vice president at Black & Decker who had patents for electric drills that he invented in his early career. However, that was 30 years ago. Part of assessing accomplishments is to look at the extent of the accomplishments and the recentness of them. A simple way to assess accomplishments is to just use overall performance review ratings. Bettis Laboratory, which designs nuclear propulsion systems for the navy, came up with a human capital metric wherein the human capital score of 0 to 100 was modified by the performance review score. So let's say you have a highly skilled employee with the right traits, but this same person is only mediocre in her current job. She might have her competency score of 82 multiplied by .5 (mediocre performance), so she ends up with a human capital score of 41. Similarly, a new employee with few demonstrated competencies gets a human capital score of 15 that gets multiplied by 1.5 for high performance, and his 15 becomes 22.5, showing a higher worth because of his good performance. The weak link in this overall system is the level of subjectivity that went into the performance review. Another problem is that it only looked at the current year's performance, so any past accomplishments were not considered. In spite of the flaws, it ended up being a practical metric that was not too hard to track and was more comprehensive than a measure that just looked at a person's traits, relationships, and competencies as a way of assessing his or her value. A separate dimension or something else that might be considered part of an accomplishment rating is credentials. Credentials include education certificates or other pieces of papers that certify competence. These are usually required for most jobs, so this factor could be easily left off the human capital analytic since it would be assumed that everyone in the job has the required credentials. I've seen some organizations that want to give points for impressive degrees from impressive schools, but there is always debate about issues like comparing the value of an MBA from UCLA to one from Harvard or Notre Dame.

Position

The final factor that might be considered when constructing a human capital metric is the easiest and most objective to measure—the level of the person in the organization. A certain percentage of the human capital score is allocated to the level of the person on the org chart. The logic behind this is that higher-level people certainly get paid a lot more than lower-level people and so they should get a higher human capital score. Also, the impact of losing a high-level leader or technical professional is usually much greater as well. I worked with a hospital that did not have an HR vice president for a year while they were doing a search, so this created a big human capital gap in the workforce, particularly in the vice president position. Calculating position is simply a matter of assigning points to the various levels in your org chart. People at the top get the highest scores and those at the bottom get the lowest.

FORMULA AND FREQUENCY

The first step in constructing a good human capital analytic is to establish the requirements for each job in the organization. What this means is identifying the traits, competencies, credentials, and important relationships needed for each job. In addition to identifying competencies, the level of competency is also extremely important to document in the job description. There is a big difference between needing a basic understanding of a topic and being considered one of the leading experts on a topic, or having done something well thousands of times. If I am getting a knee replacement, I want the surgeon who has done hundreds of them, not the guy who took a course on joint replacement in med school but has never done one. Assuming that human capital requirements have been defined for each job, measurement involves assessing employees against the requirements to determine whether gaps exist. If the gaps are due to people not having the right traits for the job, this can only be addressed by selecting new people who do have the traits and moving the existing people out or at least into jobs they are better suited for. Gaps in competencies can be addressed with both hiring and development strategies.

A straw man human capital analytic looks like the one that follows. However, as with many of the metrics in this book, the submeasures and weights need to be agreed upon by your own organization based on the nature of the work you do, the availability of data, and how sophisticated you want to get.

Traits	20%
Competencies	30%
Technical knowledge and skills	15%
Nontechnical knowledge and skills	15%
Accomplishments	20%

Position   20%
Relationships   10%

Regardless of how you calculate the human capital analytic, there are two basic ways to make the gauge move: gaining or losing people through hiring and turnover, or developing them through training, mentoring, job assignments, or other factors.

VARIATIONS

A common variation I see is a human capital metric that also includes measures of key HR processes like recruiting, selection, training, leadership development, and managing performance. The human capital analytic at ERDC that I mentioned earlier is designed this way. Personally I think it clutters up the data too much. I would prefer to have different metrics that look at whether the organization had the right mix of people and another analytic that looked at how well HR processes were being performed. The folks at ERDC believed that the two were inseparable. We can't say we are doing a good job selecting the right people if we have big gaps in our human resources. In other words, part of assessing HR processes is seeing how the processes lead to the organization having the right mix of talents and skills. This is something for you to think about and discuss. Another reason I like separating the two types of measures is that the CEO and other key executives need to monitor the human capital analytic that looks at gaps in the workforce. However, generally it is only the HR vice president who is responsible for the HR processes.

Another common variation is to include only an assessment of competencies in the human capital analytic and not to assess the values of traits, relationships, or accomplishments. This might be a good way to start constructing the metric, but I would not leave it at that.

A crude variation used by one military client is just to count the number of people in each job or trade (e.g., welders, pipefitters, mechanical engineers, etc.) and compare that number to the HR plan that spelled out the number of people needed in each job category. The only way to have a gap is if you are short of people. What I love about this is its simplicity. What I hate about it is that it says nothing about the real gaps in human capital that are caused by incompetent or barely competent people who happen to be in needed jobs. Some of the welders, for example, were barely competent, whereas others were so competent they could do the work of three guys. ERDC employed a more meaningful assessment by not just indicating how many of this and that specialty areas were needed in the workforce but also by indicating levels of competence that were needed:

- Entry-level
- Journeyman
- Expert

TARGETS AND BENCHMARKS

The overall target for the human capital index is that the organization has zero gaps. However, this is probably unrealistic, so a reasonable "green" zone might be 80 percent or above. In other words, if the organization has 80 percent of the talent it needs, it can probably achieve most of its other goals. What this does not take into account is gaps that could occur in the near future as the organization moves into new markets or fields. Consequently, the data from the human capital index needs to be drilled into for details, and the high-level analytic needs sensitive "warning lights" that light up when gaps appear in strategic or vital areas for the business.

BENEFITS OF DATA

The benefits of having an accurate measure of human capital are enormous. Having an assessment of the gaps in your workforce can enable the organization to:

- Target recruiting and selection to fill current and future gaps.
- Strategically assess the value of training on different topics.
- Evaluate the true value of each employee to the organization.
- Assess the impact of employee turnover.
- Integrate a number of key HR processes.
- Improve the integrity of succession planning.

CHAPTER **17**

The Workforce Happiness Index

WHY AN ORGANIZATION MIGHT TRACK THIS

Questions Answered

- Do employees look forward to coming to work?
- Are employees happy with their boss?
- Is the work employees do satisfying?
- Do employees enjoy the people they work with?

Why Is This Information Important?

If you run a call center that operates 24 hours a day and employees spend most of that time taking calls from angry customers, can you really expect the employees to be happy? If you run a garment plant in downtown Los Angeles that makes $200 blue jeans and your employees are working their fingers to the bone all day, can they be happy in a job like that? As an employer, do you even care? First of all, I think as an employer you should care a whole lot about the happiness of your employees. If labor is a big cost item on your balance sheet, employees' satisfaction with their jobs probably influences every other measure of performance. Study after study has demonstrated the links between business success (sales, growth, profits, etc.) and employee satisfaction. Other studies have shown that the work environment and work itself do not have to be pleasant or interesting for employees to be happy. Yet many executives with air-conditioned offices, access to healthy food, a comfortable chair, and an intellectually stimulating job where they get to sit down all day are far from being happy with their fat salaries and cushy jobs.

Organizations have entire departments and a corporate officer dedicated to measuring various aspects of financial performance. Even the smallest of companies has a finance person who tracks sales, expenditures, and taxes and who reports on achievements and problems to the boss. Financial metrics are tracked daily in some cases, and at least weekly or monthly in others. Real-time decisions are made based on changes to key metrics like cash flow, sales, orders, and expenses.

Yet more and more organizations today are driven by people, not just investments in raw materials and equipment. In fact, even an airline, which has some pretty expensive equipment and raw materials (fuel), finds that labor costs are one of the biggest items on their list of expenses.

In recent years, companies have become more concerned about tracking the satisfaction or engagement (the newest buzzword) of their employees. I'm told that both are important but that they are different. Later in the book there is a chapter on measuring employee engagement by tracking distractions (Chapter 19). An employee working 80 hours a week on an important project who takes phone calls and responds to e-mails at all hours of the night might be highly engaged, but not very satisfied with her job. Conversely, I recall working with a group of bored, talented engineers at a big oil company who were very happy with their jobs because of the short hours and big paychecks, but they were not at all engaged in their work or the organization's mission. The work they had to do could be done by a smart high school graduate and these were all A students from the best engineering universities in the country, so they were bored to death. Most put in the minimum effort possible and found they could get all their work done in only a few hours a day. The rest of the time was spent trying to look busy and attending meetings they didn't need to attend. As the economy improves and more companies start hiring, employers need to start paying more attention to the happiness of their employees as well as their engagement or they will go elsewhere.

WHAT MAKES EMPLOYEES HAPPY?

We tend to equate happiness with achievement of key milestones or accomplishments in life: getting that promotion to vice president you've waited for, getting married, having your first child, buying your first house, taking a trip around the world, or finally getting that PhD. However, day-to-day happiness does not seem to be influenced much by achievement of major milestones either at home or work. In fact, some of the happiest countries on earth are populated by a lot of poor people. Denmark is the happiest country, although it is far from being a poor one. Citizens there have access to excellent health care and a great education, and almost everyone makes about the same amount of money, so you choose your profession based on what you like and are good at, versus what is going to make you the most amount of money. Family and friends are very important, and the country values healthy eating and taking care of children and the elderly. There is virtually no crime, so safety is also a component of happiness. But what about the climate? And have you ever seen the size of the houses and apartments Danes live in? In California we have one of the best climates on earth and live in big houses with lots of room, and yet many people are miserable. Singapore, with its tropical climate, little or no crime, and booming economy, is the unhappiest. One of the biggest reasons Singaporeans are unhappy is because of work. Only 2 percent of the country's workers feel engaged by their jobs, according to Gallup. Others blame the school system that discourages students from thinking for themselves as individuals. America rates much better on job satisfaction, but still 70 to 75 percent of Americans are disengaged from their jobs. Although this is a lot better than Singapore's 98 percent, it is alarming to think that three-quarters of the people we pay on a daily basis to come to work are not really bringing their best game to the workplace each day.

TYPES OF ORGANIZATIONS WHERE THIS METRIC IS APPROPRIATE

Any organization that spends at least 20 percent of its costs on people in salaries, benefits, and facilities needs to think about measuring workplace happiness. Many of my clients find that personnel are 50 percent or more of their costs. Any organization that has a lot of employees probably cares about measuring this as well. Even if people are only 15 percent of your total expenses, if you have 20,000 employees you probably need to track this metric. If you work for a small organization of less than 15 people, you are probably really out of touch if you can't measure employee happiness by watching and talking to your people each day. However, this is tough to do if you have 150 people or 150,000 of them. Another factor to think about is how important employees are to your overall performance. If you run an aluminum plant and the manufacturing process is highly automated, how people feel about their jobs may have little bearing on the quality and quantity of aluminum produced. However, if you run a hospital, the satisfaction of your nurses and other patient-facing employees can have a major impact on both health outcomes and patient satisfaction. So, in summary, you might want to consider tracking this index if:

- Employee costs make up a big part of your expenses.
- You have so many employees that you can't gauge their happiness by talking with them.
- Key outcomes like revenue, growth, and quality products and services are dependent upon employee behavior.

HOW DOES THIS IMPACT PERFORMANCE?

FedEx and GE are both big believers in three key performance indices. At FedEx they are:

1. People—employee satisfaction and engagement
2. Service—customer satisfaction
3. Profit—or other financial metrics, depending on the job

Managers are held accountable for the satisfaction of their employees, and individual contributors are held accountable for the satisfaction of their team. Everyone has customers, and everyone has some way of contributing to the financial health of FedEx. Jack Welch, former CEO of GE, was fond of saying he only really cared about three key metrics to evaluate the health of GE:

1. Employee engagement
2. Customer satisfaction
3. Cash flow

Both of these wildly successful companies seem to understand the formula that says that if you first take care of your employees, they will take care of the customers, and they will make money for the shareholders. Pretty simple stuff, but organizations tend to have 100 times more precision in their efforts to measure financial performance than they do for measuring employee satisfaction or customer satisfaction.

If you look at companies like Southwest Airlines, Purina, and Google, you will find senior managers who understand the impact satisfied and engaged employees can have on the bottom line. All three of these companies lead their competitors on just about any measure of performance, and most attribute a lot of their success to their employees. Of course, having happy and incompetent employees will not make any organization more successful, but it seems that at these top-ranking companies a small minority of employees are incompetent, whereas at many other organizations a huge percentage of the employees aren't happy or engaged.

Happiness not only makes you a better employee, it can add years to your life. Four factors in the analytics for Realage.com are

1. Marriage

2. Friends

3. Spirituality

4. Pets

Being married actually adds years to your life, or maybe it just seems like life is longer. Having close friends whom you see often adds a few more years. Believing in something or having passion for a spiritual interest helps. In fact, all of these factors can add up to nine years to your life span, whereas not smoking only adds three or four years. So how does this relate to work? Well, many people meet their future spouse at work, and some still work with their spouses. My neighbors Paul and Susan both work as accountants from their home office. Most of us have friends at work as well. In fact, often that is where people meet most of their friends once they leave college. Work is also something that you can have passion for and find spiritual fulfillment through. I have been working for the last couple of years for AltaMed, which is California's largest community health care provider dedicated to serving populations that have a hard time affording health care. Many of the doctors, nurses, and other patient-focused employees get a tremendous amount of satisfaction helping their patients.

Also, having a dog or cat can add happiness and years to your life. Some companies like Purina allow employees to bring their well-behaved dogs and cats to work with them, and many even attend meetings with their owners. The company headquarters in St. Louis has a beautiful park in the center of the campus called the Barking Lot where employees can take breaks and let their dogs run and play with others. Badly behaved dogs or owners are banned.

In fact, Gallup's research suggests that a good boss and friends at work are important factors for engagement and satisfaction as well as workplace happiness. This seems to ring true for most of us who have had good and bad bosses, and jobs with lots of friends and jobs with none of them. The work itself is sometimes a big factor as well. Getting to do something you are really good at and have a passion for is important as well. Stephen Lundin, Harry Paul, and John Christensen's book *Fish* is a great lesson on how to make boring and even unpleasant work fun.[1] The employees at the Pike Place Fish Market in Seattle have found an innovative way of making work (selling fresh fish) more enjoyable, and they are much happier because of it.

A CULTURE OF WEIRDNESS AND FUN

Online shoe company Zappos in Henderson, Nevada, is known for both its business savvy and its highly engaged workforce. People love working at this company that rewards creativity, laughter, and weirdness. In fact, if you are really normal and boring, you probably won't fit in well there.

Zappos is so confident that employees will be happy working at their company that they offer new employees a check for $2,500 to quit after the first 30 days on the job, no questions asked. It will pay you to leave. Surprisingly, almost no one takes the offer. Zappos uses this offer as a test to see if employees really like working there and are happy.

Southwest Airlines is always mentioned as a great place to work as well, and if employees are not really happy, they sure fake it well. Year after year, Southwest continues to grow and remain profitable, while other airlines struggle with labor problems and possible bankruptcy.

Another company that was recently named the best company in America for work/life balance is Nestlé Purina in St. Louis. Companies that make it onto *Fortune*'s annual list of the best employers get around 80 percent employee satisfaction. Purina has 97 percent employee satisfaction and also beats any company in its industry on key measures like sales, profits, customer satisfaction, and innovation. Purina also recently won the Baldrige Award, given out by the U.S. president to the best-run American companies. Having happy, engaged employees seems to translate to better business performance.

COST AND EFFORT TO MEASURE

Both the cost and effort to measure employee happiness or satisfaction should be low, but could be both expensive and challenging depending on your approach. A navy client of mine with 5,000 employees spent $150,000 to have a well-known survey and research firm conduct its annual employee survey. The vendor promised a 70 percent-plus return rate because the survey was only 12 questions and employees had multiple ways of responding to the survey—mail, e-mail, or telephone. My client convinced his commanding officer to spend the money, and it turned out to be a bad decision. Only 17 percent of the employees responded to the survey after multiple reminders, so the organization wasted $150,000 because the data from a sample that small was not even useful. When focus groups were held to find out why no one responded to the survey, the basic sentiment was, "You guys have been doing these surveys for years, and we never even hear the results of the survey, and nothing ever gets better around here." In other words, don't bother measuring something if you are not going to try to improve it.

Another client replaced an expensive annual survey with a daily system of measuring employee happiness or stress that cost less than $1,000 for an entire year. The bottom line is that you don't need to spend hundreds of thousands of dollars to have a reliable and frequent way of measuring employee satisfaction.

HOW DO I MEASURE IT?

Before I explain how you should measure employee satisfaction or happiness, it is important to understand how *not* to measure it. As with any measure discussed in this book, it is important to measure employee satisfaction as frequently as possible (monthly would be a minimum) to detect when subtle changes occur, particularly declines in performance. It is also important to understand that the typical metrics are probably not accurate or useful unless they are part of a suite of measures that roll into an analytic. You could just borrow use the analytic used by *Fortune* magazine to identify the best employers in America each year. Rather than reinvent the wheel, why not use their analytic? Good question. The *Fortune* metric and assessment approach is designed to do an annual evaluation of employee satisfaction, not to be used to monitor and manage employee satisfaction on an ongoing basis. Take a look at the metrics and weights that go into determining the best companies from an employee point of view.

The selection of the best employers is based on two annual surveys. An employee satisfaction and engagement survey is worth 65 percent of the assessment, and a "culture" survey is worth the remaining 35 percent. The culture survey asks about hiring, pay, benefits, perks, opportunities for advancement, diversity, and a variety of other things. So 100 percent of the assessment is subjective and based on surveys. In previous versions of the "Trust Index Assessment" by the Great Place to Work Institute, there were a number of hard objective metrics like job growth, average pay, turnover, and other factors to offset the survey. However, a lot of companies fell off the list in the last few years because in our economy they had no job growth, salaries were flat or declining, and other measures such as training hours probably showed lower levels. Sadly, I think the older version of the assessment was more valid, because at least 35 percent of the index was based on objective measures and not a survey. However, the Great Place to Work Institute is a business, and a business does not make money by discouraging companies from applying to be on the list and paying the prerequisite fees for participation in the survey.

While everyone will acknowledge that happy and engaged employees are a prerequisite to good performance on all sorts of key success metrics, 99 percent of companies rely on annual surveys as their only measure of employee satisfaction or engagement. The three major problems with this are:

1. Surveys are notoriously unreliable.
2. Most people don't fill them out (or if they do, they are not honest).

3. Surveys can only be done a few times a year or people will protest ("Didn't we just fill out one of these stupid surveys a few months ago?").

Surveys are also just a measure of someone's opinions. Many distrust the anonymity of surveys as well and may report being ecstatic about their company and job, in case someone decides to get rid of the employees with a "bad attitude." Measuring anything once a year does not allow you to manage the aspect of performance being measured. Imagine managing the financial results of a company if you could only measure key metrics like income and expenses once a year. Yet that is exactly what most organizations do when tracking employee satisfaction.

NET PROMOTER SCORE

Well-researched employee surveys like those conducted by Gallup and others do have their place and are an excellent way of taking the pulse of the organization once a year. Gallup's 12 questions are likely to provide enough details to diagnose the causes of problems and develop action plans for improvement. A recent trend is to avoid asking 12 to 50 questions on employee surveys but to only ask one: "On a scale of 1 to 10, would you recommend (company name) as a great place to work?" Those who score 8, 9, or 10 are called your "promoters" and are likely to talk about how great their job and employer are to anyone who will listen.

The logic of these one-question surveys is that employees are much more likely to answer a survey if it is only one question, and the 10-point scale provides a wide enough range to capture diverse opinions. The biggest problem with these one-question surveys is knowing what to do if you get a score of 3? Unless you start asking follow-up questions, you have no idea why you got a low score and what to do about improving it.

Whether a survey is one question or 50, it can only be administered periodically. Employee happiness changes almost hourly, depending on what is going on and how they feel about it. You could have been having a good day until you got an e-mail an hour ago or heard some bad news in a meeting. Consequently, it is important to frequently take the pulse of employee satisfaction levels and identify and manage problems before they become worse.

USING SOCIAL MEDIA TO TRACK EMPLOYEE HAPPINESS

Happiily, a company based in Vancouver, British Columbia, has created a web and mobile application that provides managers with a near real-time dashboard of their employees' engagement and sentiment. The product, also called Happiily, provides a secure, anonymous way for employees to quickly and easily respond to questions customized by their employer about four aspects of their work life: the person they work for, the people they work with, the work they do, and the organization overall.

Each employee's answers are anonymously aggregated on a web-based dashboard that a manager accesses daily. Within seconds, managers can see the dips and spikes of employee sentiment and zero in on the issues most in need of being addressed.

This is one of the best tools I have seen in recent years as a practical and easy way of measuring employee satisfaction. Companies that get daily or weekly data on employee happiness can actually manage this important aspect of performance rather than just look at annual survey results and wonder why scores went down from last year. The cost of Happiily ranges from $25 to just $5 per month per active user, which is actually quite reasonable when you consider that annual employee surveys often cost over $100,000 and provide you with a once-a-year report.

An even lower-tech approach used by several of my clients is to have employees drop a red, yellow, or green marble in a vase at the end of the day, indicating how they felt about the day at work. Another company uses poker chips and coffee cans to track employee happiness on a weekly basis. Lake Arrowhead Hospital in California clips a stoplight chart to your biweekly time sheet, asking employees to indicate how they felt during that time.

All of these low-tech approaches are definitely less expensive, but they all suffer from the anonymity problem—others may see which marble or chip you are dropping in the bowl or can. The Happiily approach capitalizes on the fact that most employees are using various forms of social media many times throughout the day anyway so are used to communicating this way.

FORMULA AND FREQUENCY

Having designed employee satisfaction or happiness indices for many large corporations and government and military organizations, I can present you with a straw man model that can be tailored to your own organization. Regardless of how you customize the individual metrics and weights in your own index, it is important to include mostly metrics that can be tracked at least monthly. All but the annual survey are metrics that can be tracked at least monthly in the formula shown next. A few annual metrics are okay. It is also important to mix subjective metrics like surveys with objective metrics like job growth. A suggested analytic might look like the following:

Employee opinions and perceptions	34%
Annual survey (10–20 questions)	15%
Daily or weekly survey (1–4 questions)	15%
Complaints, grievances, and absenteeism	4%
Stress	33%
Hours worked and overtime	15%
Unused vacation time	5%
Employee assistance data	3%
Absenteeism	10%
Objective factors	33%
Turnover	10%
Job growth	5%
Internal versus external promotions	5%
Training hours and money spent per employee	3%
Travel (if relevant for a big percentage of employees; assign weight and adjust other factor weights as appropriate)	
Pay and benefits versus industry	10%

Objective metrics are assigned a weight of 66 percent of the analytic, but the problem with most of these individual metrics is that they are not solely measures of employee happiness or satisfaction. Absenteeism definitely relates to stress and happiness, but sometimes people just get sick and it in no way relates to their job satisfaction. The same can be said of hours worked. I have a number of clients at R&D organizations who work long hours because they love the project they are working on so much. Having to attend training all the time might be a dissatisfier for one employee and something that makes another happy and feel valued. This is why it is important to have at least a third of your metric be composed of measures of employee perceptions and opinions.

VARIATIONS

If the previous model is too complex, you might boil it down to a few key metrics. One client constructed an index that included a quarterly survey of one-fourth of the employees, turnover, percent of new employees from referrals, and percent of internal promotions versus external hires. A consulting client measured billable hours (too many are bad and too few are stressful), a one-question survey done quarterly for all employees, and travel percentage, which is viewed the same way as billable hours. Too much travel is very stressful, and very little travel is not good either. I find that about 10 days a month is my max before I start getting stressed out. Another client (a government R&D lab) came up with an interesting metric. The boss noticed that morale was way down when money was tight, travel restrictions were in place, and there was not enough work in the lab. He also noticed the opposite was true when there was plenty of work from paying clients and budgets were eased up for travel and conference attendance. So he measured the amount of work the lab had on a monthly basis and the amount of money that was being spent on training, travel, meetings, and so on as an employee satisfaction measure. He was not a big fan of surveys, and this objective measure turned out to be a very good and easy way of assessing employee satisfaction. The bigger challenge was defining the red, yellow, and green ranges, because too much work could also be stressful.

TARGETS AND BENCHMARKS

Setting a target for the overall index should be based on targets set for the individual metrics. Most organizations track many of the individual measures I list, so it should be possible to get industry averages and benchmarks to use in crafting targets based on comparative data. The overall index should probably define the bottom of the green zone as 80 percent. The companies that make it to the top 10 of *Fortune*'s annual list of the 100 Best Companies to Work For generally have employee satisfaction levels of around 80 percent. As I mentioned earlier, a few companies like Purina are higher than 95 percent satisfaction. The red or poor performance zone would probably be anything less than 50 percent, with yellow in between these two figures.

BENEFITS OF DATA

The key to measuring a dimension as complex as employee happiness is to construct an index that is based on a number of different individual metrics that are each assigned a weight based on factors like data integrity and the degree to which they are a true measure of employee happiness. For example, absenteeism is not a clean measure of employee stress or happiness, because sometimes people just get sick. Similarly, an employee may work long hours because he does not have much of a life outside of work and loves his job. Because of factors like this, it is important that an employee satisfaction or happiness index comprises a number of different individual measures.

Employee happiness is becoming increasingly important as a predictor of business performance. Important studies as well as anecdotal data suggest that people who love their jobs perform at 120 percent, and those who hate their jobs and employers do just enough to avoid being fired. Smart organizations realize that a factor like employee satisfaction needs to be accurately measured and managed just like financial performance. What this means is that you need to figure out how to measure employee happiness frequently, be able to analyze the data to determine the causes of high and low scores, and develop actions and improvement initiatives to make your organization a better place to work.

Just as the financial health of a company cannot be assessed by a single metric, employee satisfaction should be measured using a suite of individual measures combined into an index like a FICO score. The dreaded annual employee survey is a practice that is quickly falling by the wayside as new companies like Happiily are developing tools for tracking employee happiness daily and providing enough analytical data to help improve this important performance dimension.

NOTE

1. Stephen C. Lundin, Harry Paul, and John Christensen, *Fish: A Proven Way to Boost Morale and Improve Results* (New York: Hyperion, 2000).

CHAPTER **18**

The Culture Index

WHY AN ORGANIZATION MIGHT TRACK THIS

Questions Answered

- Do people really understand our values?
- Can they recognize when decisions and behavior are consistent with the values?
- Do leaders exhibit the values in their behavior and decisions?
- Do employees believe the organization really operates according to the values?
- Do our values and culture stay the same through changes in leadership and in bad times?
- Are we systematically managing the culture to ensure it stays positive?

Why Is This Information Important?

Your organization has a set of values and a culture whether they were engineered or not. Most organizational cultures tend to revolve around the personal values of the founders, even if the company has been around a long time. Young companies tend not to think much about culture because they are too busy focusing on customers and shareholders. As companies age and the founders retire or die, they tend to become more inward-looking and often want to make sure that the values that made them great in the beginning still characterize the company.

Southwest Airlines is one of those rare companies that has maintained its culture of humor, focus on the customer, and efficiency long after founder Herb Kelleher stepped down as CEO. 3M is also a company that has been through leadership changes, yet stays focused on the core value of innovation. Everyone is watching Apple now

239

that Steve Jobs is gone. He clearly was a huge part of the culture of Apple, and it's hard to imagine that the company will be the same without him. Hopefully Apple has promoted new leaders who have the same values as Jobs and they will be able to maintain the company's culture of focus and innovation.

Most mature companies tend to see a major culture change in a negative direction when the founder steps down. Changing culture and values tends to be gradual, and once you realize you've lost the wonderful culture you used to have, it is too late. Although challenging, it is possible to measure culture so you can zero in and fix problems and make adjustments before things go too far south.

Organizational culture can be a major asset or a damaging liability that hinders all efforts to grow and become more successful. Measuring and managing it is something few companies do well.

The importance of culture cannot be underestimated. In fact, I remember reading a great quote that said, "Culture eats strategy for lunch." In other words, a negative culture will ensure the failure of your strategy. Sadly, the inverse is not true—a great culture does not ensure the success of a stupid strategy.

Book after book acknowledges that corporate culture can be a major asset or liability. Yet almost no organization has a way of tracking its culture. Any metrics I have seen are worthless ones, like how many people have attended corporate culture training or can recite the generic list of vague values.

I just finished reading an excellent book called *What Really Works: The 4+2 Formula for Sustained Business Success*, by William Joyce, Nitin Nohria, and Bruce Roberson.[1] Although the book is more than 10 years old, the findings are based on extensive reviews of hundreds of winning and losing companies over a 10-year period. One of the top four characteristics that most correlated to total shareholder return was a performance-focused positive culture. Given this research, as well as most people's anecdotal data, it would seem foolish for an organization not to measure and manage its culture just like it does other important aspects of performance.

TYPES OF ORGANIZATIONS WHERE THIS METRIC IS APPROPRIATE

Culture is important in any large organization of more than a few hundred employees. If your employer is a small company with 75 employees, the leaders probably know all the employees by name and assessing culture can be done by just talking with people. If your employer is an organization of thousands or tens of thousands, it is unlikely that leaders can get a good gut feeling for the culture by talking with a few people and observing behavior in the workplace. Measuring culture is also more important in an organization that has had some turnover in its leadership. This is particularly true when new leaders have been brought in from the outside.

I recall working with Discover Card in Chicago for several years. Discover's president and most of is leaders were formerly with Sears, before Sears spun off Discover as a separate company and sold it to Morgan Stanley. Many of the old Sears values still permeated Discover Card, and it was a culture characterized by hard work, honesty, and loyalty. Most people had that strong Midwest work ethic, even at Discover facilities in Delaware, Utah, and Arizona. When parent company Morgan Stanley decided it was time for a new leadership team it brought in an executive from the old MBNA, which at the time was one of the most successful credit card companies in the United States. It later got bought out by Bank of America, and executives probably saw the writing on the wall and decided to leave while they still had the chance. The new president of Discover Card was very different from Tom, the retiring one. First of all, he was really young, as well as aggressive and innovative. He brought in a few of his cronies from MBNA, and pretty soon the culture of Discover Card started changing to be more like that of what used to be MBNA. Not all of this was bad, but it was viewed as such by many of the older employees. In fact, some of the new values were clearer and easier to see than the old ones.

The new executive team brought in a team of consultants who crafted a new set of values that spelled D-I-S-C-O-V-E-R:

Doing the Right Thing

- Displaying integrity and performing to the highest ethical and business standards.
- Being accountable for your own actions and results; acknowledging and learning from mistakes.
- Encouraging the personal growth of others.

Innovation

- Finding ways to be first to market.
- Promoting continuous improvement.
- Encouraging prudent risk taking and having tolerance for honest mistakes.
- Recognizing and rewarding truly inventive initiative and risk taking.

Simplicity

- Providing clear and direct messages.
- Working to streamline workflow.
- Making efficient use of resources and time.

Collaboration

- Promoting cooperative efforts with others and being a team player.
- Working toward the most effective, mutually satisfactory solution.
- Developing positive, professional partnerships with colleagues and customers.

Openness

- Communicating openly and honestly with others; fostering an environment of trust.
- Providing and accepting ideas and feedback.
- Listening to, understanding, and appreciating others' viewpoints.

Volunteerism

- Recognizing and supporting the needs of our communities.
- Committing time and energy to the company's volunteer activities.
- Assisting and supporting team members and customers in achieving company, team, and individual goals.

Enthusiasm

- Exhibiting a clear understanding and commitment to the company's vision, mission, values, and business strategies.

- Displaying a high energy level and going the extra mile.
- Fostering a creative and fun environment that recognizes and celebrates achievements.

Respect
- Encouraging and valuing the opinions of team members and customers.
- Honoring and respecting diversity of people, their ideas, and their work styles.
- Promoting and demonstrating a balance between work and home life.

If your company is going through a change in leadership it is vitally important to measure your culture. Regardless of whether you want to keep things the same or if you want to change the culture and get rid of some of the old values, it is important to measure and manage this effort. If the founders still run your company, and the values are so ingrained in the way the organization functions, you probably don't need to bother with this metric unless you are planning a big growth spurt. Whether growth is organic or coming from acquisitions, you probably want to make sure that the culture stays the same, so it needs to be measured. What is ironic is that almost all organizations talk about the importance of their culture as a key to their success, yet almost none of these same organizations measure or manage this dimension of performance. Where I do see measures, they are worthless. In this chapter you will learn about some useful measures to include in a culture index.

HOW DOES THIS IMPACT PERFORMANCE?

The most direct influence of culture is on employee satisfaction and engagement. I recall seeing how the changing culture of a client of mine that used to be on the *Fortune* list of the 100 Best Companies to Work For impacted employee morale. People used to love working at this company and were fanatically devoted to its success until the CEO left to teach at Harvard Business School and the new management team installed a new culture focused on cost control, process improvement, and outsourcing of noncore functions. Not only did employee satisfaction and engagement deteriorate but so did growth, profits, new products, and stock price. To suggest that culture has an impact on all measures of a company's success would not be much of a stretch. Even relationships with suppliers and vendors are impacted by an organization's culture. Back in the 1970s and 1980s, the culture of the Big Three automakers was to bully their suppliers and ask them for as many perks as they could get away with. This impacted the culture of their suppliers, who lost some self-respect by always backing down and giving in to demands for price cuts, jobs for kids, Super Bowl tickets, and other less savory requests.

PETS BEFORE PROFITS: PURINA'S CORPORATE CULTURE

One of the best-run companies I've ever worked with is Purina, part of food giant Nestlé. Its culture revolves around the idea that pets are always more important than profits. This value made decision making easy in a time when there have been several pet food scares due to tainted raw materials.

A few years ago when a number of dogs and cats died from bad pet food, Purina pulled all of its products from all retail shelves just to be sure; it later found out that almost none of its pet food was bad. The move cost the company millions, but company president Terry Block wanted to make sure no dog or cat died because the company was worried about losing money. This decision communicated the value loud and clear to all employees and customers.

Another value that characterizes Purina is innovation. About a third of its sales every year come from new or enhanced products, which would seem to be a tough challenge in the pet food business. Purina is also known for its positive work/life balance, with 97 percent employee satisfaction (the best companies in America typically get 80 percent satisfaction, and average companies get 50 percent). In 2010 Purina was awarded the coveted Malcolm Baldrige National Quality Award, while also being awarded best place to work in St. Louis, and best company in America for work/life balance. And, by the way, Purina also has the best financial and market share results of any company in its industry.

Many of the metrics proposed in this book are important for some organizations but not for others. Culture, on the other hand, is something that all large organizations need to measure and manage because of how important it is for success.

COST AND EFFORT TO MEASURE

Depending on how sophisticated your approach to gathering culture data is, this metric is probably going to require at least a medium amount of time and cost to measure. Most of the data that does exist on culture tends to be pretty useless, so new metrics will have to created, along with data collection plans. Where the cost goes from medium to high is when an organization needs to rewrite its values as a first step in measuring compliance with them. Discover Financial Services spent about a year working with consultants from Senn Delaney to craft the set of values you read about earlier and communicate them to employees. Of course, you can do this on your own without lots of consultants, but it still will take time, and sometimes you need an outside viewpoint to get an honest assessment of your existing culture and values before deciding on what you want them to become. When you consider the importance of measures of culture to your overall success, the payoff is worth the investment if you can get an accurate read from reviewing the data on a regular basis, allowing you to manage the culture.

HOW DO I MEASURE IT?

Before you can measure your culture and values, you need to make sure people understand them. Most company values I see are a generic list of vague words or phrases that no one would object to but no one understands either. Some of the values I see on brass plaques and wallet cards are:

- Leadership
- Perseverance
- Trust
- Integrity
- Teamwork
- Customer focus

- Risk taking
- Diversity
- Communication
- Growth
- Competence
- Excellence

I am guessing that a few of yours are listed here if you are like most companies and put almost no thought into defining your values and culture. The first step in measuring your culture is to make sure that people understand what your values are, which means that they can easily recognize behavior and decisions that are inconsistent or consistent with those values. Some examples of some innovative and clear values of companies are:

- Democracy—Namaste Solar
- Fitness—TRX
- Training—Hopkins Printing
- Weirdness—Zappos

Toms Shoes is another company with a clear and unique culture which it calls "one for one." For every pair of shoes sold, Toms donates a pair of shoes to a needy child. One of the unusual ones that Discover has on its list of values is volunteerism. Giving back to the community by volunteering time and money is a big part of the culture at Discover, and this value is not only unusual, it is easy to see in behavior and resource allocation. Beginning with a clear and well-thought-out set of values that define the culture you aspire to become is the first step.

If you have a set of values like the generic words and phrases I have listed previously, but your people like them, then you need to begin by defining example behaviors that show those values and examples that show the opposite. For example, consider the Discover value of respect. Some behaviors that demonstrate respect are waiting your turn to talk in meetings and showing up on time, whereas showing up to meetings late and interrupting others are disrespectful behaviors. Early on in its culture change initiative, people at Discover started fining one another a dollar when they observed a behavior inconsistent with the values. Show up to a meeting late, put a dollar in the coffee can. Interrupt someone, put another dollar in. The dollars not only served as a good reminder to follow the values, but counting them gave the company a measure of the degree to which behavior in the workplace was consistent with the values. Of course, sometimes it would backfire and people would come into meetings announcing that they were putting $10 in the kitty because they planned on violating all the values during the meeting.

Assuming you have a clear and well-communicated set of values, you can now begin constructing a culture index. As with most complex dimensions of performance, it is impossible to measure your culture with a couple of metrics. Rather, you need to construct an index, like your FICO score, that allows leaders to look at a single gauge to measure culture and drill into details if the gauge shows yellow or red performance.

The key dimensions in a culture index are:

- **Knowledge**. Do people know what your values are and can they recognize when your behavior and decision making is consistent with those values? This is best measured via a test that could be anonymous. You are not measuring individual employees, only how well the values have been communicated. I prefer measuring knowledge versus process measures such as training or orientation sessions conducted, because people could attend these sessions and not remember a thing. The knowledge that should be tested is not memorization of the values but whether employees can identify behaviors and actions that are consistent or inconsistent with the values.

- **Perceptions**. These are opinions about the real values and culture of the company, collected via anonymous surveys or focus groups held off-site and facilitated by outsiders. Questions should focus on identifying what the real values and priorities are versus what is stated. For example, a lot of companies talk about diversity, but tend to hire people who look and think like them and who graduated from the same six universities where they always recruit. Perceptions can be measured with a survey or with focus groups, and a sample of the workforce can be surveyed monthly or quarterly.

▪ **Behavior**. This refers to incidents of good and bad actions and employee behavior related to the values. For example, if health and fitness is one of your values, you might measure the number of employees who get an annual physical or work out in the company gym. If one of your values is work/life balance, you might measure how many employees work while they are on vacation. If your value is accountability, you might track how many employees are disciplined or fired for poor performance. Some companies, like Purina, recognize employees with on-the-spot rewards when behavior is observed that demonstrates their values. Counting the number of people recognized could also be a behavior measure. Or the opposite: Discover Financial Services counted dollars in the coffee cans to measure bad behaviors.

▪ **Decisions and resource allocations**. The real values of an organization are often best understood by looking at how they make decisions and commit resources. The Purina example of taking all their pet food off retail shelves before finding out their food was not tainted is a perfect example. Discover might look at how employees are given time and other resources for volunteerism. One company I read about expects all employees to spend eight hours a month on community service. It gives them four hours off from work with pay and expects them to donate the other four hours. Measuring decisions and resource allocation might involve a quarterly or monthly documentation of major decisions that have been made and resource allocations, and coding them as neutral, for the values, or against them.

Each of these four dimensions is assigned a percentage weight based on its relative importance and the integrity of the data in each category. It is also important to measure culture at least once a quarter; monthly would be preferred. An annual metric on any aspect of performance is mostly useless, because things can go south in a lot faster than a year.

VARIATIONS

According to research done by a company called Critical Metrics in the spring of 2012, the vast majority of companies that have any measure of corporate culture do nothing more than a survey of perceptions. The lure of this is that it is cheap and easy. There are many downsides to using this as your only measure, however. First, many employees will probably not complete the survey because they are already over-surveyed and they have lots of work to do. Second, employees who do fill out the survey may not be honest, especially if it is done electronically and there is no way to ensure anonymity. People may tell you a politically correct answer for fear of being labeled as someone who is not a team player. The other problem with relying on a culture survey is that surveys can only be done every so often (usually once a year), making it impossible to manage a measurement that only occurs once a year.

A variation that one of my clients uses is a one-question survey done monthly on one-twelfth of the population that asks on a 1–10 scale the degree to which the company operates according to its stated values. Along with the survey, they also do random anonymous knowledge tests of a sample of employees once a month and count the number of employees recognized for behavior consistent with the values. These three measures track perceptions, knowledge, and behavior, and the amount of effort needed to collect the data is minimal.

FORMULA AND FREQUENCY

As with most of the indices described in this book, the formula outlined here should be viewed as a generic straw man that needs to be customized and tailored to fit your own organization:

Knowledge	20%
Test scores	15%
Training attendance	5%
Perceptions	25%
Surveys	15%
Focus groups	10%
Behavior	20%
Decisions and resources	35%
Decisions and policies	20%
Resources	15%

TARGETS AND BENCHMARKS

As with most of the metrics in this book, your own targets would need to be set in relation to your baseline and other comparative data you might gather from others. However, if less than 80 percent of your employees don't understand the values and less than 80 percent don't perceive that the company really operates according to its stated values, I consider that the red range. If between 80 and 90 percent understand the values and related behaviors, I would code that as yellow or still needs work, and green should probably be 90 percent or better. The same sorts of ranges would apply when setting targets for the perception data. If less than 90 percent of your workforce thinks the values are not really followed, that is a big problem. When setting targets for the submetric that relates to decisions by senior management and commitment of resources, the red, yellow, and green targets should be in the same ranges.

BENEFITS OF DATA

The biggest benefit of this data on culture is that you can actually manage it. Very few organizations measure and manage their culture, and yet they all say it is vitally important. By tracking culture using the three types of measures I have mentioned, you can implement the right countermeasure to improve it. If most people don't understand the values, then a good training program should solve that problem. If, on the other hand, everyone understands the values but thinks the organization does not really follow them, then that is a much bigger problem. Changing perceptions takes time and cannot be done with a training program. The fastest way to change perceptions is to have the leaders start making decisions and committing resources in such a way as to communicate the values.

Take Discover Financial Service's value of volunteerism, for example. If all the leaders suddenly started volunteering more of their time, encouraging their direct reports to do so, and committed more company resources to charity and community groups, perceptions would probably start to change regarding the degree to which the company really believes in volunteerism. Another benefit of measuring your culture is that it will reveal programs and efforts that may be a waste of time. One client was appalled that no one remembered the organization's values, so he posted them in front of all urinals and on the back of all bathroom stall doors. Several months later, people still couldn't recall them even though many looked at them seven or eight times a day. Organizations often embark on culture change initiatives without any way to measure their success or failure. This metric will help you fine-tune your efforts and zero in on approaches that really work.

NOTE

1. William Joyce, Nitin Nohria, and Bruce Roberson, *What Really Works: The 4 + 2 Formula for Sustained Business Success* (New York: HarperBusiness, 2003).

CHAPTER **19**

The Distraction Index

WHY AN ORGANIZATION MIGHT TRACK THIS

Questions Answered

- Are employees doing what I hired them to do?
- Are employees engaged in their jobs?
- Are employees being utilized to achieve the greatest value?
- Are employees focused on achieving key results most of the time?

Why Is This Information Important?

The single biggest cost in many organizations today is people. Between salaries, benefits, vacations, and bonuses, personnel is a huge line item on most balance sheets. As with any expenditure, it is important to track what value is derived from these costs. Organizations spend a lot of time and money making sure they hire the best and brightest, but they rarely have any data on whether those employees and managers are spending time on valuable activities. Distractions are also a key factor in employee engagement. Being allowed the time to focus on completing your job responsibilities has a lot to do with one's job satisfaction.

Start-ups are almost always lean and focused on a few key activities that really matter, like marketing, manufacturing, and delivery. If you have a good product or service and watch your numbers carefully, the company grows and becomes more prosperous. The people you hired in the beginning are now bosses of hundreds or thousands of people and your org chart gets more complicated each year, as the need for new departments and positions arises. You hired people because they were good salespeople, accountants, operations managers, or HR professionals, but now they are being asked to spend time on a lot of other things. As organizations go from birth to maturity to middle age, they tend to become flabby and fail to spend enough time on the things that made them successful in the beginning.

TYPES OF ORGANIZATIONS WHERE THIS METRIC IS APPROPRIATE

Small organizations or those with low labor costs compared to total operating expenses probably should not bother with this metric. In a small business, there is no time for all these distractions, and employees and managers tend to spend most of their time on overall job responsibilities. Large corporations, universities, and government organizations tend to have high payroll costs and to be the worst at distracting their employees with administrative duties and management programs. Hospitals and other types of health care organizations could probably benefit from a metric like this but slightly modified. One hospital I worked with just asked people to track their time in two categories: delivering health care and other. Most of what comprised the "other" category had to do with filling out paperwork to get paid. Of course, there are hundreds of people whose jobs in a hospital have only indirect links to the delivery of health care, so this metric might only apply to the doctors, nurses, technicians, and others who are the direct health care providers.

Organizations with a flat organizing structure will also find little use for this data. In these organizations where there are only a few layers between workers and the senior leaders, the vast majority of the staff are focused on major job responsibilities. For example, a call center I worked with has about 85 percent of its staff on the phone as either individual customer service representatives or supervisors who also take tough calls. They can't take big groups of people off the phones for meetings and special programs, so they probably would not need to have the distraction index on their corporate scorecard.

HOW DOES THIS IMPACT PERFORMANCE?

The distraction index is a leading indicator of many different output and outcome measures. If employees are distracted from focusing on their main job responsibilities, it will impact:

- Productivity and efficiency
- Quality
- Customer service
- Costs
- Profits
- Turnover
- Employee engagement

The most immediate impact of having employees distracted from their primary jobs is that it affects their level of engagement. I prefer not to do surveys to measure engagement, because they can only be done once or twice a year and many of them include ridiculous questions like, "Do you agree with the company vision and understand it?" or "Can you see how your job helps contribute to the company mission?" or "Does your boss model the company values in his or her behavior?" The answer to all of these questions is obviously "yes." Most employees are very frustrated by having to spend more and more of their workday on what they probably view as activities that are a waste of time. If you want your employees to be engaged, make sure they are in the right job and make sure they spend most of their time doing their job. If you are intent on measuring engagement via a survey like Gallup does, I encourage you to continue with this, but look at it as an annual study, not a measure that is used to track and manage engagement on a weekly and monthly basis. You will probably find that engagement scores on your survey get better as you improve performance on the distraction index.

I recall working years ago for Discover Card in suburban Chicago, helping them develop a scorecard linked to their new strategic plan. When it came time to develop the People section of the scorecard, the typical measures of employee satisfaction and turnover were suggested. Then the tone of the meeting changed and everyone started getting engaged and emotional. I recall one guy who suggested, "We need a metric that tells senior management how much time people spend doing their jobs versus spending time on all these improvement initiatives we have around here like strategic planning, activity-based costing, business process improvement, and balanced scorecard." Someone else chimed in: "Yeah, it's not just these three-letter management programs, it's all these administrative activities we have to spend time on like budget meetings, sexual harassment training, and other stuff—it's getting out of hand." Before I knew it, I thought I might have a mutiny on my hands, since I was one of the enemies, taking up their time with a balanced scorecard meeting. After listening to their comments, I realized that this was an important factor linked to organizational success. Organizations need to spend time doing things that make customers continue buying their products and services. After discussing this with the team, they agreed that some amount of these nonjob activities were necessary, but the majority of the group agreed that these activities were taking up too much of people's workdays. The problem was no one had any data or facts—all we had were strong opinions and perceptions that too much time was spent on these activities. I suggested that a study possibly be done to determine the extent of the problem, but the group disagreed. "If we do a study that is a one-time event, it might lead to a temporary reduction in these programs or activities, but it would be short-lived. We need an ongoing performance measure that leaders can track every week and month. As soon as you kill one of these programs or activities, three new ones spring up."

COST AND EFFORT TO MEASURE

This metric is extremely easy to measure and requires no additional costs. If employees already complete weekly or biweekly time sheets, data collection requires sorting time into several categories. If no one completes time sheets or records on time, then a time tracking system will need to be developed, which usually is a one-page form or electronic request for employees to submit their work hours sorted into predetermined categories.

HOW DO I MEASURE IT?

Data for the distraction index comes right from employees' time sheets. Employees are asked to sort their time into three general categories:

1. **Job**. Activities directly associated with your job and why you were hired: preparing financial reports, reviewing contracts, making a presentation to a prospective client, debugging software, delivering a training program, or whatever the main function of your job is.

2. **Admin**. Activities that all organizations need to spend some time on, including budgeting, contracting and procurement, recruiting and hiring, attending compliance or regulatory training, participating in audits or certification activities, sales or project review meetings, and learning about new policies or software.

3. **Programs**. Management or improvement programs that tend to have three-letter acronyms such as BSC, ABC, MBO, CRM, TQM, ERP, BPI, and so on. These programs might also include generic training programs that everyone is forced to attend, or motivational events.

In order to make it clear to employees, many organizations that have adopted this metric provide a one-page cheat sheet or job aid that helped people decide how to sort their time. For example, Cold Regions Research and Engineering Laboratory (CRREL), which is part of the army, provides employees with a two-column list of meetings, programs, training, and programs that fall into the categories of "Administration" and "Management Programs."

Organizations like law firms, consultants, and engineering firms will find it very easy to track this data because it is basically unbillable hours. Hours billed to client projects are those associated with doing one's primary job, whereas administrative time and participation in internal management programs cannot typically be charged to customers. Many of these firms require employees to track time in 10- to 15-minute intervals, so employees learn to become very adept at tracking their work activities. These types of firms tend to get highly accurate data to feed into the distraction index. Other types of organizations may require a new process of tracking time or filling out time sheets if this is not currently done. Asking people to do this once every two weeks is likely to produce inaccurate data, as employees are likely to forget what they did over the previous 10 days. If you need to start collecting time sheet data and have not done so in the past, I recommend only tracking activities or events that take at least an hour. Going from not filling out a time sheet to a system of recording time in 15-minute intervals will be too much to handle for most people, and they will view this task as just one more distraction.

FORMULA AND FREQUENCY

Most organizations track distraction levels on a weekly or biweekly basis or as often as employees submit time sheets. Only asking for data on a monthly basis is probably a waste of time, because most employees won't keep good records and will just guess when filling out their time sheet. The formula is as follows:

$$\text{Total hours of admin time} + \text{Hours of program time}$$
$$\div \text{Total work hours} = \text{Distraction index percentage}$$

The number is better expressed as a negative factor by showing the amount of time employees are distracted, because this tends to be more dramatic and gets more attention.

VARIATIONS

The most common way of calculating this index is to sort time into the three categories previously described. Other alternatives used by clients who adopted this index include:

- Billable versus unbillable time
- Job, training, administration, time off
- Job, regulatory and legal, other
- Client projects, marketing, admin

I have also seen the distraction index be one of the key metrics in an employee engagement index. This is quite logical, because being distracted from doing your job is a major frustration for most employees, and this is a measure that can easily be tracked every day and week, compared to surveys that can only be done a few times a year. Another variation is to use the distraction index as one of the submeasures in a productivity or efficiency index. Other measures might include outputs divided by labor-hours and labor cost divided by total cost.

TARGETS AND BENCHMARKS

Most clients that use this metric have a target range of people spending 70 to 80 percent of their time doing what they were hired for. In other words, no more than 10 to 15 percent of time should be spent on administrative activities, with the same amount of time spent participating in management and improvement programs. Targets for improvement should be based on current baseline levels, however. Several clients found that professionals and managers routinely spend only about a third of their time on regular job responsibilities, so they had a way to go to reach the targeted green zone of 70 percent job, 30 percent other.

BENEFITS OF DATA

There is always a cost in collecting data, but luckily this measure requires almost no cost or additional time from employees. Training employees to have the discipline to track their time at work accurately may require some patience, but it will quickly become a habit and you probably won't get too much resistance from them. In fact, most are glad to track their time in these categories if the result is fewer management programs, meetings, and task forces and less time on administrative activities. The biggest benefit of having data on how employees spend their time is that you now have hard facts and data on the cumulative effect of all the programs and requirements that seem to exponentially increase as organizations grow larger. This is a good statistic to keep an eye on as you track growth in revenue, to make sure it does not get out of hand. Data from the distraction index may cause you to refrain from starting new initiatives, practices, or programs until others are completed or dropped. Data from this metric may also lead to the development of policies that minimize disruptions and distractions. For example, one large corporate client only allows one major management program at a time to be implemented. Every few years, the client implements a new program or process, and this has led to a long trend of improving performance as well as helping its employees avoid getting burned out. Employees have no choice but to participate in mandatory training and meetings and to complete paperwork required by payers or regulators. Filling out tax forms each year is an administrative chore we all have to do that distracts us from more important things.

Another important lesson to be learned from this data is that certain employees tend to participate in all the important improvement initiatives, whereas others don't participate in any of them. Many of my clients have a core group of 20 to 30 people who always are the first to volunteer to work on improvement initiatives. This is great, since they are almost always highly competent people, but it is really not fair that others get to avoid these responsibilities. The participants are often overachiever types who still manage to get their job responsibilities done well. The fallout is that these people get burned out. Eventually the 60- to 70-hour weeks lead to health problems or problems with personal relationships. Data from the distraction index can be used to balance participation in improvement programs across the entire workforce, rather than having these programs completed by only a small minority of people. Lack of participation in any of the organization's improvement initiatives is not a behavior you want to drive with this metric. Spending zero time on administration or management programs would not be considered healthy.

A distraction index that shows people are spending 30 percent or more of their time on nondirect job responsibilities means that employee engagement will tend to go down and stress levels will increase. The consequence of spending too little time on improvement programs or administrative requirements might be regulatory problems, lawsuits, and failure to meet improvement goals. All organizations need to spend some time on administration and on improvement. The key is to keep this time balanced with getting your job done. This measure helps you do just that.

CHAPTER **20**

The Corporate
Wellness Index

WHY AN ORGANIZATION MIGHT TRACK THIS

Questions Answered

- How healthy are our employees?
- Does our corporate wellness program really work?
- Are there health and wellness programs that we offer that are a waste of money?
- Do employees care about their health?
- Are we doing things that might encourage employees to be unhealthy?

Why Is This Information Important?

About every 10 years some new business fad emerges that promises to save millions, improve performance, and transform the culture of your company into one focused on excellence. Many will recall previous fads like TQM, Six Sigma, CRM, Lean, knowledge management, reengineering, learning organization, and others. Years later, it's hard to believe we wasted so much time and money on consultants, meetings, and training programs that failed to produce the kind of sustained results promised by the salespeople.

Is corporate wellness yet another one of these fads? I don't think so. As a purveyor of many of these business programs over the years, I've become a little cynical and jaded when something new comes along that promises anywhere from two to six dollars in return for every dollar invested. However, I think a healthy organization is increasingly important in today's world of double-digit annual increases in employer health care costs. I also think that programs that encourage employees and partners to become healthier have few bad side effects and many corollary benefits.

I remember doing a study for a navy shipyard client on the characteristics of its best managers, and Mike stood out among all the others I interviewed and studied. First of all, Mike had the best performance of any of the project superintendents, and his priorities were a little different than his average-performing peers. "My priorities are, number one, my health; number two, my family; and number three, my job," Mike explained. "I make sure to always hit the gym five days a week from 5:30 until 7:00, have dinner with my family every night, never work weekends, and don't take my work smartphone with me on vacations."

Mike looks about 10 years younger than his actual age, and is viewed as an anomaly by others who are typically at least 30 pounds overweight, work 70-plus hours a week, don't get enough sleep, and routinely make excuses for poor performance on their projects. Sadly, I have not met too many Mikes in my 30-plus years of consulting. Imagine if you had an entire company of people like Mike. Think of what could get accomplished in an eight-hour day.

In case you haven't read the newspapers or watched the news in the last five years, this is the first time in over 100 years where the current generation of children may have a shorter life expectancy than their parents. Life spans had been dramatically increasing for many years, but now seem to be going in the other direction, if we can trust predictive metrics like diabetes and obesity in young people. As an employer you may not be responsible for the health of your employees, but it certainly has a major impact on your performance. Absenteeism and its lesser-known cousin presenteeism cost millions every year. For those of you who aren't in HR, presenteeism means coming to work even though you are sick. Many companies I work with actually encourage this and reward people for coming to work with a migraine or bad sinus infection. Being unhealthy impacts productivity and other key measures of performance. All employers want to have a healthy workforce, but few do much to try to create one or measure if their efforts are making a difference.

Most big corporations today have some sort of wellness program, but many of these programs are not even marginally successful and are not used by the vast majority of employees. Bolting a wellness program onto a company that fundamentally does not care about the health and well-being of its employees is doomed to failure. If the company frowns on people who exercise at lunch, work an eight-hour day, and refuse work assignments when they are already fully committed, a wellness program is probably going to be a waste of time. In spite of what is on the values plaque in your lobby, most corporations today value long hours, 24-hour-a-day accessibility of employees, checking in daily while on vacation, people who went to the same five schools as the leaders, and being a "team player" (i.e., don't rock the boat).

Some companies actually do have a culture that promotes health and wellness, such as food giant General Mills. Among other things, the company has Fitness Fridays and walking meetings, and employees go cross-country skiing on the Minneapolis campus.

Having healthy employees often boils down to bottom-line cost savings for employers. A healthy culture seems to make more sense at a company like Patagonia that makes clothing and accessories associated with outdoor fitness-related activities, or TRX, where "fitness" is one of its core values. Johnson & Johnson is another company that does a good job of promoting health and wellness as part of its culture, as does MD Andersen Cancer Center. On the other hand, I worked with a major pharmaceutical company that claims to promote health and wellness but encourages the use of prescription drugs and has a high-stress culture that rewards being a workaholic.

TYPES OF ORGANIZATIONS WHERE THIS METRIC IS APPROPRIATE

Any organization that spends 20 or 25 percent of its costs on people should probably consider this metric, as well as large organizations that have more than 1,000 employees. Organizations with corporate wellness programs should definitely consider tracking this measure to see if their efforts are making any difference. Even a small organization might consider an employee health analytic if the organization values health and wellness. I worked with the Jackson Hole Airport in Wyoming to help develop performance metrics, and one the team decided on was employee health. Airport CEO Ray Bishop is in amazing health, and his level of fitness is certainly that of someone at least 10 years younger. With only about 75 employees including all the Transportation Security Administration agents, Bishop wanted a comprehensive measure of employee health that would be easy to implement, so he elected to have employees go the web site Realage .com and enter data on their own lifestyle, family, and current health statistics. The three major factors that are assessed in Realage.com are family history and genetics, lifestyle (diet, exercise, sleep, etc.), and current health statistics like blood pressure and LDL/HDL ratio. Based on all this data, the web site computes your physical age versus your chronological age. By making use of this free web site, Jackson Hole Airport has a simple yet comprehensive analytic to use in assessing the health of its workforce.

Most organizations of any size pay for the health insurance of their employees. Even firms like Starbucks and UPS that have a mostly part-time workforce provide excellent health insurance for their employees. The healthier employees are, the less insurance will cost and the more productive employees will be. A healthy workforce boils down to huge cost avoidance. Employees will accomplish a lot more at work if they are fit and healthy like the guy Mike I mentioned earlier. Mike's success was due to many things, but being healthy was certainly one of those factors.

HOW DOES THIS IMPACT PERFORMANCE?

If your organizational results are dependent on employees and their behavior, their health will impact your company performance. If you work for a hospital, airline, retailer, pharmaceutical firm, government, military, or even many manufacturing companies, you will no doubt find that the health of your employees costs you a great deal of money. Another important way health impacts performance is that you avoid losing key employees to sickness or even death. I recall working for a big aerospace client that had two of their top vice presidents die of heart attacks in one year. Both of these guys were in their fifties and had worked at the firm since college. The company had invested a lot of time and effort grooming them and turning them into high-performing executives, and now they were gone. The previous CEO was a major proponent of health who had only vegan food served in the executive lunchroom, exercised regularly, and did a lot to encourage health from all his employees. When he retired, the culture of the company moved away from a focus on health.

HALFHEARTED APPROACHES TO WELLNESS

If you examine most of the wellness programs in the corporate or government world, you'll find that they include a minimal workout facility or discounts at a local health club, one healthy food choice option in the company cafeteria (which almost no one eats), exercise clubs like lunchtime walking or yoga, annual health screening and physicals, drug testing for new employees, Weight Watchers or similar programs, posters with tips on improving health, and online health assessments. The vast majority of employees don't take advantage of any of these wellness programs. In fact, the ones who do are usually people who are already very healthy, or who don't have a lot of work to do and can find time to participate in these activities at work. Most managers I encounter don't even take a lunch hour, let alone find time to go to the company gym or walk with a bunch of others.

WHAT REALLY WORKS: TOUGH POLICIES

Radical and innovative approaches seem to be the ones that produce real results, even though most of these programs or approaches are controversial. Blue Cross Blue Shield of Maryland and Nationwide Insurance were among the first companies to have completely smoke-free workplaces. Smoking employees were given 90 days to quit and offered whatever counseling or help they needed. Blood tests make sure that there is no nicotine in their blood, so the company can verify that employees are actually quitting smoking.

Other companies were slow to follow Nationwide because of fear of lawsuits, but now it is common to find companies that refuse to hire smokers. There is enough data to indicate that smokers cost a company thousands more in health care costs. Most companies at least make smoking employees pay extra for health insurance and discourage them from smoking on company property. In the not too distant past it was common to see groups of smoking employees huddled outside of entrances puffing away. One of my clients built a shed hundreds of feet away from the buildings where employees had to go to smoke. The "smokehouse" was unheated and the cold and the distance made most employees really think twice about how badly they wanted to smoke at work.

ESAB, a company I worked with a few years ago, also has a radical approach that really works. Employees are given a very thorough annual physical and lifestyle assessment. Based on results, they are sorted into three categories: (1) extremely healthy, (2) average health, and (3) unhealthy or high-risk. Unhealthy or high-risk employees are not given company-paid health insurance. Those in the average health category get minimal coverage, and the extremely healthy employees get the best coverage, which pays for doctor visits as well as dental, vision, and family care, and so on.

The program has caused some major behavioral changes to occur in many of the employees. In fact, two of the executives were found to be in the unhealthy category even though they were avid exercisers, so they were on strict diets to try to reduce their blood pressure and bad cholesterol. The company offers all kinds of programs and assistance to help employees get healthier and then obtain company-paid insurance, and there are much higher levels of participation than in typical corporate wellness programs.

WHAT REALLY WORKS: IN-HOUSE HEALTH AND WELLNESS CENTERS

HHI Healthcare Solutions has a really innovative approach: on-site health and wellness centers for employees and their families. Employers pay for only catastrophic health insurance and run their own health centers that handle most of the medical needs of employees. HHI builds, staffs, and manages these on-site facilities, which often include full gyms and access to nutritionists, doctors, dentists, trainers, and full spa services. Rather than having to take a day off from work to get an annual physical or have a root canal, employees can see HHI doctors and dentists on-site and get back to work in a few hours. Employees can also get in a workout with a trainer at lunch, get a massage, or get a facial. HHI's centers look much more like a spa or health club you might see at a Four Seasons or Ritz-Carlton than an industrial-looking rehab facility or clinic from the old days.

A common cause of absenteeism is having to deal with childcare or eldercare issues. Taking your mom or dad to the doctor, attending to an ill child, and other related issues force most people to take a few days off to deal with them. Realizing this, HHI centers often include both childcare and eldercare facilities so that you can bring both your dad and your daughter to work and know that they will be well taken care of.

The whole focus is on prevention, and the in-house facilities lead to increased levels of employee satisfaction, greater productivity, and savings of around 20 percent in hard dollars spent on health insurance. Real cost savings are much higher when you factor in all the time lost from work that's spent dealing with health issues. SAS, regarded as one of the best employers in the United States, has compelling data that shows that it gets $1.41 back for every dollar it has invested in its on-site health center. HHI also has a sister company that gets prescription drugs from Canadian pharmacies, saving employers an additional 25 to 30 percent over what they would pay for prescriptions filled in the United States.

WHAT REALLY WORKS: HIRING THE RIGHT PEOPLE

More and more companies are finding that hiring people with the right values is a key to maintaining their culture. Disney's philosophy is to hire the smile and attitude versus hiring for specific skills and knowledge. Southwest Airlines hires people with a good sense of humor, and Purina hires people who love animals. It is also possible and probably a good idea to hire people who value health and fitness. Some people really value wellness and do everything possible to be as healthy as they can; others do not.

An effective way of making sure that fitness and health are part of your culture is to attract and hire people who already embrace this as one of their personal values. Forward-thinking companies today use web sites and social media to communicate their culture to prospective employees so as to attract people who already embrace the same values as them. Purina has dramatically reduced its recruiting costs and improved its pool of qualified job applicants by communicating the company culture and values and only receiving résumés from individuals who already have the same values.

COST AND EFFORT TO MEASURE

This metric I would say is medium to high in cost and effort to measure. Of course, you can spend next to nothing and use the approach of Jackson Hole Airport and just have employees log on to Realage.com, but the data is subject to integrity problems since you are relying on employees to enter it themselves and to report what the web site calculated for their real age. To develop a metric that has good integrity, much of the data should not be based on self-reporting. We are all notoriously unreliable in recalling our own behavior, especially bad behavior. I read recently that according to a survey, about 65 percent of Americans report that they have a healthy diet. I also recall reading that about the same percentage of Americans are overweight, and that a third of Americans are considered obese. Seems to be a pretty big disconnect in this data. The approach to measuring health and wellness I am advocating in this book goes way beyond surveys and counting behaviors like people who signed up for the lunch walking program or annual 5K run. In order for your corporate health analytic to have any integrity, at least 40 to 50 percent of it should be made up of hard objective health measures like waist size, resting heart rate, and cholesterol ratios. In order to get this data people have to go somewhere for a physical and blood test, and that is expensive. However, they should be doing that at least once a year anyway, and insurance usually pays for all or most of an annual physical, so it may not end up costing a lot to get this data.

Aside from the cost factor, you may face a battle in gathering this data in the first place because of privacy laws (HIPAA). As long as individual employee data is not revealed there is nothing illegal or improper about getting group averages for body mass index (BMI), blood pressure, glucose, or other health metrics. In organizations with hundreds or thousands of employees there is usually less concern that someone will see their personal health data, but this might be a concern that requires some effort to overcome. I have a client who refuses to go in for a company physical because she does not want to be told that she has to lose weight and quit smoking.

HOW DO I MEASURE IT?

Regardless of your approach to employee health and wellness, it is important to have ongoing measures that provide feedback to management on the effectiveness of the entire effort as well as individual components. Most company scorecards do not include any measures of the health of their workforce, or if they measure anything at all, the metrics are pretty useless.

For example, one big corporation I consulted with measures the percentage of employees who get an annual physical at one of their quarterly health drives where a big van pulls into the company parking lot and runs tests on volunteering employees. The logic is that if employees get an annual physical they will receive information that might cause them to change their behavior and adopt more healthy habits. My brother gets an annual physical from his employer and routinely ignores all the advice provided and discredits the importance of metrics like blood pressure, BMI, HDL/LDL ratios, and other health stats that may show he is a heart attack waiting to happen. He pops his statin drug and hopes for the best.

Other useless metrics I've seen are the number of people participating in company wellness activities, such as exercise groups, weight loss or quit-smoking programs, or health fairs. Some very healthy people don't participate in these programs and prefer to exercise at their own gym or at home; maybe they don't want everyone at work to know they are in a weight loss program if that's the case.

AltaMed Health Services Corporation, one of the largest independent Federally Qualified Health Centers, has a comprehensive employee health analytic on the CEO's dashboard that includes individual metrics such as health risk assessment completion, EAP utilization, web-based sponsored wellness program participation, health coaching participation, biometric screenings completion (self-reported and performed on-site), and number of clicks on health information web sites. Targets for participation and/or completion of such components are set on a yearly basis to benchmark annual participation improvement rates.

Counting participation in wellness programs is fairly useless, so how do executives measure the impact of their efforts and the overall health of their workforce? The answer is a corporate health analytic. Just like your credit score is made up of many individual measures to provide an overall assessment of your credit worthiness, a corporate health analytic should consist of a mixture of metrics.

Constructing a good health or wellness analytic involves first deciding what factors you are going to include. An important and objective factor that should be measured is *knowledge*. A prerequisite to having a healthy lifestyle is knowing what to do and not do. Most of us know that smoking is bad, drinking and driving is bad, and eating too much red meat and saturated fat is bad, but I think it is shocking how little most people know about health and wellness beyond some basic facts. In fact, a popular segment on *The Dr. Oz Show* is the quiz on common health myths. Whenever I watch this segment, the audience—and often me, too—get about half of the questions wrong. There are many myths about health that come from old wives' tales (chicken soup will help cure a cold), propaganda from advertisers (vitamin C in orange juice helps prevent colds, or high-fructose corn syrup and sugar are the same thing), or just from reading too much stuff on the Internet. Measuring people's knowledge simply involves giving them a test that should focus on testing actual knowledge that people can use in daily life to live more healthily. For example, show four fast-food choices and ask people to select the one with the choices lowest in calories. A health knowledge test might cover a wide range of topics, such as diet, exercise, stress, diseases, common illnesses, psychological factors, and understanding key health statistics. Results from the knowledge tests are not only a good measure, but they also allow you to identify knowledge gaps in the workforce. These gaps can then be alleviated by offering training to improve employees' knowledge of health.

A second dimension that should be included in a comprehensive wellness analytic is *beliefs* or perceptions. These are different from knowledge. These are attitudes about health that would be measured via an anonymous survey. You could create a series of statements and have people indicate the degree to which they agree or disagree with them. For example, some of the attitudes or perceptions might be things like:

- People who exercise extend their lives by exactly the same amount of time they spend exercising, so I would rather be doing something more fun.
- Diet and exercise just don't work for me because everyone in my family is fat—it's just genetics.
- Vegetarians always look pale, drawn, and unhealthy. Humans are designed to be carnivores.
- Wearing a seat belt makes it more likely you will die in a crash because you won't be thrown free of the vehicle.

I'm sure you can think of dozens more of these statements that we have heard people espouse. A big part about changing attitudes or beliefs is getting people the knowledge that changes their minds. Even knowledge is often not enough, because beliefs and attitudes are entrenched and most people don't radically alter them as a result of one article or training program. By getting a baseline on the health attitudes and beliefs of your employees you can develop a change management strategy for beginning to modify those beliefs.

The third dimension that might go into your health analytic is family history or *genetics*. Having a family history of diabetes or heart disease is not a guarantee that you will get these diseases, but you are probably more likely to get them if you are not extra careful. If everyone in your family is obese, you probably stand a greater chance of becoming that way than the typical person. If both your parents were alcoholics, you probably need to be a little more careful with your alcohol consumption than some of your peers. Genetics is one of the three factors assessed in the Realage.com analytic, but it is given less weight than lifestyle or current health statistics because genetics just show tendencies, not certainties. Just because your grandparents all lived well into their nineties is not a guarantee that you will do the same. Genetic data on large groups of employees might help an employer craft a wellness program around certain predispositions. I would recommend giving genetics a very small weight in your wellness index, because there is nothing you can really do about them, and if you wanted to leave this factor out entirely it would not be a big deal; I think you can still have a robust analytic without genetic data. This data is also subject to integrity problems, because respondents are relying on memory and whether they were even told about the health of their relatives. I just recently found out that my mom's father died of heart disease in his late forties. Yet my mom is 87 and still going strong.

The fourth dimension is *behavior*. Behavior is a huge determinant of current and future health, but it is very hard to measure accurately. Some behaviors, like going in for an annual physical, are easy and quite objective. Others, like measuring what people eat or how much they drink, are probably very unreliable if we rely on people's verbal reports. Most of us cannot remember all the details of what we eat on a daily basis. Behavior like anger or feelings of depression can only be measured via surveys or instruments. Some organizations have become more diligent in measuring behavior than simply relying on verbal reports. I mentioned my client, community health care leader AltaMed, earlier. Many of AltaMed's employees are participating in the 10,000 steps program wherein employees are encouraged to walk 10,000 steps a day. Different departments are competing with each other on who can do the best, and the company is giving prizes to the winning team. Of course the real prize is that everyone will probably lose weight and improve their health. All participating employees must use pedometers, and their daily activity is tracked and recorded automatically on their computers. The company wellness director can get daily data on the percentage of employees who logged the 10,000 steps and the average number of steps per employee. This is only one behavior, but technology makes it much easier to get objective data. Of course, this method is not foolproof either. I know of someone who thinks the company wellness program is a joke and moves his pedometer back and forth all evening while doing 12-ounce curls with his other hand and watching ESPN. He goes back to work the next day with his 10,000 steps logged and the company nurse is continually puzzled that his weight continues to increase.

The final and most objective type of data to include in your wellness analytic is *health statistics*. This is data collected via blood sample, lab analysis, and testing done by doctors, nurses, or medical technicians. There are a wide variety of tests and procedures that might be done, and the comprehensiveness of the data might vary by the level of the employee. My dad was an executive at what is now Target and used to be Dayton Hudson. He got sent to the Mayo Clinic in Rochester, Minnesota, for a three-day physical every other year, so in three days Mayo collected lots of data and did lots of tests to assess my dad's health. Even a one- or two-hour hour physical like the one I get results in statistics on close to 75 different variables. While this data is the most objective, it is also the most personal. People may prefer to go to their own doctor for a physical and not report the results to their employer. A guy I know seems to be in great health, but he is a binge drinker and does not want his employer to know this. Another guy I know smokes pot every day and does not want this information to get to his employer. To get around privacy concerns like this, many employers have agreed to only measure a dozen or fewer key health statistics like blood pressure, cholesterol, and BMI, although the last one is touchy for some folks, especially in light of recent reports on better ways to measure body fat (waist-to-height ratio) than BMI.

VARIATIONS

Some variations I have seen involve tracking a few simple health statistics such as absenteeism, disability claims, annual physicals completed, and participation in company wellness programs. The level of complexity of your health metrics depends a lot on how big the organization is, how much it pays for health insurance and absenteeism, and whether health is one of your core values. Even just tracking absenteeism is better than nothing, and this is a metric on which you can get lots of comparative data from others in your city or industry. What I would avoid is just tracking participation in company-sponsored wellness activities and programs. You might have very few people work out in the company gym or eat the healthy choice in the cafeteria, yet you could still have a very healthy workforce. They work out at home or at their own gym and bring their own lunch. I also think you can leave genetics out of the index without doing much harm, because this data is notoriously unreliable and nothing can be done about it.

FORMULA AND FREQUENCY

I would lower the weight of the lifestyle and behavior metrics if they are all based on self-report or interviews and questionnaires. I would also lower the weight of the behavior measures if the measures are counts of activities like participating on company wellness programs. In a company that gets a very low score for health literacy and knowledge and beliefs, I might put an initially high weight on these factors, since the first step toward changing behavior is changing knowledge and attitudes, and then with time gradually shift more of the weight to the outcome measures of behavior and health outcomes. The weights shown below are for a company where employees already have good beliefs and attitudes about health and know quite a bit about it:

Knowledge of health and wellness	10%
Beliefs and attitudes—health and wellness	10%
Genetics and family history	10%
Behavior and lifestyle	30%
Health statistics and data from physicals	40%

TARGETS AND BENCHMARKS

Individualized targets for knowledge and beliefs would have to be set based on your baseline levels. Targets would not be set for genetics or family history, because nothing can be done to change them; they are just information that provides data on the overall health of the workforce. Comparative data and well-researched standards can be used to assess behaviors. For example, sleeping eight or nine hours a night would be green, six or seven hours would be yellow, and less than six would be red. Health statistics will also be easy to set target ranges for, since data exists for large populations about what good levels of blood pressure, glucose, and other factors look like. Of course, these target ranges change all the time with new research and often as a result of lobbying from pharmaceutical companies to sell more drugs.

BENEFITS OF DATA

In today's world of tight budgets and reduced spending on any program that does not contribute directly to the bottom line, it is easy to dismiss wellness programs as something nice to do when there are extra profits to invest in things like this. In the last few years, most companies have severely cut budgets for training, travel, new software, and lots of other things viewed as nonessential. Wellness programs, if properly designed and executed, can bring an ROI as high as six to one, according to an article in *Harvard Business Review*.[1] It would be difficult to find another investment with such low risks, such a high payback, and so many side benefits.

NOTE

1. Leonard L. Berry, Ann M. Mirabito, and William B. Baun, "What's the Hard Return on Employee Wellness Programs?," *Harvard Business Review*, December 2010.

About the Author

Mark Graham Brown has been consulting with business and government organizations since 1979. His clients include Nestlé Purina, Pfizer, the U.S. Navy, AltaMed, Sysco, the New Zealand Defence Force, and the City of Los Angeles. He has been a top-rated instructor for the Institute for Management Studies in the United States and Europe for 13 years and is the author of numerous other books on measuring and managing performance. Mr. Brown has his own consulting practice in Manhattan Beach, California, and may be contacted via his web site: www.markgrahambrown.com.

Index